# RADIO'S NEW WAVE

*Radio's New Wave* explores the evolution of audio media and sound scholarship in the digital age. Extending and updating the focus of their widely acclaimed 2001 book *The Radio Reader*, Loviglio and Hilmes gather together innovative work by both established and rising scholars to explore the ways that radio has transformed in the digital environment. Contributors explore what sound looks like on screens, how digital listening moves us, new forms of sonic expression, radio's convergence with mobile media, and the creative activities of old and new audiences. Even radio's history has been altered by research made possible by digital and global convergence. Together, these twelve concise chapters chart the dissolution of radio's boundaries and its expansion to include a wide-ranging universe of sound, visuals, tactile interfaces, and cultural roles, as radio rides the digital wave into its second century.

**Jason Loviglio** is Associate Professor and Director of Media and Communication Studies at the University of Maryland. He is the author of *Radio's Intimate Public: Network Broadcasting and Mass-Mediated Communication* and co-editor (with Michele Hilmes) of *The Radio Reader: Essays in the Cultural History of Radio*.

**Michele Hilmes** is Professor of Media and Cultural Studies at the University of Wisconsin, Madison. She is the author or editor of several books on broadcasting, including *Radio Voices: American Broadcasting 1922 to 1952, Network Nations: A Transnational History of British and American Broadcasting,* and *The Radio Reader: Essays in the Cultural History of Radio* (with Jason Loviglio).

# RADIO'S NEW WAVE

## Global Sound in the Digital Era

*Edited by Jason Loviglio and Michele Hilmes*

**Routledge**
Taylor & Francis Group

NEW YORK AND LONDON

First published 2013
by Routledge
711 Third Avenue, New York, NY 10017

Simultaneously published in the UK
by Routledge
2 Park Square, Milton Park, Abingdon, Oxon OX14 4RN

*Routledge is an imprint of the Taylor & Francis Group, an informa business*

*Library of Congress Cataloging in Publication Data*
Radio's new wave : global sound in the digital era / edited by Jason Loviglio and Michele Hilmes.
   pages cm
   Includes bibliographical references and index.
   1. Radio broadcasting. 2. Digital communications. 3. Web 2.0. I. Loviglio, Jason, editor of compilation. II. Hilmes, Michele, 1953– editor of compilation.
   HE8694.R25 2013
   384.54—dc23
   2012048873

ISBN: 978-0-415-50975-6 (hbk)
ISBN: 978-0-415-50976-3 (pbk)
ISBN: 978-0-203-12467-3 (ebk)

Typeset in Bembo and Stone Sans
by EvS Communication Networx, Inc.

Printed and bound in the United States of America by Publishers Graphics, LLC on sustainably sourced paper.

To the unsung radio artists of the past, who may at last achieve recognition in the digital present. And to today's sound artists who are making radio's new wave.

# CONTENTS

# ACKNOWLEDGMENTS

A book like this one truly represents the work of many. We would like to thank our patient and perceptive editor, Erica Wetter, who first envisioned a book that would update our previous collaboration to look at contemporary radio scholarship and practice. Our wonderful contributors inspired us and made this book possible; we learned as much from them as we hope our readers will. And thank you, readers, for closing the loop and allowing us to contribute to the rising interest in radio and sound studies found everywhere today.

Jason Loviglio would like to thank his wonderful colleagues Rebecca Adelman, Donald Snyder, and Fan Yang and students, current and former, in Media and Communication Studies and American Studies at the University of Maryland, Baltimore County. John Jeffries, Dean of the College of Arts, Humanities, and Social Sciences at UMBC, has generously supported this work in many ways. Thanks to Rachel Buff for intellectual and spiritual sustenance. And as always big thanks to Anne Wolf, the best person I know.

Michele Hilmes thanks her students, current and former, at the University of Wisconsin-Madison who take a lively interest in soundwork and have helped to build up this field. Many of them are quoted or included in this volume. The Institute for Research in the Humanities at the University of Wisconsin and research grants from the Hamel Family provided intellectual and material support. And finally I thank my husband Bruce, whose patient encouragement and provision of many cups of coffee are indispensable ingredients in all that I do.

# INTRODUCTION

## Making Radio Strange

*Jason Loviglio and Michele Hilmes*

A little more than a decade ago, we embarked on a project that was hailed at the time as a landmark in radio studies. *The Radio Reader,* a collection of essays on the past, present, and future of American radio, signified to many readers that, at last, radio had achieved the status of a legitimate field of study, on a par with the visual and literary arts, a medium in its own right. Radio had arrived. The authors whose work we selected for that volume hailed from a wide range of disciplines—American studies, history, literature, communication and media studies, cultural studies, political science, journalism—but all had discovered in broadcast radio a significant cultural technology whose intersections with the broader currents of twentieth-century American history had for too long been ignored. However, as disparate as our backgrounds and individual interests were, all of us who contributed to that volume were confident that we knew what radio was: sound waves streamed over the electromagnetic spectrum, carried by an infrastructure of stations and networks and transmitter towers, pulled out of the air by the electronic devices in our cars and stereos and portable receivers: broadcast radio.

That was in 2002. Since then, radio has changed. Somewhere around 2004 we entered the era of what is now commonly termed "web 2.0." Thanks to breakthroughs in digital compression and data speed, the places, spaces, and modes of media use expanded dramatically. Mobile media devices proliferated. While the digital transformation of radio began with streaming audio in the late 1990s, highlighted by the introduction of the iPod in 2001, it took a few more years for radio to evolve into something strange: materialized, diversified, de-spatialized. Podcasting made its debut in 2004, combining the mobility of the iPod with digital syndication software and web-based subscription. With the rise of Wi-Fi, the debut of the astonishing iPhone in 2007, and the rapid proliferation of smartphones, tablets, e-readers, and digital radios, our aural universe exploded. Boundaries began to blur. Computers became ever smaller, lighter, cheaper, and more powerful; connection grew ever faster and easier, especially as Wi-Fi spread and gave us access to the new "cloud," as in cloud computing, all around us. The very concept of radio shifted; radio's new digital interfaces gave sound forms a new visibility, literally and figuratively. New sound forms emerged. Radio took on a truly global reach, across a digital soundscape expanded far beyond the local and national spheres permitted by traditional broadcasting. Old gatekeeping devices—like licenses, spectrum allocations, limited reception areas, specialized equipment, FCC regulations—receded and diminished in importance, as thousands of streaming internet "stations" sprang up and podcasting proliferated.

Radio might have refused to adapt and become an obsolete art, stuck in the ad-ridden format rut of recycled pop music that characterized so much of commercial broadcasting, dominated by conglomerates, relegated to the oblivion it sometimes seemed to deserve. Instead, it has blossomed into new relevance, driven largely by an expanding independent and public sector, worldwide. Digital tools and technologies have allowed the production and reception of sound to extend far beyond radio's former secondary place in the media universe. Sound is now cutting edge. This can be seen in the high spirits of the Radiovision Festival, started in 2011 by the legendary free-form radio station WFMU in Jersey City and dedicated to exploring the limitless horizon of sound's intersection with the digital. One of the speakers, Jim Colgan of SoundCloud, a DIY audio site, expresses it this way: "The places where you can listen to audio, have a relationship with audio, are increasing exponentially." He points especially to the advent of podcasting as "a moment where we saw this whole other channel, beyond the terrestrial airwaves."[1] Radio's enhanced and expanded status can be seen in the young audiences that pack the touring stage shows of two of the new radio's biggest hits: Ira Glass's *This American Life,* and Jad Abumrad and Robert Krulwich's *Radiolab.* When that venerable institution National Public Radio changed its name to simply NPR in 2010, it provided a sure indication that radio has moved onto new stages and platforms. Rather than fade away, as predicted so often in its history, it has expanded to encompass a far greater reach and range of practices.

This volume is dedicated to exploring the evolution of radio as a concept and as a practice, to look at places where change is occurring and where the new possibilities opened up by radio's evolution enable new understandings of its past. In selecting our focus for this volume, we were looking for ways to make radio strange: to think about it in new ways, to look for the irruption of new voices across old borders, to call attention to the new sounds and forms that comprise aural creativity. Radio has expanded beyond its formerly national boundaries, still a medium of local specificity and intimacy, but increasingly defining its audience not through geography but through cultural affinity.

Radio has revived some of the forms thought lost long ago: documentary, feature, poetry, drama. Radio has also encountered new problems, as its economics shift and it moves from being a mass medium to one of infinite digital niches.

Much has changed in radio studies, too, since *The Radio Reader* was published. Academic presses, journals, and conferences boast an impressive number of monographs, articles, and panels exploring radio's national histories, transnational connections, and local communities. Radio scholars are finding homes in departments, associations, and conversations built around the burgeoning field of sound studies as well as those dedicated to studying television, film, music, and literature. And new scholarship has taken advantage of a wealth of digitally available sounds, transcripts, audience response, and other documents previously available, if at all, in remote, scattered, and sometimes private archives. Radio's new materiality has had a tremendous impact on how scholars discover, assess, and share the sounds that comprise a good part of the primary source material of radio history. The global digital archive gives scholars new access across geography and across time; radio programs from the past once hidden in remote archives are now available instantly, everywhere; new work that once would have aired briefly and disappeared from memory now can be found and experienced again and again.

*Radio's New Wave* highlights these changes, introducing readers to what's new in radio studies at the same time that it introduces new directions in radio soundwork in the US and across the globe. Broadly shared access to both the digital archive of radio's past and the multifarious present is as big a part of the scholarly and creative renaissance as it is for radio's release from strictly technological, institutional, or practical limits of the pre-digital era. The new materiality of radio has meant that local radio can be heard globally, invisible sound can be seen and managed on screens, and formerly evanescent sounds can be archived, distributed, and re-worked. In this new era, comparative and collaborative radio scholarship has become vastly easier to accomplish across the boundaries of nation, language, culture, and time.

*Radio's New Wave* is organized into three sections: "The Digital Soundscape," "Radio's New Sounds," and "Radio's New Histories." However, the essays in each section address themes that cut across sound production, local practices of listening, and technological convergences, providing readers with opportunities to make serendipitous connections of their own. Together they represent the simultaneous development of the field of radio studies and its evolving, hard-to-pin-down object of study. Also, they demonstrate the exciting ways that globalization and digital convergence are interacting with local conditions, communities of interest, and stubborn problems of political economy to generate radio's new wave: a transformation from talk of platforms to practices, from national systems to local reception, from radio programming to digital soundwork.

In section I, "The Digital Soundscape," Kate Lacey, Jason Loviglio, Michele Hilmes, and Elana Razlogova explore the broad terrain of radio's intersection with the digital, looking at evolving institutions, technologies, and practices across history to the present. Kate Lacey analyzes how listening as a cultural practice has changed over time, both in the way that it happens and ways in which it is understood. She argues that "Listening in the digital age needs to be understood in the context of an ongoing 're-sounding' of the public sphere that began with the revolutionary recording and radio technologies of the late nineteenth century." Jason Loviglio takes up the theme of radio's role in the public sphere by tracing the discourse of "crisis" that has surrounded US public radio since its inception, and that, as he argues, symbolically provides "the tiny vibrating crystal through which can be heard the death rattle of liberalism and the first vocalizations of the neoliberal order." Michele Hilmes examines the new materiality of radio that, after a century of ephemerality, has now turned radio into a screen medium. She claims that "radio must now be understood as *soundwork:* the entire complex of sound-based digital media that enters our experience though a variety of technologies and forms." Elena Razlogova's critical examination of "serendipity" in free-form DJ playlists and on internet radio recommendation algorithms depends upon the Google site search feature of WFMU's radio logs as well as music blogs, YouTube, and torrent sites, to trace a history of "symbiosis between the algorithmic resources and radio DJs" of broadcasting's past.

In the next section, "Radio's New Sounds," four scholars take a more specific approach to digital innovations, moving away from radio's structures to an examination of the soundwork being produced across geographies and cultures. Ece Algan's study of the interplay between mobile phones and radio among Turkish youth goes beyond simplistic notions of technological convergence to get to the place where political economy, local culture, and new communication technology interact. She argues that, "due to increased commercial gains and opportunities, convergence can result in disrupting—or even destroying—earlier participatory cultures" for youthful users in Şanlıurfa, Southeast Turkey. Dolores Inés Casillas's focuses on the "bi-national perspective" evident in the music, news, and caller responses of California's Spanish-language radio stations, where "on-air dialogues between callers and radio hosts…foster local station loyalty precisely because the bulk of these on-air conversations rest on national and transnational matters." Bill Kirpatrick's exploration of the popular animus against non-normative, "Crip" voices on the radio is informed by free, public, and online sources that document popular responses to contemporary radio like web forums and Facebook "fan" pages. His study reveals "the overwhelming ocularcentricity of present scholarship on disability and representation, but more importantly it reveals much about both radio sound and social constructions of disability." Virginia Madsen traces the long-submerged history of the radio feature, examining the roots of its documentary impulse and cinematic power in light of the recent irruption of radio's new digital potential "to create dialogues, sustain conversations between the past and the future, offer an 'ecology of the pod' to the radio *documentaire de creation,* as well as creating a fertile ground for new forms in the present to interact with the old, to mix and create new hybrid forms for the future."

Section III provides four examples of Radio's New Histories—historical work that draws on the digital archive increasingly available to scholars, enabling revelations of once obscure forms and practices that point to radio's long transnational heritage. Alejandra Bronfman analyzes the play of domestic and transnational forces in 1940s Caribbean radio, arguing that its highly contested hybridity should be understood "as precisely a site through which to work out conflicts over the politics of empire in the 1930s." Susan Smulyan and David Goodman's chapter examines tensions around the re-voicing of US serial dramas for audiences in Australia and beyond. Their transnational analysis, conducted on two continents, convincingly demonstrates that "domestic American entertainment radio from radio's golden age had an international history after World War II that needs to be understood as a significant and influential form of American influence and Americanization abroad, alongside the much better remembered international histories of American film, television and music." Derek Vaillant's exploration into French responses to US radio's market-friendly version of public service in the interwar period likewise shows how "the international rise of radio broadcasting elicited self-reflexive commentary assessing comparative, international technological development, cultural change, and power relations within and across the borders of nation-states." And Alex Russo's exploration of the "musical clock" format show in the 1930s and 40s draws attention to a little-studied forebear of later forms that "both embody and respond to cultural anxieties around industrial-era time discipline."

We hope that together these essays provide a sense of radio in all the strangeness of its present-day moment, freed from a specific apparatus, the physical limits of the electromagnetic spectrum, and decades-old predictions of its imminent demise. In its new materiality, mobile screens, and digital algorithms, radio continues to be both familiar and strange, keeping time and passing it; declaring crisis and regulating it; and connecting listeners to the complex geographies of empire and colony, migration and nation; public and private. We also hope that these essays invite more conversations and more scholarship that engage with the affordances of new soundwork, digital archives, and global connectivity. We hope that readers of this book will attend to Kate Lacey's injunction to "listen out," for the strange and insistent sounds of radio's new wave.

## Note

1. Amanda Petrusch, "Radio's Star, Never Killed, May Lead the Way to New Frontiers." *New York Times*, October 19, 2012, C28.

# SECTION I

# The Digital Soundscape

# 1

# LISTENING IN THE DIGITAL AGE

*Kate Lacey*

Radio in the digital age is arguably becoming more prolific, more fragmented, more manipulable, more mobile, more global, more personal. It is carried on a wider range of platforms and is less differentiated from other media than it seemed to be in the analogue age. But through all these contradictory and complex changes, and across all the variety of formats, one of the key threads of continuity that sustains the definition of radio is the construction of a dispersed and privatized public through the act of listening. The act of listening itself, however, is rarely problematized. And yet listening, as a cultural practice, is also subject to change and re-definition. This means that we do not just listen differently in different times and places, but that the way in which listening is experienced, and how it is configured and valorized as an activity in the public sphere is historically contingent. Listening is not changed *by* media technologies, but it does change *in relation* to changing technological constellations. And so the question arises about how to make sense of the continuities and changes in listening as radio rides its latest wave.

When digital radio was first mooted as a commercial prospect in the 1990s, it was sold on the promise of "superior sound" and "compact disc clarity" that would provide a new and improved listening experience.[1] Digital signal processing would eliminate the static, hiss, pops, and fades associated with analogue radio. Another selling point was the possibility for "mere" sound to be accompanied by text or pictures. However, the dominant practice of listening to radio while doing other things—like driving or housework—ensured, as the editor of BBC digital radio, Steve Mulholland, put it in 1997, that "while the visual can underpin or embellish audio, it must never detract from it."[2] Alongside claims for improved quality in transmission and enhanced delivery of information, came claims for increased quantity of provision. The digital delivery system would overcome the limitations of spectrum scarcity, and promised a "revolution" in access to the airwaves that would democratize them and see a rise in the diversity and creativity of radio programming, whether commercially or community orientated.[3] The most recent developments in "hybrid radio" are still being promoted in similarly confident terms. The RadioDNS project, a collaboration across public service and commercial broadcasters and associations that was launched in 2010 to more closely connect broadcast radio and the internet, simply declares its open technology to be "enhancing the listener experience, and making radio better."[4]

Promises of perfected sound and aspirations for a technologically re-invigorated democracy also accompanied the emergence of analogue recording and radio transmission into the public sphere in the late nineteenth and early twentieth centuries, and have tended to characterize each subsequent generation of hardware.[5] The early market leader in delivering online radio streaming in the mid-1990s, for example, in calling itself "RealAudio," put a marker down about the sound quality and realism of its transmissions,[6] despite the fact that dial-up connections and limited bandwidth often meant poorer audio quality than on-air reception by most conventional measures. Meanwhile, reports of one of the earliest internet radio stations, reveling in a name that belied its expectations to make a global impact—"Radio Technology for Mankind"—emphasized the expectation that "the data stream" would provide immediate, indiscriminate, and perpetual access to public performances in political and cultural life:

> [P]erformances at the Kennedy Center for the Performing Arts, speeches and debate from the floors of the House and Senate, broadcasts of luncheon speeches from the National Press Club, recordings of famous authors reading their works as well as the internet subscribers' favorite radio talk show, "Geek of the Week."[7]

Intriguingly, this ambitious list is remarkably similar to the one provided by Thomas Edison to the *Scientific American* in 1877, when forecasting the uses to which his newly invented phonograph could be put:

> [F]or taking dictation, for taking testimony in court, for reporting speeches, for the reproduction of vocal music, for teaching languages […] for correspondence, for civil and military orders […] for the distribution of the songs of great singers, sermons and speeches, the words of great men and women.[8]

A similarly rich and ambitious menu was also widely predicted by the pioneers of the early radio industry. The Marconi Company, as just one example, was reported in 1922 to be hoping to popularize its "wireless telephone" in London by broadcasting "music, speeches and news of various kinds […]

weather forecasts [...] sermons by eminent ecclesiastics [...] important election-eering speeches and [...] fairy tales for the children to listen to when they are going to bed."[9]

But more than just recording and redistributing public and creative events, the novelty of these first internet radio stations was seen to lie in a new level of interactivity, with listeners able "to retrieve biographical data about the speak-ers and send them comments by electronic mail." In addition, all these online "broadcasts" could be "transmitted globally, stored, searched, and augmented with text and picture files. The station's creator, Carl Malamud, hoped that this new, accessible archive would be a useful tool in holding those in public office to account: "Imagine, they wouldn't be able to say, 'No, I never said that,' because it's all recorded."[10] Here at the very beginning of the internet radio revolution, we once again see familiar tropes from earlier rounds of tech-nological innovation: the collapse of time and space through mediation, the dream of a universal archive reproducing and recalling lived experience in all its plenitude, the immediacy of face-to-face communication achieved through mediated form, the collapse of barriers to share in the central concerns of the life of the nation, the fantasy of a comprehensive surveillance system applied in the service of accountability and public scrutiny.

The persistence of all these hopes for *true* communion and community through communication is fascinating, but it would be a mistake to think that there is nothing new, or that there are not newly urgent questions that arise with each new incarnation of the debates.[11] By the same token, however, to get caught up in each new moment without a sense of what went before, is to run the risk of missing the bigger picture. Listening in the digital age needs to be understood in the context of an ongoing "re-sounding" of the public sphere that began with the revolutionary recording and radio technologies of the late nineteenth century.[12]

The recurrence of claims to realism in the transparency and "fidelity" of recording and transmission techniques going right back to the earliest days of phonography and wireless broadcasting, are symptomatic of a newly consti-tuted listening public learning to have *faith* in the ability of these radical new forms of mediation to afford a reliable representation of and access to "the real." The indiscriminacy of the microphone in picking up all sounds within its range, and the indiscriminacy of the radio transmitter in transgressing national and social boundaries produced new requirements on the listener to be dis-criminating in their listening, and to find new ways to accommodate listen-ing practices and everyday routines to the new sonic landscape. The liveness and domestication of radio demanded a new sensibility that could recognize and accept the personalization of the institutional address as both intimate and impersonal in the same moment. In other words, a public mode of listening had to be learned and developed in private space. All these techniques of listening have long since been naturalized, but they are, nevertheless, techniques that had to be constructed and appropriated over time.

Certainly the first wave of audio technologies—the telegraph, telephone, phonograph, and radio—did represent a radical transformation of the conditions of auditory perception, but centuries earlier it had been writing that was really the first media technology to enable the acoustic and temporal limits of public space to be extended; and the phonetic alphabet that was the first system of "recording" or at least representing, the sounds of speech. However, it was the widespread application of print technology in the modern era that allowed for the irresistible "de-auralisation" of public life.[13] The constitution of the modern public sphere was achieved through the development of an "audience-oriented" subjectivity[14] through the act of (mostly silent) reading, and the representation of the public back to itself as an imagined community, abstracted and disembodied. The authority and logic of the written word combined with the hegemony of "Cartesian perspectivalism"[15] to privilege the eye over the ear, and to render the experience of mediated public life if not an entirely silent, at least a significantly muted, affair. Moreover, it represented a shift from the group-oriented intersubjectivity of the audience to the interiorized subjectivity of the individual reader.[16]

The possibility of recording and transmitting sound certainly accelerated the experience of time and space compression, afforded new forms of mediated interactivity, new kinds of data storage, new levels of mimetic realism. These new forms of representation and new communicative contexts developed in relation to new ways of listening, and enabled new ways of commodifying the act of listening. But, more significantly than any of this, the new sound media involved, gradually, but insistently, the accommodation of a *listening* public alongside, if not quite in place of, a *reading* public.

There *is* no public, in the modern sense, outside of representation. The modern public, forged in the age of print, had encountered itself through the disembodied and alphabeticized word.[17] The restoration to the public realm of representation of the sounds of the human voice—with all its traces of embodied particularity, its emotional inflections, its intimate immediacy—therefore signaled a radical shift in terms of the access to, and experience of, public discourse. However, what this shift might mean for public life was bitterly contested. Although it is rarely acknowledged in this way, many of the debates through the twentieth century about whether these new "mass" media of communication were a force for democratization or for standardization and control hang on the extent to which *listening* was acknowledged as a critical activity like reading, or was associated simply with passive and uncritical reception.

The appropriation of the term "audience" rather than "public" in relation to audiovisual media is telling in this regard. "Audience," with its etymological roots in the act of listening plain to see (though almost always overlooked) and carrying with it the image of an embodied collectivity of listeners (though almost always thought of as spectators), is generally located in the realm of consumption, entertainment, and passivity. It is commonly opposed to the idea of "the public," associated with critical activity of individuals *producing* and participating in political and public culture. This in turn is tied up with the idea that political agency is measured in terms of "voice"—in terms, that is, of speaking up, casting votes, being heard. The agency involved in *listening* to voices in the public sphere meanwhile is, more often than not, entirely ignored. Even when listening *is* considered as an activity in modern mediated culture, it is almost exclusively in terms of listening *in* to particular voices, genres, or programs. This is true not only of broadcasting and commercial organizations with an interest in ascertaining the size, reach, and reactions of the audience listening to (or "consuming") particular outputs, but also of academic research interested in describing and analyzing the active audiences and their negotiation of the meanings of specific texts.

This (re-)invention of the listening public is part of what McLuhan identified as the shift from the linear visual logic associated with the age of print to the experiential acoustic logic of the electronic age.[18] If the former was associated with rationality, objectivity, abstraction, linearity, individualism, and nationalism, the latter is associated with partiality, involvement, experience, simultaneity, collectivity, and globalism. The characteristic impact of the electronic age is in treating the eye as an ear, offering immersive, mythic, and networked communication. If acoustic metaphors resonate through discussions of electronic and digital culture, then "listening" rather than "reading" might seem the appropriate term to encapsulate engagement with digital and electronic "texts." For example, in its immediacy, informality, and interactivity, a digital form like tweeting aspires to the conditions of talk or chat, and makes the condition of permanent and pervasive receptivity more like listening than reading, a listening out for connection to the world.

Listening is a rich concept for histories and theories of communication, bringing together as it does notions of embodiment, intersubjectivity, liveness, and sensory perception with notions of an active and critical disposition. With the dominance of the written and printed text, we have become accustomed to the idea of "reading" all sorts of non-literary texts. But in the digital age, when the very idea of a stable and finite text is increasingly problematic, and when multimedia texts call on more embodied and immersive modes of perception, "listening" becomes a more appropriate term than "reading" for engagement with all media in the age of convergence, not just those that deal exclusively in sound. Thinking through the question of listening to radio in the digital age, then, might have implications beyond radio itself.

Before returning to a discussion of listening to digital radio specifically, there is, first, an important distinction to be made between "listening in" and "listening out." While both "administrative" and "critical" audience research has been concerned primarily with the act of listening *in* to particular texts in particular contexts, it is also possible to listen *out* in a way that is not tied to or pre-determined by particular texts or voices. This is a kind of anticipatory disposition that is defined by openness. In other words, it is a *public* disposition, attentive to, but not determined by what is being listened to. The indiscriminacy of "listening out" is, in fact, the necessary corollary of the indiscriminacy of public address. Herein lies the political agency and ethical responsibility of listening—for without a listening public there would be no *call* to find a public voice. Moreover, without a listening public open to give those voices a "hearing," there can be no guarantee of the plurality of voices or the exercise of the freedom of speech.

"Listening out" in this sense need not be a critical disposition in relation to acoustic representation only (in much the same way as we no longer regard "reading" as a critical activity restricted to the written word). However, this conceptualization of listening does provide some insight into debates about radio's "new wave," particularly in relation to the politics and ethics of listening in relation to the new forms of digital radio. The implications can be seen particularly acutely in relation to the prolific output out of contemporary digital culture.

By 1998, when websites like the BRS radio directory were already acting as portals to thousands of online radio stations (both terrestrial re-broadcasts and dedicated online radio),[19] the first generation of customizable radio stations was being reported. Imagine Radio, for example, allowed listeners to "become their own disk jockeys" by selecting and rating tracks from a series of formatted stations. The stations that resulted could, in turn, be "shared."[20] Some claimed that these "stations" were more like online CD jukeboxes, and so hybrid forms began to emerge, such as Puremix, that allowed for listeners to choose a preferred mix from a wide range of streamed music channels, but interspersed with familiar broadcast elements like disc jockey talk and news on the hour.[21] Around the same time, software like Winamp and Shoutcast or RealSever Basic 8, was becoming more widely available, enabling people not only to personalize radio stations, but to re-broadcast them to friends and develop a listening network.[22] Peercasting took this a step further, with every listener in a decentralized file-sharing network also becoming a broadcaster, a trend that became more "mainstream" with the take-up of "podcasting."[23]

Although the most prominent of these developments in personalization and networking centered on music, there were developments in talk radio and other formats too. Audible was one of the first providers of downloadable speech audio files, and remains one of the largest. In 2008 it was bought by Amazon, and is now the leading online provider of audiobooks and other speech-based material. Interestingly, its promotional gambit is "to establish literate listening as a core tool for anyone seeking to be more productive, better informed, or more thoughtfully entertained."[24] The BBC even experimented with personalized radio drama in 2001, producing a half-hour play with some

94 billion narrative routes. Taking as its theme Einstein's theory that God does not play dice with the Universe, Nick Fisher's *Wheel of Fortune* was made up of twenty-three minute long segments each ending in a narrative junction affording the listener three options about how to continue listening.[25] More recently, there have been experiments to emulate the microblogging phenomenon of sites like Twitter with spoken word versions like Audioboo, an audioblogging platform that offers mobile, locative, and interactive audio file sharing, because, as their tagline has it, "sound is social."[26] These new sites, like the leading social sound sharing app "SoundCloud," allow people not only to record and "share sound with the world," but to *track* the numbers and location of people listening around the globe.[27]

The trend to personalized and networked listening took another turn with the arrival of stations like Last.fm that use a combination of audio fingerprinting and collaborative filtering to enable the station to "learn" about an individual listener's musical tastes and so tailor a playlist to suit not only the listener, but also the record labels for whom such sites provide valuable market research.[28] Pandora radio, floated for $2.6 billion in 2011,[29] goes even further, based on its claim to a "scientific" analysis of musical tastes and preferences with its "musical genome project" that plays music listeners' requests "and more music like it."[30] In 2008, the "smart radio" application "Stitcher" set out to do the same for news and information, aggregating content from various newsfeeds and podcasts according to previous choices and settings.[31] Sites like these claim to be "discovery" services—although the implication is always that listeners can be reassured that their discoveries will be safely within the realm of the familiar.

Again, there are precedents in the analogue age. Radio caused genre-specific stations and formats to proliferate long before television followed suit in moving away from "mixed programming." This sort of specialization and audience fragmentation was "sold" on the promise of increased choice, though Andrew Crisell was one of many critics who judged the choice involved in such listening decisions to be "an often timid, conservative faculty."[32] Similarly, Susan Douglas identified a tendency in format radio to cultivate and pander to "a safe, gated-in listening."[33] Even earlier, Horkheimer and Adorno had located "the regression of the masses" in "their inability to hear the unheard of with their own ears" because of the way in which the culture industry offered up only pre-digested fare.[34] And, indeed, this pessimism about the lack of courage or wherewithal to escape the comfort zone of conformity and deference was already part of Kant's famous answer to the question "What is Enlightenment?".[35] In other words, the latest constellation of institutional, psychological, and algorithmic mechanisms that are in play to direct listeners to familiar, homely sites are not evidence in themselves for a narrative of decline from some past age of cosmopolitan listening.

Nevertheless, the contemporary developments in digital radio—personalization, networking and specialization—represent arguably heightened forms of privatization of the public potential of listening, working to reproduce a model of "listening in" to more of the same, more of what is already familiar, rather than "listening out." These new textual and algorithmic strategies combine with quite familiar psychological and pragmatic strategies on the part of the listener to develop convenient and manageable (and often quite limited) "repertoires" of listening in amid the global cacophony. This generally conservative application of a radical new technological potential is compounded by the fact that there is a good deal of re-circulation of content within and between sites, so that the apparent proliferation still condenses around familiar central distributors.[36] The flipside of this, is that the dispersed and disaggregated audience, for all the talk of personalization and fragmentation, might then still be sharing in some sort of common culture and conversation, especially with the way rankings, recommendations, hit-rates, and advertising direct listeners towards a concentration of popular, trusted, or fashionable sites, followed by the "long tail" of more niche options—albeit these niches in aggregate are emerging as a bigger market than the "mainstream."[37] Personalized and social sound media are not separate from the mainstream, for they share in, comment on, or reproduce more conventionally mainstream sources of news, music, and other material, while the mainstream in its turn picks up, reproduces, and comments on what is "trending" in the social media.[38]

Nevertheless, a focus on the new forms of "listening in" often leads to celebratory analyses of the proliferation of platforms, the profusion of personalized stations, the convergence with other media forms, the possibility for listeners to produce, share, comment on, and manipulate media materials, and the convenience of listening on mobile devices which "produces" new forms of encounter. This is connected to the longstanding cultural bias which privileges the productive activity of "speaking up" over the receptive "passivity" of listening. In other words, the proliferation of forms and formats for individual expression is assumed to be coterminous with a plurality of voices, which in turn is taken to be the marker of a properly functioning communicative democracy. The celebration of interactivity in the digital age is, in these terms, a celebration of the opportunities for listeners to do more than "just" listen.

This is nowhere clearer than in the way in which the conventional divide between broadcaster and listener is being re-described. There are various portal sites for internet talk radio, many of which use a version of YouTube's famous tagline, "Broadcast Yourself." Countless websites claim to be able to make an individual voice (or an individual's choices) heard by millions, holding out the promise to their users that they will be able to "Talk to the World."[39] Apart from the question about whether there is really such a large and willing audience for these individualized soundbites, there is an odd contradiction at play here as it speaks to the desire both for a decentralization of broadcasting to the point where every individual has a voice, and at the same time to the desire for each individual voice to be precisely at the center of a network of millions. The rhetoric of decentralization in other words openly mobilizes narcissistic fantasies of propagandistic power in a radical move that at the same time promises to strip broadcasting of its heritage as some sort of collective endeavor.

Participants in personalized radio stations are generally invited to categorize their speaking or listening into generic types, such as sports, lifestyle, comedy, and so on. As far as politics is concerned, these genres might be further disaggregated with labels such as "liberal," "conservative," or "libertarian," or be even more precisely distinguished by issue, event, or even individual electoral candidate.[40] The interpretation of this degree of genrification is ambivalent. On the one hand, it can be read as a symptom and reinforcement of social and political fragmentation or even polarization. On the other it could potentially encourage users to dip into forms of radio and types of opinion which are new, unfamiliar, or anathema to them. To this extent, there is a surprising echo here of an ambivalence in the approach of the early BBC in an era of monopoly rather than proliferation, and where broadcasting was unequivocally understood as a public, rather than a consumer good. On the one hand, the Reithian ideal was to have mixed programming on a single service in order to allow listeners to be surprised—and enlightened—by encountering ideas and voices to which they might not otherwise have chosen to listen. People, in other words, were invited to listen out for the unexpected, to listen out for things that might challenge their preconceptions and widen their horizons. On the other hand, listeners were continually chided for listening "indiscriminately." "Proper," responsible listening was selective, intentional, concentrated, and critical. People, in other words, were invited to "listen in," on purpose and with purpose to a choice of programs. And yet within a framework of public service the two ideas are not entirely mutually exclusive: it is how the balance is struck between listening out and listening in that is the issue.[41]

This is because a proliferation of voices and sounds online is not in and of itself a sign of a well-functioning democratic public sphere, for not only does proliferation not equate straightforwardly to plurality, but it might also erode any sense of a collective public forum. Certainly critics have long expressed concerns about the fragmentation of the public into "sphericules" and isolated or entrenched media enclaves.[42] These critiques tend to mourn the loss of a common public space of conversation, normally organized at a national level. There are several things to be said about this. First is that even the classical bourgeois public sphere was made up of multiple published interventions, not all of which were read by everybody. The narrative of decline from a shared common space can be read, then, either as a deep-set nostalgia for the lost shared acoustic space of the ancient city states (for which read "face-to-face" encounter) and a distrust of the politics of representation altogether; or it is a nostalgia for the shared national cultures aspired to by the national press and network broadcasting that have begun to occupy a less dominant space within the new media landscape. But to focus only on mediacentric explanations is to overlook other potential explanations, such as the declining trust in conventional media and politics, and a wider withdrawal into the private sphere, or the generalized shift from broad class-based politics to identity or issue-based politics.

Second, concerns about the fragmentation of the public sphere tend to read a fragmentation of the (listening) public off a fragmentation of "the text." The logic of specialization that has characterized the history of radio since the days of the national networks to the current trend for customized stations is read as a specialization of the audience, and therefore of the public. But a public is not constituted in relation to particular texts, but rather, as Michael Warner has it, in the *reflexive circulation* of discourse, a "concatenation of texts through time."[43] In a multimedia universe, this concatenation of texts is put together by users travelling between sites and across platforms. In other words, the identification of increasingly specialized radio stations, for example, does not necessarily mean that listening can be mapped in the same way. An individual station might be closely circumscribed in various ways, but its listeners will rarely be tuning in only to that one site, and will identify not only as listeners but also as viewers, readers, users, and contributors. Indeed, recent empirical research of online audience activity confirms "overlapping patterns of public attention rather than isolated groups of audience loyalists."[44]

Third, and perhaps more significantly, the fragmentation of the public sphere is less of a problem if plurality, rather than consensus, is taken as the guiding principle. In other words, it is not only the *number* of voices or contributions which matters, but the *variety* of voices and the variety of ways in which those voices are able to speak that matters—the possibility of both inter- and intra-discursive contestation, as Lincoln Dahlberg has put it.[45] This element matters because the power dynamics that privilege certain voices and ways of speaking offline are, of course, replicated online. And this is where the question of listening out becomes so important.

First of all it is only through listening out for difference that a plurality of voices can register—this is the role, in other words, of audition as audit. Freedom of expression is necessary, but not sufficient, to ensure plurality. The vagaries of (conditioned) individual choice and the conditions of the marketplace, as well as more direct instances of censorship and control, might lead to a multitude of similar voices, or the marginalization or silencing of certain other voices. It is only in listening out for difference that plurality can be identified and secured. This is reinforced by the idea that the "freedom of listening" is something that inheres in the communicative spaces *between* speakers, whereas the freedom of expression was historically conceptualized as an individual property right.[46] It is this privileging of the freedom of expression over the freedom of listening that is an important factor in the widespread celebration of new forms and platforms of expression and interactivity. And it is the extension of the idea of "expression" to include any form of contribution to the production of content, rather than the content itself that lies behind Jodi Dean's blistering critique of the de-politicization of the public sphere under the contemporary conditions of communicative capitalism. She critiques the "fantasy of abundance" and the "fantasy of participation" in the digital age in order to account for the lack of political response despite all the apparent proliferation of debate.[47] In other words, the performance of participation is valued over everything else. To speak up is the thing, regardless of whether anyone is listening.

Secondly, there is also the question of whether there is a plurality not only of voice, but also of listening. In terms of radio, the proliferation of voices on air resonates within an increasingly privatized and personalized public sphere. The techniques of producing personalized programming and the rise of earphone culture together privilege listening as an intensely private, rather than a public activity. Indeed, in the digital age, there is a sense in which the act of listening is rendered increasingly obscure. The new "activity" of the listener in personalizing and intervening in the "production" of digital radio is most commonly conceptualized as actions in response to, or in advance of, the act of listening, not the act of listening itself. In an echo of the dominant formulations of the analogue age which (mis)conceived the listening public as a passive mass audience, the activity of listening, as a mode of active reception anterior to and separate from measurable *expressed* response is once again elided as audience activity is understood in terms of "speaking up" whether that be via posts to websites, preferences registered, personalized stations created, or comments tweeted. Moreover, listening in in this sense of online or digital activity is conveniently open to surveillance, measurement, and commodification by both corporations and digital savvy individuals.

The privatization of the act of listening has profound implications for the public sphere if we accept that communication is about both the production and distribution of content, *and* its reception and critique. An open, public listening position is critical at every level; not, as is commonly assumed, only at the level of reception. Listening out is a *productive* act, since it is generally only in the expectation of finding an audience that people are moved to express themselves at all. This is not unrelated to the description of the contemporary media age as an "attention economy," where producers of content compete in the media marketplace for the scarce and therefore valuable attention of an audience.[48] However, the economistic frame privileges attention as listening in, an activity belonging to the private realm of consumption, and a "passive" sort of attention that can be easily swayed or caught (despite being clothed in the politicized rhetoric of "choice"). The idea of listening out, on the other hand, reserves a sense of responsibility and intentionality to the concept of "attention." It also, therefore, raises questions about the ethics of listening in the digital age.

To listen out for otherness, for plurality, can be conceived, therefore, as a civic obligation. Lisbeth Lipari has argued that ethics itself arises out of this difficult commitment to engage with difference, this "listening otherwise," as she calls it, which involves, "a transcendence from self-in-separation to self-in-relation."[49] While Lipari is concerned with the private sphere, this obligation to listen otherwise intersects with a civic obligation in democratic societies to be well informed in order to form grounded opinions, deliberate well, and participate in public and political life. It is not for nothing that we speak of giving someone a fair "hearing." Similarly, Susan Bickford's conceptualization of "political listening" is about having the courage to listen to difference, neither refusing to listen, nor simply opposing or blithely accepting difference, but being open to and respectful of other voices.[50] Listening out in this sense is not about the search for consensus or conformity, let alone the confirmation of already given tastes and opinions. Nor is it about the erasure or disregard of conflict or different interests. It is, rather, about the need to *attend to* others and otherness and, as Chantal Mouffe puts it in her discussion of agonistic pluralism, how to ensure an adversary's right to express a contrary opinion is not negated, but *listened* to.[51]

The openness of listening out, then, is about keeping channels of communication open across ongoing difference and conflicting interests. It is, therefore, a difficult, challenging, and risk-laden responsibility at the best of times. It is arguably more of a challenge at the end of a broadcasting century in which the listening public has been persistently constructed as a commodified audience made up of self-interested individual consumers controlling privatized soundscapes and listening in to sounds targeted at particular demographics or communities of the like-minded. But at the same time it is precisely the experience of living in a media age that produces and heightens the requirement, the context, the responsibilities, and the possibilities of listening out.

Media ethics is generally considered a question of media production. The recent "ethical turn" in media studies has, significantly, acknowledged the importance of the ethics of reception.[52] Though the recent innovations in digital radio raise important questions about the ethics of listening, they are not necessarily questions that can or will be answered at the level of media policy, institution, or text. Once upon a time the "civic ambition" of radio, whether commercial or public service, was expressed in terms of a certain kind of centralized programming and a certain idea of "proper" (undistracted and discriminate) listening in.[53] Radio in the digital age is radically de-centered and dispersed, and under these conditions it is increasingly necessary to detach the question of the ethics of listening from particular media productions and producers. Cultures of communication, after all, exceed the set of activities—productive *and* receptive—that cluster around particular media texts at particular moments. Listening out is a civic as much as a media practice. It is the practice of being open to the multiplicity of texts and voices and thinking of texts in the context of, and in relation to, difference, and how they resonate across time and in different spaces. Despite the increasing sophistication of techniques by search engines, advertising, and personal recommendations to attract listeners to sites similar to those just visited, or to devise more or less familiar playlists, or to retreat into a personalized and privatized soundscape, a culture and practice of listening out would go a long way in protecting the digital environment as a place of wide horizons and diversity.

## Notes

1. Andrew Pollack, "Next, Digital Radio for a Superior Sound," *New York Times*, July 11, 1990; Steve Crowley, "Bringing Radio Up to Date: New Digital Technology Can Sound as Clear as Compact Discs," *Washington Post*, June 3, 1990.
2. Quoted in Anne Karpf, "Value Addled Services: Digital Radio May Have Set the Technofreaks Ablaze. But Does it Offer Anything for the Average Listener?" *The Guardian*, December 3, 1997.
3. Nigel Powell, "Tuning In for a Digital Revolution," *The Times*, February 19, 1998; Raymond Snoddy. "Africa Set to Go Radio Gaga," *The Times*, June 26, 1998; Stephen A. Booth, "Radio That Bytes," *Popular Science*, November 2000, n.p.
4. http://radiodns.org/. For discussions of contested definitions of radio in relation to its more recent technological incarnations, see, David A. Black, "Internet Radio: A Case Study in Medium Specificity" *Media, Culture and Society* 23, no. 3 (2001), 397–408; Chris Priestman, "Narrowcasting and the Dream of Radio's Great Global Conversation," *The Radio Journal: International Studies in Broadcast and Audio Media* 2, no. 2 (2004), 77–88 ; Kate Lacey, "Ten Years of Radio Studies. The Very Idea," *The Radio Journal: International Studies in Audio and Broadcast Media* 6, no. 1 (2008), 21–32; Ariana Moscote Freire, "Remediating Radio: Audio Streaming, Music Recommendation and the Discourse of Radioness," *The Radio Journal: International Studies in Audio and Broadcast Media* 5, no. 2/3 (2008), 97–112; Andrea Baker, "Comparing the Regulatory Models of Net-Radio with Traditional Radio," *International Journal of Emerging Technologies and Society* 7, no. 1 (2009), 1–14.
5. There have been, however, notable exceptions to this general trend, as standards of sound quality are defined not only by taste and technology, but also by the marketplace. Examples would include the "delay" in introducing radio on FM in the US because of objections from established AM stations and plans for FM television and the prioritizing of quantity over quality in relation to the commercial digital radio multiplexes currently operating in the UK. See Stephen Lax, "Digital Radio and the Diminution of the Public Sphere," in *Media and Public Spheres*, ed. Richard Butsch, 109–21 (New York: Palgrave Macmillan, 2007), 118. The widespread adoption of the "compressed" sound of mp3 players, along with other forms of miniaturization, is another example of the adoption of a "good enough" aesthetic.
6. Part of the Real Networks Corporation, based in Seattle. RealAudio was launched in 1995, followed by RealVideo and then RealPlayer. http://www.realnetworks.com (accessed August 6, 2012).
7. Peter H. Lewis, "Internet Radio Station Plans to Broadcast Around the Clock," *New York Times*, September 19,1994.
8. Quoted in Friedrich Kittler, *Gramophone, Film, Typewriter* (Stanford, CA: Stanford University Press, 1999), 78.
9. Mr. Godfrey Isaacs, managing director of the Marconi Company, quoted in "The New Wireless Era. Marconi Telephone Plans," *The Manchester Guardian* May 6, 1922, 9.
10. Lewis, "Internet Radio."
11. For the best discussion of the history of communication in these terms, see John Durham Peters, *Speaking into the Air: A History of the Idea of Communication* (Chicago: University of Chicago Press, 1999).
12. This is the problematic I pursue at greater length in *Listening Publics: The Politics and Experience of Listening in the Media Age* (Cambridge, UK: Polity, 2013).

13. James Carey, "Walter Benjamin, Marshall McLuhan, and the Emergence of Visual Society," *Prospects* 11, no. 1 (1986), 29–38.
14. Jürgen Habermas, *The Structural Transformation of the Public Sphere: An Inquiry into a Category of Bourgeois Society* (Cambridge, MA: MIT Press, 1991), 28–29.
15. Martin Jay, *Downcast Eyes: The Denigration of Vision in Twentieth Century French Thought* (Berkeley: University of California Press, 1993), 68.
16. Walter J. Ong, *Orality and Literacy: The Technologizing of the Word* (New York: Routledge, 1982).
17. The term "alphabeticized" here refers to the invention of the phonetic writing system (the first technology of sound recording, offering a graphical reproduction of the spoken word that could be sonically reproduced in being read aloud). See Ong's *The Presence of the Word: Some Prologomena for Cultural and Religious History* (1967; Global Publications: 2000), 87; http://ssips.binghamton.edu.
18. Marshall McLuhan, "Visual and Acoustic Space," in *Audio Culture: Readings in Modern Music*, ed. Daniel Warner (New York: Continuum, 2006), 67–72.
19. BRS stands for Broadband Radio Service. The BRS Media company launched its online radio directory in 1995. As www.web-radio.fm it links to over 10, 000 radio websites, and over 5,000 webcasting sites. http://get.fm/about (accessed August 6, 2012).
20. Rachel Lehmann-Haupt, "Internet Radio: Listeners Take On Role of the Deejay," *New York Times*, November 5, 1998.
21. Sean Dodson, "Internet Thrilled the Radio Star: Sean Dodson Tunes In as the UK's First Ever Personalised Radio Hits the Airwaves," *Guardian Online*, November 16, 2000.
22. John Gilroy, "Online Broadcasting Up Close and Personal," *The Washington Post,* November 16, 2000.
23. Peter Rojas, "Pirates of Peercasting," *The Guardian*, July 25, 2002. The term "podcasting" has been attributed to *Guardian* journalist, Ben Hammersly, writing in 2004. See Richard Berry, "Will the iPod Kill the Radio Star? Profiling Podcasting as Radio," *Convergence: The International Journal of Research into New Media Technologies* 12, no. 2 (2006), 143–62, 143.
24. Audible Press Centre http://www.audible.co.uk/press-centre (accessed March 17, 2012).
25. "Bets on for interactive drama," *BBC News Online*, September 19, 2001, http://news.bbc.co.uk/1/hi/entertainment/tv_and_radio/1552369.stm (accessed February 20, 2012).
26. Audioboo.fm (accessed March 17, 2012).
27. http://soundcloud.com/ (accessed March 17, 2012).
28. Dominic Timms, "The New Pioneers: Niche Stations Using Imagination and Innovation are Driving the Use of Online Radio," *The Guardian*, August 18, 2003.
29. "Online Radio Firm Pandora Floats for $2.6bn in New York," *BBC News Online*, June 15, 2011, http://www.bbc.co.uk/news/business-13780371 (accessed February 20, 2012).
30. Pandora, "About the Music Genome Project," http://www.pandora.com/about/mgp (accessed March 27, 2012).
31. http://stitcher.com (accessed March 17, 2012).
32. Andrew Crisell, "Radio: Public Service, Commercialism and the Paradox of Choice," in *The Media: An Introduction*, ed. Adam Briggs and Paul Cobley (Harlow, UK: Pearson Education 2002), 121–34, 121.
33. Susan. J. Douglas, *Listening In: Radio and the American Imagination* (London: Time, 1999), 348.
34. Max Horkheimer and Theodor Adorno, *Dialektik der Aufklärung: Philosophische Fragmente* (Frankfurt: Fischer, 1988), 42–43.
35. James Donald, "Kant, the Press, and the Public Use of Reason," *Javnost: The Public* 10, no. 2 (2003), 45–64, 48.
36. Tim Wall, "The Political Economy of Internet Radio" *The Radio Journal: International Studies in Audio and Broadcast Media* 2, no. 1 (2004), 27–44.
37. Chris Anderson, *The Long Tail: How Endless Choice is Creating Unlimited Demand* (London: Random House, 2010).
38. Henry Jenkins, *Convergence Culture: Where Old and New Media Collide* (New York: New York

University Press, 2006); Pablo J. Boczkowski, *News At Work: Imitation in an Age of Information Abundance* (Chicago: University of Chicago Press, 2010).

39. Live 365 promises its subscribers that their personal stations will be "immediately available to millions of listeners," http://www.live365.com; "Talk to the World" is the tagline of the Spreaker audio platform, http://www.spreaker.com (accessed March 17, 2012).

40. See, for example, the search options on the Tunein website, http://tunein.com/radio/Talk-c424725/ (accessed March 17, 2012).

41. This was a recurring debate in other radio systems, including the American radio of the 1930s, as David Goodman has discussed fully in *Radio's Civic Ambition: American Broadcasting and Democracy in the 1930s* (New York: Oxford University Press, 2011).

42. Elihu Katz, "And Deliver Us From Segmentation," *Annals of the American Academy of Political and Social Science*, 546, no. 1 (1996), 22–33; Todd Gitlin, "Public Sphere or Public Sphericules?" in *Media, Ritual and Identity,* ed. Tamar Liebes and James Curran (London: Routledge, 1998), 168–74; Cass Sunstein, *Republic.com* (Princeton, NJ: Princeton University Press, 2001); Scott W. Campbell and Nojin Kwak, "Mobile Communication and Strong Network Ties: Shrinking or Expanding Spheres of Public Discourse?" *New Media and Society* 14, no. 2 (2012), 262–80.

43. Michael Warner, "Publics and Counterpublics" *Public Culture* 14, no. 1 (2002), 49–90, 62.

44. James G. Webster and Thomas B. Ksiazek, "The Dynamics of Audience Fragmentation: Public Attention in an Age of Digital Media," *Journal of Communication* 62, no. 1 (2012), 39–56.

45. Lincoln Dahlberg, "Rethinking the Fragmentation of the Cyberpublic: From Consensus to Contestation," *New Media and Society* 9, no. 5 (2007), 827–47.

46. Kate Lacey, "Listening Overlooked: An Audit of Listening as a Category in the Public Sphere," *Javnost: The Public* 18, no. 4 (2011), 5–20.

47. Jodi Dean, "Communicative Capitalism: Circulation and the Foreclosure of Politics," *Cultural Politics* 1, no.1 (2005), 51–74.

48. Thomas. H. Davenport and John. C. Beck, *The Attention Economy: Understanding the New Currency of Business* (Boston, MA: Harvard Business School Press, 2001); Patrick Crogan and Samuel Kinsley, eds., "Special Issue: Paying Attention," *Culture Machine* 13 (2012).

49. Lisbeth Lipari, "Listening Otherwise: The Voice of Ethics," *International Journal of Listening* 23, no. 1 (2009), 44–59, 45, 53.

50. Susan Bickford, *The Dissonance of Democracy: Listening, Conflict, and Citizenship* (Ithaca, NY: Cornell University Press, 1996).

51. Chantal Mouffe, *The Democratic Paradox* (London: Verso, 2000), 80–107.

52. Roger Silverstone, *Media and Morality: On the Rise of the Mediapolis* (Cambridge, UK: Polity, 2006); Nick Couldry, *Listening Beyond the Echoes: Media, Ethics and Agency in an Uncertain World* (London: Paradigm, 2006); Jonathan C. Ong, "Where is the Cosmopolitan? Locating Cosmopolitanism in Media and Cultural Studies," *Media, Culture and Society* 31, no. 3 (2009), 449–66.

53. Goodman, *Radio's Civic Ambition*.

# 2

# PUBLIC RADIO IN CRISIS

*Jason Loviglio*

> Only a crisis—actual or perceived—produces real change.
>
> Milton Friedman[1]

> Crisis, however, is something that public broadcasting has never been able to escape.
>
> *Broadcasting Magazine*, 1973[2]

## Introduction

One of the earliest and most persistent viral hoaxes to circulate through American email inboxes at the dawn of the internet age featured the alarming claim that National Public Radio (NPR), the US public radio network, was on the verge of elimination through federal de-funding. The email message's origins were sincere: In 1995, a Florida undergraduate, concerned about culture war rhetoric, responded to a very real proposal in Congress to radically defund public radio, television, and the arts with an email petition to voice support for the institutions. Later versions added the subject heading "Save Sesame Street!" and contrived references to NPR news reports of the impending budget cuts. In various forms, the message bounced around the internet for years, until finally petering out in the late 1990s. The coda to this hoax, of course, is that in the decade since this email petition has petered out, the threats to eliminate NPR funding have become increasingly serious, generating new rounds of internet discourse.[3]

I begin with this bit of internet history because it so perfectly captures NPR's paradoxical relationship to crisis and growth, and its odd resilience in the face of technological change, political controversy, and federal budgetary austerity. More broadly, it crystallizes two seemingly contradictory patterns in US public radio's modern history: its nearly constant state of crisis and its impressive rise in audience, market share, membership donations, corporate underwriting, and cultural significance; all this at a time when other print and broadcast news media are hemorrhaging consumers, reporters, foreign desks, red ink, and relevance.[4] NPR is now one of the dominant cultural institutions in the country, yet a routinely threatened one. It has grown at a phenomenal rate over the four decades of its existence despite, and perhaps because of, a pattern of crises. In its propensity to provoke and survive threats real and imagined, exaggerated and implicit, NPR has come to exemplify the precarious and contested status of US public institutions in the twenty-first century. In what follows, I will explore the persistent trope of crisis in NPR's transformation from a marginal, underfunded network to a central US cultural institution.

In the larger project from which I take this essay, I explore modern public radio in terms of "the long march of neo-liberalism," arguing that it has become a key cultural institution in the evolving structure of feeling of the neo-liberal era. The story of public radio, it argues, is the tiny vibrating crystal through which can be heard the death rattle of liberalism and the first vocalizations of the neo-liberal order. Public radio in the US is an institution mired in and thriving upon some of the very contradictions that characterize this long political and cultural moment, whose origins in the early 1970s match up almost exactly with those of NPR and the modern era of public radio.

## Radio Broadcasting and National Crisis

To understand this particular contradiction, it is important first to acknowledge the history of the symbiotic relationship between crisis and broadcast journalism. For nearly a century, the newscast has been the defining electronic ritual in evoking and assuaging a state of crisis. From its origins in "wireless telegraphy," electronic news has had the quality of what J. L. Austin calls "a performative act," in that it conjures a state of affairs in the act of uttering it.[5] In 1912, when the *Titanic* sent its wireless distress signal and the *Carpathia* responded, saving hundreds of lives, radio's connection to the modern experience of the making of news was born. By the 1930s, newscasts, drawing on radio's "everywhere-ness, all-at-once-ness, and never-ending-ness" helped to evoke and assuage the crises that they reported.[6] The imagined community of Benedict Anderson's newspaper-reading public became, in the simultaneous reception of the radio news bulletin, a community drawn together *in a state*, in both senses of the term: a people in crisis *as* a nation-state.[7] FDR's massively popular, highly choreographed, and sparingly used radio addresses were among the first and most effective uses of the performative and regulatory power of radio to create and manage the crisis in the very utterance of it.

Take for example, the May 27, 1941 Fireside Chat, which he used to declare an "Unlimited National Emergency," a broadcast which simultaneously created and regulated a state in crisis.[8]

Radio's historical relationship to crisis reaches its strange zenith in the *War of the Worlds* panic broadcast of October 1938. Its resonance at the time and ever since has much to do with the way this Halloween trick merely exaggerated the power that every radio newscast had to put the country in a state of shared receptivity to crisis, and in so doing, create a mode of reception that characterized radio listening in general. Invasions from Germany (and Mars) became the stuff of breathless news bulletins in the late 1930s, crash courses for radio networks and audiences for US entry into World War II, a long crisis that helped to institutionalize the centrality of the radio news bulletin. Since World War II, the electronic mass media's relationship to coverage of national and international crises has been as powerful, if often unpredictable. In the 1960s, of course, TV coverage of civil rights protests, anti-war demonstrations, and warfare itself became a key window on the most challenging moments of that tumultuous decade.[9] From radio panics from Mars to "the television war" in Indochina, to "the Twitter Revolution" in Iran, the history of crisis is always also a history of the media that "regulate" the crises even as they help utter them into being.

## NPR's Origins in Crisis

Even in this context, NPR's origin stories are uniquely tied to the story of national crisis. The station's flagship news program, *All Things Considered* was born coincidentally but consequentially on May Day, 1972, in the midst of the teargas and chaos of a massive anti-war demonstration in DC. Reporter Jeff Kamen interviewed protesters, questioned motorcycle cops, and opined that "Today in the nation's capital, it is a crime to be young and to have long hair."[10] This broadcast and its place in NPR lore helped to define an enduring, if misleading, reputation for liberal, anti-establishment bias, which persists to this day, part of the political instability at the heart of the crisis/growth paradox.[11] *Morning Edition* began on the first morning of the Iranian hostage crisis in 1979, quite by chance (unlike ABC's *Nightline,* which began in direct response to the unfolding hostage crisis). NPR's overall audience skyrocketed during the first Gulf War in 1990–91 and has kept growing since, with predictable growth spurts in times of national crisis. Nicols Fox, writing for the *American Journalism Review* puts it baldly: "Public radio owes a lot to the firm of Cheney, Schwarzkopf & Powell. The Gulf War—like Watergate, Iran-Contra and Tiananmen Square—brought the news-hungry to a halt at the NPR signal."[12]

The size of the network's audience spiked after the attacks of September 11, 2011, as well, resulting in enduring gains for the network and helping to justify the addition of new foreign bureaus and correspondents in more of the world's hot spots. The attacks also helped to spin off the Sonic Memorial Project, Story Corps, and to revive the popularity of first-person non-fiction narratives, particularly stories of trauma and resilience, in audio formats.[13] Unlike CNN and other electronic news outlets, which require fresh infusions of shock and awe to get their ratings bumps, NPR tends to hold a good chunk of its new audience post-crisis.[14] NPR has grown in audience, revenue, and national stature during a period when other electronic and print news outlets have been in free-fall. In an era of genuine crisis for traditional journalism and in the tumult of its own impossible situation, NPR evolves and thrives.

NPR's pre-history is also one of existential crisis. In Jack Mitchell's deft telling of the machinations that preceded passage of the 1967 Corporation for Public Broadcasting Bill, the words "and radio" had to be surreptitiously added with Scotch tape in the text of the "Public Television Bill" the night before the House vote. The legislation primarily focused on the creation of a public television service, PBS, and directed more than 80% of the funding to it.[15] Since then, the lore of narrow escapes has grown and with it, an anxious sense of being at odds with the world it is charged with reporting on. The tensions between crisis and evolution, political peril and rightward drift, are heightened by the quixotic origins of the network: "puny resources," a mission to provide an alternative to the status quo; and vast ambitions "to cover events in a first-rate fashion."[16] As early as 1983, Robert Siegel, then head of news, worried if "we are really describing the country that voted for Ronald Reagan." The concern, that NPR was "too liberal" for its public, has been a constant and very productive anxiety. The pivot away from its liberal past has become a defining ritual, a reflexive response to each new crisis. Liberalism, always a difficult term to pin down, is in this ritual a floating signifier, unmoored to any fixed meaning. Liberalism is NPR's besetting sin, its origin story that no amount of atonement or pivoting or maturing can seem to redeem. And yet each fresh crisis brings new chances for redemption, for reinvention. Just as neo-liberalism feeds upon liberalism's liver all day long, only to see it regenerated overnight, so NPR endures round after round of "maturation" from its naïve origins in liberalism, only to encounter a new crisis.

It is impossible to separate the network from the stories it has told, and from the storytellers who lent those stories their trademark mix of gravitas and whimsy. Had the Public Broadcasting Act focused solely on public television, it is hard to imagine the soundscape of the American professional middle class over the last 40 years. What would all those car radios have been tuned to during all those hours of commuting? How would the experience of the crises of the past four decades, from Watergate to 9/11 to the economic crisis of 2008 have been different without coverage by *All Things Considered*? Trying to imagine the structure of feeling of the "most highly educated" citizens, "our educators, our mainline clergy, our writers, our artists, our high-tech workers, our social service providers, and our professionals" without the voices of

Susan Stamberg, Garrison Keillor, Terri Gross, Nina Totenberg, and Ira Glass is nearly unthinkable.[17]

That said, the unthinkable—professional middle-class life without public radio—is something we're asked to consider with surprising regularity, as public broadcasting is frequently taken hostage during congressional budget stand-offs. In the lull between these moments of legislative brinksmanship, NPR, the flagship institution for what is now a splintered and diverse array of distributors, producers, stations, and independent creators, has demonstrated a genius for creating its own existential crises of leadership, financial solvency, and philosophical orientation. Less apocalyptically, the ritual *noodging* of the member station on-air fundraising pledge drives often conjure a world without public radio, a reminder of the tenuousness of the revenue stream that powers the whole enterprise. Turning to listeners for financial support began with the 1984 "Drive to Survive," a watershed in NPR's pivot from public to private funding, about which more later.

The discourse of narrowly averted catastrophes and structural insecurity has been a crucial part of how NPR has been understood by journalists, policy makers, listeners, historians, and the network itself. At the same time, the network's growth and transformation into a more market-based organization with increasingly mainstream political instincts and up-market "listener-members" has been described by these same sources as a natural maturation, an inevitable process of "growing up." Anthropomorphic metaphors of public radio ("Our baby is born," its "painful wounds," its threatened "life") from public radio producers and historians map the clichés of physical and psychological development onto its story.[18] This convergence of narratives of crisis and evolution is key to the logic of neo-liberalism and to the remarkable, unstable success of public radio over the last 40 years. Nicols Fox's 1995 article "NPR Grows Up," reinforces this parable as does McCauley's emphasis on NPR's growing "voice," "body," and "soul."[19]

A general hostility to the vast political-cultural complex known as "the sixties" seems to be at the heart of some of the impatience which attends most accounts of the inevitability of NPR's maturation into something more politically, aesthetically, and organizationally conservative.[20] Confronted with the crises of the "real world," NPR resembles the proverbial liberal who, once mugged, becomes a conservative, older and more sensible. Nobody has limned the contours of the cultural and political shift better than Barbara Ehrenreich in her 1990 *Fear of Falling,* still the best account of the professional middle class shift to the right in the 1970s. The right-wing working-class reaction to the excesses of liberalism are, Ehrenreich argues, largely a fiction narrated by the New Class of media workers, as cover for their own rightward drift, middle-class anxiety, and ambivalent feelings toward the unstable politics of change that characterized "the sixties."

Indeed, from the perspective of the twenty-first century, there is something impossibly quaint about NPR's early years. The founding "Principles" for the network, articulated by Bill Siemering, its first president, sounds dated despite and because of its universalizing idealism:

> National Public Radio will serve the individual: it will promote personal growth; it will regard the individual differences among men with respect and joy rather than derision and hate; it will celebrate the human experience as infinitely varied rather than vacuous and banal; it will encourage a sense of active constructive participation, rather than apathetic helplessness.[21]

These principles betray the network's philosophical parentage: the individualism and pluralism that marked the overlapping logics of Cold War liberalism and Great Society optimism. These in turn sired the neo-liberal cult of "personal growth," an emergent meme in the therapeutic culture of the 1960s and 1970s and a key feature of NPR's appeal throughout its four-decade history. The high-flown idealism of this rhetoric, combined with the paltry funding from the CPB and the political upheaval of the early 1970s, meant that NPR began from an almost unsustainable position.[22] Also, the original mission to be an alternative service, a complement to mainstream journalism, clashed with the ambitions of the journalists who built the network into an increasingly professional and influential operation.[23] After four decades of economic boom and bust, each wave attended by market-based policy shifts, it is hard to imagine a cultural institution navigating this historical terrain and still retaining some notion of the public interest outside the confines of market rationality.

And from the other side of Watergate, the bombing of Cambodia, the oil crisis, and inflation, it is hard to imagine how the upstart network could have remained small, alternative, and committed to the values of joy, personal growth, and active constructive participation. As in the past, American crises got the media they deserved. And the news media got all the crises they could wish for. In the dominant narrative, NPR's programming evolved to tell the stories that were exploding around it, creating newer, larger audiences that required the network to re-conceptualize its audience and to re-calibrate its mixture of amateurish immediacy with its growing professionalism.

## Neo-Liberalism and the Shock Doctrine

> The history of the contemporary free market, best understood as the rise of corporatism—was written in shocks.[24]

In order to understand NPR's seemingly paradoxical history of crisis and growth, it is useful to think of the network as embodying—and giving voice to—some of the central political contradictions of its time. Born in 1970, NPR, like neo-liberalism, emerged from the ashes of the Great Society liberalism and matured during the following decades, "the long march of the Neoliberal Revolution," as Stuart Hall has dubbed the era."[25]

Straddling competing assumptions about public service, buffeted by partisan attacks, and chivvied by untenable funding formulas, public radio's struggles exemplify many of the challenges that beset liberal institutions starting in the 1970s. At the same time, public radio networks have embraced commercial approaches to marketing and audience research, new developments in satellite and digital technology, and entrepreneurial funding formulas; such innovations, efficiencies, and privatization schemes, of course, are exemplary of the neo-liberal "reforms" that mark this era.

Over the last 40 years, public radio has served as an expression of, a balm for, and an ideological state apparatus of the neo-liberal changes in the political economy and in social and cultural experience. Public radio programs, series, podcasts, and features from NPR, PRI, and American Public Media, like *All Things Considered, Morning Edition, Radio Lab, Planet Money, This American Life,* and *Marketplace* have shaped a distinctive style of storytelling, in tune with the interiority of the neo-liberal sensibility. The structure, tone, characters, and thematic preoccupations of these stories hail the modern neo-liberal subject, offering succor for "the ghastliness of life exhaustively ordered by the market and measured by market values."[26] At the same time, they provide a model of interiority, irony, and political quietism that corresponds with market rationalities and the exigencies of the neo-liberal subject.[27] The network's approach to fund-raising, audience research, technology, and news and cultural affairs programming exemplify many of the contradictions of neo-liberalism as a period of historical change, an ideology, and a structure of feeling.

Naomi Klein has identified the vital connection between the power of shock and the workings of neo-liberal policies at home and abroad, or "the intersection between superprofits and megadisasters." The metaphor of shock belongs to economist Milton Friedman, "the grand guru of the movement for unfettered capitalism." The unfettering of capitalism at home and abroad, along with an aggressive foreign policy, and a fresh contempt for human rights, are part of the "shock treatment" ushered in during the 1970s and continuing into the twenty-first century. "Only a crisis—actual or perceived—produces real change," enabling "the politically impossible to become the politically inevitable." Neo-liberal ideas that are already "lying around," come in handy at these pivotal moments of crisis, reasons Friedman.[28]

The Shock Doctrine is more than just a handy metaphor for understanding NPR's unlikely balancing act on the precipice of federal defunding, embarrassing lapses in leadership, and competing digital news and audio platforms. It is also a way to tune in to the neo-liberal logic that defunding critical public institutions can go from "politically impossible to politically inevitable" in the wake of a crisis. The process of NPR's privatization has had a *longue durée*, beginning with its creation as a public service with Great Society ambitions and austerity budgets. In 40 years, the politically inevitable solution of privatization has unfolded in a series of economic spasms within the network and political and cultural crises in the US. Modern public radio began in crisis and its growth from a marginal service to a truly national one is inextricably tied to its financial growing pains, technological change, and the neo-liberal logic that attended them.

## Air Superiority: NPR and Satellites

"We wouldn't do it that way now—and yet, we would," Linda Wertheimer remarks in 1995, looking back to *All Thing Considered*'s chaotic, gritty debut. Like the network itself, Wertheimer is keen to preserve the legacy of public radio's insurgent, immediate amateurism even as NPR becomes increasingly sophisticated, influential, and professional. Attempts to emphasize continuity at NPR often take the form of banal universals, like "telling stories," "a sense of connection and friendship with our listeners," terms that sound as if they've been cross-referenced with the psychographic profiles of their most coveted listeners.[29] In times of war, the pressure to describe the country in ways that harmonized with the increased patriotic rhetoric and diminished tolerance for dissent was often compelling.[30] Fox places the Gulf War's critical role in the network's growth into context:

> The Gulf War—like Watergate, Iran-Contra and Tiananmen Square— brought the news-hungry to a halt at the NPR signal. According to Arbitron, the war fattened its audience by 14 percent, inspiring NPR marketers to put out a T-shirt boasting "Air Superiority."[31]

Fox is not the first to attribute NPR's 1990s growth to its "air superiority" during the Gulf War, but he makes it clear that this is but one among many fortuitous crises for the network. National crises presented not just an increased audience for news per se, but a relative advantage for NPR compared to rival news sources. And in the case of the Gulf War, this in turn fostered a sense of identification at the network, not just with crisis, but with the militarization inherent in national crises and the role of the press in reporting them. This crucial slippage, between NPR and the nation it serves becomes most apparent in moments of national crisis, or in moments when the rhetoric of national crisis has been most successfully mobilized as part of a political movement.

The network's pioneering use of satellite technology was a key feature of its move into mainstream, big-time journalism and its eventual "air superiority" over its rivals. Public broadcasting was one of the early adopters of satellite technology in the 1970s and NPR was quick to ensure that it could "piggyback" on the advances made by its richer sibling, PBS. As early as 1975, NPR officials were anticipating the advantages that satellite uplinks and downlinks could bring the network. These advantages included multi-program distribution, improved sound, two-way transmission, and substantially lower rates for national distribution than with AT&T's telephone lines.[32]

Most crucially, satellite multiplexing enabled the segmentation of "audiences by age, religion, political orientation or race and ethnicity." As Russo and Kirkpatrick put it,

> discourses of taste, cultures, and audience preferences began to supplant ideals of a public interest at the same moment that centralized national satellite distribution began to offer the demographically distinctive programming that could sound local.[33]

While Russo and Kirkpatrick focus mainly on commercial broadcasting here, the changes wrought by satellite multiplexing had a similarly profound impact on NPR, an early adopter of the technology. By the 1990s, NPR found itself at the intersection of key changes wrought by satellite technology: cheap, high quality, live national distribution; audience segmentation, and "air superiority," with all that the phrase connotes in terms of the militarization of communications media in general and the news in particular. The collapsing distinctions between public interests and market forces, news coverage and military news briefs, smart coverage and smart bombs intensified with the first Gulf War and then again during the wars in the first decade of the twenty-first century.

## Private Funding for Public Radio

Unlike the national radio systems of nearly every other nation on earth, the US has looked to commercial funding to finance radio programming since the 1920s. The dearth of public funds for broadcasting and the domination of for-profit, commercially sponsored networks meant that the Federal Communications Commission (FCC) had to develop an elastic definition of its chartered mission, to serve "the public interest, convenience, and necessity." And the commercial networks in turn had to approximate a rhetoric of "civic ambition" to accommodate an essentially commercial public sphere of the air.[34] Non-profit stations, housed in churches, union halls, and universities, with a few exceptions, eked out a marginal existence during the Golden Age, using poor quality equipment, broadcasting from undesirable frequencies at obscure times of day. There was slow but sustained growth in the educational sector of broadcasting, but no dramatic transformations until the passage of the 1967 Public Broadcasting Act, which created the Corporation for Public Broadcasting (CPB) with a mandate to fund national radio and television services. Like the Public Broadcasting Service (PBS), the television arm of this new public initiative, National Public Radio drew upon annual grants from the CPB to fund its operations. The grants allowed only a very modest budget for NPR, which meant low salaries, a small staff, inferior technical equipment, and a premium on innovation. Live reports from the field emphasized serendipity, ambient sounds of the street, and the informal candor of its youthful reporters.[35]

After a series of restructurings, and a near-bankruptcy, the modern business model for public radio has come to rely on three politically and economically variable sources of revenue in roughly equal measure: voluntary donations from listener members, fees from underwriters in exchange for brief but frequent on-air acknowledgments, and grants from federal and state governments, universities, and private foundations. Because these sources are all vulnerable to the ups and downs of the larger economy, the formula does not diversify risk so much as it guarantees periodic "perfect storms" of funding shortfalls, as in December 2008 when NPR, citing the economic downturn, eliminated 7% of its workforce and cancelled two national programs, *Day to Day* and *News and Notes*, the network's lone program aimed at an African American audience.

Of these three sources of revenue, listener-membership has received the lion's share of the attention from the public radio networks, their star broadcasters, and their historians. Ira Glass, in his pitch for donations to support the podcast version of *This American Life* (which is produced by WBEZ and distributed by PRI) has called the fundraising model of US public radio "perfect." "It's the fairest way to fund anything: the people who like these stories and want them to exist, we pitch in a few bucks."[36] The system relies on seasonal fund-drives by the nearly 1,000 local public radio stations that carry NPR programming, in which the regular program schedule is interrupted and at times suspended altogether, so that local and national personalities can make their pitch to listeners to make a pledge of monetary support.[37]

Procuring large donations from corporations and charitable foundations became a focus of NPR during the presidency of Frank Mankiewicz, who took the helm in 1977 with the goal of "weaning" the network off federal funds. Importantly, this idea for reorganizing the funding for public radio did not originate with Mankiewicz; it had been "lying around" at NPR since at least 1975, only 4 years after the debut of *All Things Considered*. Mankiewicz, however, was able to produce the necessary crisis. Taking a page from Friedman's playbook, Mankiewicz spent the network into a $10 million budget hole, bringing it to the brink of bankruptcy.[38]

The crisis led to Mankiewicz's departure and precipitated a major restructuring of the network's relationship to federal funding. In exchange for a loan that would keep NPR on the air, the network agreed to a radical shift: the CPB would hereafter give funds directly to the member stations around the country who would then use those funds to purchase programming from NPR—as well as from other producers and distributors of public radio programming. Instead of drawing public funds to produce content in the public interest, NPR was now in competition with other vendors to provide a product to myriad local customers. The new funding formula also "freed up" the network to seek other forms of revenue: corporate underwriting and foundation support now that its finances were not so directly tied to public funds. Member stations found their annual grants from the CPB to be insufficient to cover the cost of buying programs and running local operations and increasingly turned to listener donations and local underwriting. This move away from direct government funding of NPR didn't insulate the network from political crises, charges of liberalism, demands for further reductions in funds to public radio, and so on. As the "Save NPR" email story suggests, it merely whetted the appetite for further cuts.

## Listener-Members

This new model—looking to listeners and corporate funders as the main source of revenue—shaped and was shaped by the shift in meaning and status of the notion of "the public interest." The notion of the "listener-member" is itself a historical construction pointing in the direction of a neo-liberal model of citizen-subject as consumer. The listener-member is the product of decades of audience research pioneered by David Giovannoni as early as 1979, when he began working on psychographic models of public radio's most ardent listeners. In McCauley's admiring account, the refinements in audience research under Giovannoni enabled NPR to shed the vestiges of its "alternative" "progressive," "leftist" past and embrace the science of "mining [the] private funds of the listeners."[39]

The rhetoric of crisis also figures in McCauley's description of NPR's listeners. Public radio's natural core audience, says McCauley, is composed of aging baby boomers whose "mythical American dream" was "shattered" when the post-war economic boom in the 1970s "came to a crashing halt." NPR hailed an audience in the throes of a generational, economic crisis, Americans whose "sense of control and direction" had been "destroyed." McCauley describes the core audience for public radio as "highly educated baby boomers, who could easily have been mistaken, at some point in their lives, for cast members of the ABC television series, *thirtysomething*." This point of reference marks McCauley's book as dated, not (only) because that television program is no longer current, but because the caricature of the liberal, educated NPR listener has become, in the 10 years since his book's publication, at least as iconic as *thirtysomething* ever was, and needs no such analogies by way of introduction. But McCauley's sense of impending danger is as timely today as ever: "America's public radio system must, *as a matter of survival*, focus its programming and fundraising efforts on the highly educated thirtysomething (now fiftysomething) audience that covets its programs most."[40] Thus public radio and its (now sixtysomething) audience find themselves joined together in complementary crises: shattered baby boomers turn to NPR in search of their lost "values" and public radio turns to highly educated boomers as listeners and as a source of scarce vital funds.

Public radio's embrace of audience research was key to its growing success in the last two decades of the twentieth century. Mining the private funds of

listeners requires attracting and keeping a set of listeners for whom the programming is meaningful. The consequences of this move—constructing and
then courting the ideal listener-member—have been dramatic for public radio's
sound and its structure of feeling. Audience researchers felt strongly that only
listeners who tuned in continuously throughout the day would make the generous donations necessary for a sustainable revenue stream.[41] For listeners to
become listener-members, a more-or-less unbroken flow of constant listening,
all day long was necessary. Likewise, corporate underwriters were more eager
to reach a stable, homogenous audience of loyal listener-members, especially
one that was skewed more to the educated and thus affluent. All these factors
militated for ever-finer audience profiles, ever-smoother programming flows,
and a narrower, more predictable sonic footprint. This audience had to be
reached not just as listeners but as "members," members of a community organized around an ambivalent but intense set of identities.

This logic, begun at the network level, soon trickled down to newly
empowered local affiliates. "Each station," according to McCauley, "could
strengthen its long-term viability by reaching out to a particular set of listeners
with a schedule of programs that spoke clearly to their values and needs."[42] The
move towards a more narrowly defined audience and a more predictable sound
echoed changes in FM music formats throughout the 1970s, as free-form rock
stations transformed into Album Oriented Rock, Classic Rock, and myriad
other micro-formats, with smaller playlists, increased emphasis on hits, and the
promise of a narrower demographic to offer to advertisers.

These listeners, who were recovering from the "shattering" disappointments
of the 1970s, required programming perched on the contradictions at the heart
of the neo-liberal structure of feeling. In order to maintain such a flow, programming needs to be consistent in tone, content, and in its psychographic orientation to those who are both "interested in social responsibility" and "likely
to continue purchasing."[43] This prescription turns out to be perfectly consistent
with the contradictions in the structure of feeling wrought by the neo-liberal
turn: a public radio service "that focused *on* the societally conscious, not a service that *was* societally conscious."[44] McCauley makes a similar point: "NPR
airs many stories *about* these [socially marginal] groups, phrased in a manner
that speaks to the sensibilities of its core listeners," that is to say, the socially
powerful *thirtysomething* folks (emphasis added, 112).

For Mitchell, this coveted audience can be broadly defined around their
social commitments as well as by their occupations:

> They work in government. They volunteer their time and talents for
> political and social causes. They care about their communities, the envi-
> ronment, and the well-being of our planet and its inhabitants. (3)

And while listeners are defined here in terms of values and community
work, rather than in terms of its income and consumption habits, the task of

psychographic research is to link the two. NPR has, most recently, chopped up its listeners into groups with names like "Team Captains," "Voracious Voyagers," and "Dutiful Aggregators," terms meant to capture the values, traits, and habits that they bring to listening, work, and of course, shopping.[45]

In the era of modern public radio, a curious logic of equivalences dominates the relationship between broadcasters and audience. McCauley puts it most starkly: "NPR news is made by people like me for people like me."[46] Mitchell, founding producer of *All Things Considered*, and historian of NPR, concurs: "the listeners we attracted were pretty much like us." The notion of NPR as a refuge for the "highly educated," "socially conscious," and idealistic listener performs an impressively efficient bit of cultural work, flattering listeners and their *dopplegängers* at the network, while attracting the up-market corporate and foundation underwriting business eager to get their messages to this demographic.

Listener-membership under these circumstances, implies a sense of partnership, one might even say "active constructive participation," on behalf of the listener with regards to the network. Such a tight sense of identity between listener and network is a critical factor in the success of membership drives, in the high regard with which listeners hold the underwriters, and in the self-consciousness with which public radio has responded to criticism. It also speaks to the self-preserving logic that Ehrenreich identifies in the conservative turn of the new class of media professionals, who invent and hail an audience who shares their interests.

## Twenty-First Century NPR

In a new century that began with an uncertain presidential election; an unprecedented attack on the homeland; two long costly wars; the devastation of the Gulf Coast by hurricanes, failed levees, and a massive oil spill; and the global economic crisis precipitated by failures of US financial institutions, NPR has won praise for the depth and breadth of its coverage. It has opened more foreign bureaus in this period, embedded more journalists with armed forces in war zones, and reaped more journalism awards. Its portion of the news media market has ballooned. It has also seen an intensification of the debates about its political bias, its leadership, and the sustainability of its public funding. Since 2000, calls to slash federal funding to NPR, PBS, and other federally funded cultural institutions, like the NEA and NEH have come thick and fast.

In 2010, the new president of NPR, Vivian Schiller enthused about "creative destruction" that was currently taking hold of the traditional news media. She had in mind the blossoming of online-only newspapers, and multi-platform initiatives, like NPR's web and mobile innovations.[47] After a right-wing ambush of an NPR fundraiser had been videotaped, misleadingly edited, and leaked to the press, Schiller was forced out by the network's board and by the very forces she had celebrated less than a year prior. Schiller's departure came hard on the heels of Ellen Weiss's 2011 resignation as vice president for news fallout from the damaging firing of longtime NPR commentator, host, and reporter Juan Williams. In October, 2011, NPR's coverage of the Occupy Wall Street movement was overshadowed by the clumsy firing of Lisa Simeone, host of *Soundprint*, a documentary show carried on NPR affiliate stations. Shortly thereafter, NPR stopped distributing *World of Opera*, an independently pro-duced program that Simeone also hosts. In a climate of intensified rhetoric of catastrophe via federal spending, these mostly self-inflicted wounds were attended by gleeful and increasingly credible threats from Republicans in the Congress to cut all federal funding. NPR entered its fifth decade of operation appearing to be not just crisis-prone, but a mechanism engineered for produc-ing crisis.

But these crises seem to have worked the familiar paradoxical magic, galva-nizing support for NPR, while providing handy cover for new calls for further privatization, further retreat from critical engagement with political contro-versy, and other reforms completely in keeping with the creative destruction model. Schiller, now at NBC News, has suggested that NPR "wean itself from" public funds in order to shed its vulnerability to further political attacks, another pivot in an endless dance of Pyrrhic victories for public radio's public-ness.[48] In its management of personnel crises and in its reporting on national crises, the move away from a supposed liberal past has proven to be a produc-tive, almost inevitable ritual. Signs of this ritual pivoting away from liberalism at a moment of danger appear in other public radio programming as well. NPR news has, in its eagerness to tell the nation a version of itself that reflects its vot-ing habits tended, naturally, to support administration policies on war, torture, and diplomacy.[49]

Nowhere has the logic of these shifts crystallized as clearly than in new programming like *Planet Money*, a collaboration between NPR News and *This American Life*, public radio's ranking heavyweights in gravitas and whimsy, respectively. Perhaps no phrase better captures the spirit of neo-liberalism, a system under which "all dimensions of human life are cast in terms of a market rationality," than *Planet Money*. Like *Marketplace* ("The business show for the rest of us"), *Marketplace Money,* and *All Things Considered* (with its perseveration on the daily ups and downs of the markets), *Planet Money* targets an audience trying to square its "socially conscious" values with its upscale habitus and political complaisance.

*Planet Money* has become a popular and influential podcast in its own right after having been incorporated into many of the episodes of *This American Life* in the months following the financial collapse of late 2008. The program, which describes itself as "a multimedia team covering the global economy," was also an opportunity for *This American Life* to move beyond the familiar territory of personal narratives, gothic family dramas, and other explorations of interior landscapes of the human heart and take on journalistic assignments more connected to the broader world of economics, politics, and policy. The collapse of the housing market, the banking crisis, and the 2008 presidential election contributed to a sense of urgency about these matters. *Planet Money*'s blend of storytelling and reporting, empathy and hip insouciance—potent extracts of the paired opposites that drive the programming of NPR news and *This American Life*—strikes just the right tone for unraveling the knotty confusion of the nation's financial problems in a way that avoids any criticism of the tenets of capitalism.

On the one hand, the concept of *Planet Money*, like that of *Marketplace*, represents the democratic idea that complex financial issues should be made plain to the public. And on the other hand, the individual programs often embrace the neo-liberal principles that flexibility, private enterprise, and efficiency are the best tools to build economic growth, fight poverty, etc. The short programs take on a single problem, often framed in terms that make clear the neo-liberal agenda: why is business so slow in India? Too much bureaucracy ("In Search of the Red Tape Factory," 2010).[50] Why hasn't Haiti managed to thrive despite the outpouring of do-gooder efforts there for decades? Not enough entrepreneurship ("Island Time" 2010). Such framing questions effectively remove from consideration any analysis that doesn't start and end in neo-liberal models of success through growth, privatization, and so on. In 2009, Adam Davidson, a member of the *Planet Money* "team" was forced to apologize for an aggressive, disrespectful interview with Wall Street critic and reformer Elizabeth Warren, which some listeners felt was diametrically opposite in tone from his "more deferential" interview with Secretary of the Treasury, Timothy Geithner.[51] His "tough" approach to Warren, at the time one of the leading liberal figures in bank reform (and now a US senator), and his general pro-market views on *Planet Money* were rewarded in 2011 with a plum columnist gig for the *New York Times Magazine* where he has published on such topics as "What Does Wall Street Do For You?"(The answer: a lot).[52] In identifying the "real victims of the LIBOR [banking] scandal" (2012), the *Planet Money* "team" equivocates: "we may never know," and minimizes: "the changes were small."[53]

In an episode of *Planet Money* devoted entirely to General Motors' early experimentation with Japanese industrial methods in the 1980s, the poor quality, low morale, and contentious labor relations are laid, for the most part, at the feet of the United Auto Workers and their surly, corrupt, and even reckless approach to their work. The hidebound corporate culture of the company comes in for a much smaller share of the criticism. The solution promised by the Japanese and modeled in its Nummi auto plant in Texas, is an intense worker loyalty to and pride in the corporation and its brands.[54] While this may not, in itself, be an unhelpful insight, it is clearly one that privileges a corporate, profit-based perspective rather than one dedicated to the welfare of workers, consumers, or the environment, three concerns central to the liberal agenda that NPR is perpetually pivoting away from. If disembedding capital from social and political constraints is the project of neo-liberalism, then—in these episodes—*Planet Money* seems bent on identifying the cultural constraints that have reined in capitalism.

If *Planet Money* represents the fullest flowering to date of public radio's neo-liberal turn, it is also true that public radio contains multitudes. It is in its very ambivalence, its un-pin-down-ability, that it has been able to simultaneously represent lost liberal values and their demise. We can even see a bit of this on *Planet Money* itself, where muckraking journalism occasionally ferrets out an especially egregious villain in the world of high finance or where a Dickensian contrast between partying mortgage dealers and underwater homeowners gesture toward the yawning gap between haves and have nots in the neo-liberal order.[55]

## Conclusion

I close with one oblique metaphor for NPR's accommodation to, and rationale for, neo-liberal experience at its most mundane and compelling: *the driveway moment*, in which the network imagines its audience spellbound by the act of listening. This, it should be said, is a conceit that thousands of listeners have been only too willing to authorize, with rhapsodic letters and emails to the producers and station managers thanking them for their specific "driveway moment." There is, of course, a series of CDs by this name available at "The NPR Shop." This conceit provides a model of privatized reception in which 27 million listeners in 27 million cars, listen in their driveways, at the end of their long commutes from professional managerial jobs that provide enough disposable income to make generous annual membership donations and to appeal to up-market underwriters.

Lingering in the driveway, prolonging the liminal space/time of driving between work and home, the archetypal NPR listeners, Team Captains, Voracious Voyagers, and Dutiful Aggregators alike, are caught up in the matrix of narrative, solitude, and dashboard, heeding the imperative to "only connect" by sitting alone in a car. This spell of non-productive pleasure, and the sense of time stolen from economic functions and domestic intimacies, is different from the vigilant monitorial reception of the citizen tuned in to an unfolding national crisis. This is reception as balm, reception as escape. Human connection, through narrative, through the gorgeously modulated voices of NPR reporters and hosts are figured in network promotions and listener testimonials as intensely *private goods*. Private listening creates the conditions for fleeting moments of empathy, a seeming luxury in times of budget austerity, cascading crises, and the neoliberal turn inward.

Even so. The last dozen years, September 11, two grueling wars, the devastation of New Orleans, and the near collapse of the economy have reinforced the importance of radio—public radio in particular—in moments of crisis. If not to model empathy as a form of public practice, then at least to bear witness to something that is happening, to make an event in the most literal terms a public one: in the case of Hurricanes Katrina and Rita in New Orleans in 2005, and Hurricane Sandy in the northeast in 2012, local community stations were sometimes the only source of information in communities devastated by floods and, prior to that, by the zombie apocalypse of corporate-run, remotely operated commercial radio stations. And if the larger lessons that NPR draws from these crises conform to Klein's Shock Doctrine, then at least for a moment, the shared ritual of listening, even in our own driveways, reminds us at moments when it is most tenuous, that something called society still exists, that public radio, like Big Bird and the post office, is worth saving.

## Notes

1. Quoted in Naomi Klein, *The Shock Doctrine: The Rise of Disaster Capitalism* (New York: Picador, 2007), xx.
2. *Broadcasting*, November 12, 1973, 26–32.
3. http://www.snopes.com/politics/arts/nea.asp, accessed July 9, 2012.
4. http://www.gallup.com/poll/155585/Americans-Confidence-Television-News-Drops-New-Low.aspx?utm_source=alert&utm_medium=email&utm_campaign=syndication&utm_content=morelink&utm_term=Politics, accessed July 10, 2012.
5. J. L. Austin, *How to Do Things with Words* (Oxford: Clarendon Press, 1962), 5.
6. Daniel J. Czitrom, *Media and the American Mind: From Morse to McLuhan* (Durham: University of North Carolina Press, 1982), 184.
7. Credit for this useful pun goes to Judith Butler and Gayatri Chakravorty Spivak's *Who Sings the Nation-State? Language, Politics, Belonging* (London: Seagull Books, 2007), 3–4.
8. Edward Miller, *Emergency Broadcasting and 1930s American Radio* (Philadelphia: Temple University Press, 2002), 78–79; Jason Loviglio, *Radio's Intimate Public: Network Broadcasting and Mass-Mediated Democracy* (Minneapolis: University of Minnesota Press, 2005), 18–20.
9. Todd Gitlin, *The Whole World is Watching: Mass Media in the Making and Unmaking of the New Left* (Berkeley: University of California Press, 1980).
10. http://www.npr.org/programs/atc/atc30/timeline/index.html, accessed July 9, 2012; see also Susan J. Douglas's account of this debut broadcast in *Listening In: Radio and the American Imagination* (New York: Times Books, 1999), 321–322.
11. It is beyond the scope of this chapter to fully engage the arguments about NPR's perceived liberal bias. However, this matter has been taken up elsewhere: Jeffrey A. Dvorkin, "NPR In 1988: 'News That Soothes.'" NPR.org (2005); Tim Groseclose and Jeffrey Milyo, "A Measure of Media Bias," *The Quarterly Journal of Economics* 120, no. 4 (2005), 1191–1237; Norman Solomon, "NPR and the Fallow Triumph of Public Radio," Alternet.org. April 11, 2002, accessed February 2, 2012.
12. Nicols Fox, "NPR Grows Up." *American Journalism Review* (September, 1991), 30–36.
13. Elisia L. Cohen, "One Nation Under Radio: Digital and Public Memory after September 11," *New Media & Society* 6 (October 2004), 591–610.
14. "Change in Audience Since 1998," http://www.npr.org/blogs/gofigure/2010/05/13/126801256/broadcast-audience-gains-a-rare-story-for-news-media, accessed December 5, 2012.
15. Jack W. Mitchell, *Listener Supported: The Culture and History of Public Radio* (Westport, CT:

Praeger, 2005), 36–37, 82. See also, Michael McCauley, *NPR: The Trials and Triumphs of National Public Radio* (New York: Columbia University Press, 2005), 21–22, 40.

16. Susan Stamberg, "Introduction: In the Beginning, There Was Sound but No Chairs," in *This is NPR: The First Forty Years* (San Francisco: Chronicle Books, 2011), 15. "NPR's Frischknect: Don't Look Back," *Broadcasting,* January 17, 1977, 65.

17. Jack W. Mitchell, *Listener Supported*, 3.

18. McCauley, *NPR*, 8, 29.

19. McCauley, *NPR,* 4, 8, 29, 33, 35.

20. See esp. McCauley, 2, 110–113.

21. Jack Mitchell, *Listener Supported: The Culture and History of Public Radio* (New York: Praeger, 2005), 55.

22. *Broadcasting*, November 12, 1973, 26–32.

23. See Siemering on NPR's alternative, complementary mission, "NPR's Frischknect: Don't Look Back," *Broadcasting,* January 17, 1977, 65. On the tension between old and new guards at NPR in the 1980s, see McCauley, *NPR*, 82–83; and Mitchell, *Listener Supported*, 90–91.

24. Naomi Klein, *The Shock Doctrine*, 23.

25. Stuart Hall, "The March of the Neoliberals," *The Guardian*, September 12, 2011, 10.

26. Wendy Brown, "Neoliberalism and the End of Liberal Democracy," in *Edgework: Critical Essays on Knowledge and Politics* (Princeton, NJ: Princeton University Press, 2005), 46.

27. For more on NPR's and *This American Life*'s portrayal of a neoliberal structure of feeling, see Jason Loviglio, "Public Radio, This American Life and the Neoliberal Turn," in *A Moment of Danger: Critical Studies in the History of U.S. Communication Since World War II*, ed. Janice Peck and Inger Stole (Milwaukee, WI: Marquette University Press, 2011); Jason Loviglio, "U.S. Public Radio, Social Change, and the Gendered Voice," in *Electrified Voices*, ed. Dmitri Sakharine (Gottingen, Germany: Vandenhoek & Ruprecht Unipress, 2012).

28. Klein, *The Shock Doctrine,* 10, 5, 7.

29. Susan Stamberg, *Talk: NPR's Susan Stamberg Considers All Things* (New York: Perigee Books, 1993), xiii; Stamberg, *This Is NPR: The First Forty Years* (San Francisco: Chronicle Books, 2011), 9–35.

30. Norman Solomon, "Spinning War and Blotting out Memory," in *War, Media and Propaganda; A Global Perspective*, ed. Yahya R. Kamalipour and Nancy Snow (Lanham, MD: Rowman and Littlefield, 2004), 47–58; Susan D. Moeller, *Media Coverage of Weapons of Mass Destruction* (College Park, MD: Center for International and Security Studies, March 9, 2004); Neil de Mause, "NPR Gives Torture Credibility: Report Treats Torture-Based Confessions As News," Mediamatters.org. October 10, 2007, accessed February 12, 2012; Jim Naureckas, "NPR Disappears Iraqi Dead," *Extra!* (New York: Fairness and Accuracy in Reporting, May/June, 2008); Steve Rendall and Daniel Butterworth. "How Public is Public Radio? A Study of NPR's Guest List," *Extra!* (New York: Fairness and Accuracy in Reporting, May/June, 2004).

31. Fox, "NPR Grows Up."

32. *Broadcasting*, January 19, 1976, 47; Russo and Kirkpatrick, *Down to Earth; Satellite Technologies, Industries, and Culture* (Piscataway, NJ: Rutgers University Press, 2012), 158; see footnote 28.

33. Russo and Kirkpatrick, 164.

34. David Goodman, *Radio's Civic Ambition: American Broadcasting and Democracy in the 1930s* (New York: Oxford University Press, 2011).

35. Douglas, *Listening In*, 320–327; Mitchell, *Listener Supported,* 67–73; Stamberg, *This Is NPR*, 9–35.

36. http://www.thisamericanlife.org/blog/2011/12/please-donate-now-to-support-the-show, accessed September 20, 2012.

37. http://www.npr.org/about/aboutnpr/audience.html

38. http://www.americanradiohistory.com/Archive-BC-IDX/75-OCR/1975-04-07-BC-0092.pdf#search="npr"

39. McCauley, *NPR*, 9.
40. McCauley, *NPR*, 5.
41. McCauley, *NPR*, 79–81; Mitchell, *Listener Supported*, 95, 133–134, 146–148.
42. McCauley, 9.
43. http://www.wqub.org/media/NPR%20Profile%20stats%202009/values%20attitudes. pdf; see also, http://www.npr.org/blogs/gofigure/2010/04/13/125900055/what-public-radio-listeners-think-and-believe
44. Emphasis added. Mitchell, *Listener Supported*, 184.
45. "Audience Opportunity Study, Summary of Key Takeaways" (Westlake Village, CA: Smith Geiger, 2010); *Public Radio Today, 2010: How American Listens to Radio* (New York: Arbitron, 2010).
46. "Like our listeners, we were intelligent, interested and curious people," McCauley, *NPR*, 114.
47. Kara Swisher, "Why Online Won't Kill the Radio Star," *The Wall Street Journal*, June 7, 2010, http://online.wsj.com/article/SB10001424052748704764404575287070721094884. html, accessed September 12, 2012.
48. "NPR's Problem With Money, 'Ownership,' and 'Politicalization,'" Beet.TV, March 24, 2012, http://www.beet.tv/2012/03/schillernpr.htmlTV, accessed on September 12, 2012.
49. David Dadge, *The War in Iraq and Why the Media Failed Us* (New York: Praeger, 2006); Neil deMause, "NPR Gives Torture Credibility: Report Treats Torture-Based Confessions as News," Media Matters.org. October 7, 2010, accessed Sept 12, 2012; Jim Naureckas, "NPR Disappears Iraqi Dead," *Extra!* (New York: Fairness and Accuracy in Reporting, May/June 2008); Steve Rendall and Daniel Butterworth, "How Public is Public Radio? A Study of NPR's Guest List," *Extra!* (New York: Fairness and Accuracy in Reporting, May/June 2004).
50. http://www.npr.org/blogs/money/2010/04/the_tuesday_podcast_in_search.html
51. http://www.npr.org/blogs/globalpoolofmoney/images/2009/05/podcast05.11.09.mp3
52. http://www.nytimes.com/2012/01/15/magazine/what-does-wall-street-do-for-you.html
53. http://www.npr.org/blogs/money/2012/07/09/156484153/identifying-the-real-victims-in-the-libor-scandal?sc=tw&cc=share
54. "Nummi," #403, 2010.
55. "Inside Job," #405, 2010; "The Giant Pool of Money, #355, 2008.

# 3

# THE NEW MATERIALITY OF RADIO

## Sound on Screens[1]

*Michele Hilmes*

A decade ago, at a radio conference held in Madison, Wisconsin, the question on everyone's lips was "what is the future of radio?" Clearly some kind of transition was in progress, but it was hard to see the way forward in the face of the enormous consolidation and conglomeration occurring in the radio business, the continued dominance of satellite-delivered music formats, and the decline of that traditional backbone of US radio broadcasting, the local station.[2] In 2003, online streaming had become widespread, peer-to-peer file sharing was rocking the music business, and low-cost digital tools for audio production were in the hands of a growing segment of the tech-savvy, but the outlook for radio as we knew it remained unclear. Radio's death was predicted as often as its survival, as the individualized listening experience of iPods, earphones, and playlists seemed poised to replace everything that had most endeared radio to its public as a live, shared medium over the previous eighty years.

Many uncertainties remain, but clearly the tide has shifted. "What *isn't* radio today?" more accurately sums up the current situation, pointing to the sense of exploding categories and expanding possibilities that the new digital sound environment has loosed upon us. Radio's present era is marked by a transformative new materiality, as digital platforms finally overcome the ephemerality that once made radio so hard to capture and assess as a cultural form; a new mobility, as radio moves across devices and into new spaces; and by a new globalism, as digital accessibility unleashes radio and extends it well beyond its former local and national boundaries. Radio has not only survived but revived, both as a creative medium and as a shared cultural experience.

So, what is radio, as I'll be using the term here? No longer constrained by the technologies, institutions, and practices of the pre-digital era, radio must now be understood as *soundwork:*[3] the entire complex of sound-based digital media that enters our experience though a variety of technologies and forms. Today radio is a screen medium: we access it through screens both mobile and static, using tactile visual and textual interfaces. Through screens we listen to soundwork both streamed and podcast, enjoying its programs live and listening again later, creating our own "radio" through playlists and algorithms. Radio crosses platforms: no longer confined to specialized receivers, it is experienced via headphones and computer speakers, on digital players, television sets, phones, and tablets; in our cars, on the subway, at the gym, walking down the street. Thanks to the variety of digital platforms and practices developed by professionals and amateurs alike, radio's archive has opened up for enjoyment and analysis as never before, as far back as the first golden age of network broadcasting but also including the previously largely inaccessible soundwork of last week, or last month, or last year.

Radio is still about music, yes, though music no longer confines itself to its former definitions and devices either; it too has become a screen-based medium. But radio is also comprised of comedy podcasts, archived discussion programs, time-shifted voice tracking, public radio newsmagazines, short and long-form audio documentaries, curatorial sites, interactive audio drama, sound installations, audio tours of urban spaces, audiobooks with or without musical soundtracks, historic sound events posted on YouTube, spoken word collections, nostalgic broadcasts of old-time radio, audio collectors' online offerings, and the hundreds of audio apps available for iPhones and tablets. To claim all these previously unconnected elements of the soundscape as "radio" would in the past have seemed ridiculous overreaching, since they derived from such different sources. Now that they have all come together on digital platforms they clearly emerge as diverse aspects of a sonic cultural landscape whose commonalities we can at last see plainly.

Radio is the art of sound. This is the title Rudolph Arnheim gave his groundbreaking study back in 1936, and his exploration of sound's protean capacities under the rubric "radio" is what prompts my appropriation of the term to cover contemporary sound's expanded universe.[4] This chapter is a preliminary attempt to limn the contours of radio's new wave, tracing its struggles with ephemerality and negotiations with materiality over time. This leads to a discussion of the implications of thinking about radio as a screen medium as well as an overview of some of the innovative programs and initiatives brought about by radio's intersection with the digital, particularly in the fields of public radio and independent sound production.

## The New Materiality of Radio

One of radio's earliest creative geniuses, the BBC's Lance Sieveking, began his 1934 book *The Stuff of Radio* with a section titled "Ghastly Impermanence of the Medium."[5] Perhaps no one is more entitled to bemoan early radio's ephemerality than Sieveking. Though he produced hundreds of original radio compositions, many of them highly experimental montages of live and recorded sound mixed through a specially designed "dramatic control board" and transmitted live over the BBC network, few were recorded and none survive.[6] For his twenty years of innovative work, only a few scripts, scrapbooks of sketches and clippings, and his long out-of-print book remain: the rest is silence. This was the fate of the bulk of radio production until the mid-1930s, and it echoes the many aspects of sound's persistent ephemerality that kept creative soundwork in a secondary cultural position through much of its history. A brief overview of radio's contested relationship with recording demonstrates how significantly sound's new digital materiality has revolutionized the ways in which soundwork is produced, distributed, presented, and preserved over space and time, leading the way into a discussion of some of the new practices that digital materiality has enabled over the last decade.

Though the BBC began to make use of recorded programs in its Empire Service in the early 1930s—long before broadcasters in the US, where the use of recordings on the air was strongly discouraged by regulation[7]—the limitations of early recording technologies placed severe restrictions on the production and preservation of broadcast texts. An art of live studio production emerged in radio in the 1920s that, for both technological and regulatory reasons, used recorded sound very sparingly.[8] The bulkiness and fragility of disc recorders in the 1930s and early 40s, combined with discs' very short playing time, meant that capturing and preserving actuality sound was well-nigh impossible. Furthermore, such recordings could not be edited. Studio producers of radio's "golden age" combined live music and performance with sound effects (mostly produced live but sometimes recorded), mixed through a control board much as Sieveking had done, and transmitted live. Shows like *The March of Time,* the closest thing to news coverage during this period, made an art of re-creating world events for the ear, from the speeches of politicians (re-enacted by a stable of impersonating actors) to sports events, to human interest stories, dramatized and performed live in the studio.

Once produced and transmitted, few programs were recorded (more typically, they might be re-performed for subsequent live broadcasts). Only the most historically or economically important broadcasts were preserved on transcription discs by radio networks and producers until the late 1930s, and despite the size of these discs only 15 minutes of programming could be captured per side.[9] Wire recorders remained bulky and problematic through the early 1940s, though they became increasingly important to BBC World Service output during the war years. A few broadcasters experimented with sound-on-film devices, too, most notably the Phillips-Miller recording system, which used 16mm film coated with gelatin and an opaque layer into which sound waves were etched with a sapphire needle. It could be played back without optical development, and allowed a certain amount of editing to be done before re-recording on disc. The advantage of this system was that up to an hour of programming could be captured on a single reel of film; it was particularly useful for lengthy speeches, or for classical music programs.[10]

Though commercial companies began to syndicate radio programs on transcription disc in the late 1930s, and the practice was developed even further by the Armed Forces Radio Service during World War II, it was not until magnetic tape recording emerged from the spoils of war in the late 1940s[11] that sound could be more easily collected and edited, and radio programs could be reliably and relatively cheaply preserved for later reference and use. However, with the debut of television at precisely this time, both audiences and home-based entertainment began a rapid shift over to that new medium (in the US, particularly), which quickly went through its own evolution from live broadcast to filmed commodity form.

In the United States, radio de-nationalized and transformed itself into a local medium for music presentation in the 1950s, drawing on a developing music industry revitalized by new durable and long-playing recording formats (the vinyl LP and 45) and studio recording techniques that allowed multi-track mixing and new creative production practices. The small remainder of radio that was not music—such as DJ patter, news, a few public affairs or educational shows—remained live, with little effort made to archive any of its staggering number of hours of output.[12] Non-music or "spoken word" recording, though it grew through the 1960s and 70s, made up only a tiny fraction of commercial record sales, dominated by comedy, poetry, and religious sermons, marketed in a special section at your neighborhood record store.[13]

Under these circumstances, radio as a creative, vital form in its own right merited Fred Allen's gloomy summary: "Radio is the only medium that died before it was born." Yet he spoke too soon, at a low point in the production of creative soundwork in the US (though a high point in the emergence of popular music, enabled by radio). The advent of National Public Radio in 1970 began turning the tide of soundwork's cultural invisibility, as its member stations debuted high-profile national newsmagazines and a variety of national and regional programs through the 1970s and 80s. Though the primary emphasis remained on news and public affairs programming, NPR's parent, the Corporation for Public Broadcasting, funded several significant experiments in programming.

One of these was Wisconsin Public Radio's nationally distributed *Earplay*, an anthology drama series launched in 1972 focused on original works by famous playwrights such as Edward Albee, Archibald MacLeish, and David Mamet; another was an ambitious adaptation of *Star Wars* for radio in 1981.[14] However, as Jack Mitchell states, "Although critically successful, *Earplay* did not attract audiences and did not revive radio drama," and as for *Star Wars*, "It probably introduced some new listeners to NPR, but its long-term impact was minimal."[15] Long-form documentary production lagged behind as well, in an NPR schedule focused on its national news magazine program *All Things Considered* above all else. As Mitchell points out, "Public radio, like all radio, builds audience through loyalty, which means giving listeners relatively consistent service 365 days a year, rather than half-hour events heard once a week for thirteen weeks and then disappearing."[16] Listeners expected continuous flow, not unique events to which, once missed, they could not return.

Through the mid-1990s, radio's problem remained its intractable immateriality: the "ghastly impermanence" no longer of live production, in this era of tape recording, but of what we might call "live listening," based on the lack of any kind of permanent visible and material record of radio's presence aside from the numbers on the radio dial. Soundwork no longer needed to be produced live, but it was distributed live and received live. Radio had no theater marquee, no headlines on display at the newsstand, no TV Guide; though its invisible signals might saturate the atmosphere all around, they could not be lastingly perceived or returned to. One way that early network radio had coped with this ephemerality was its insistence on seriality: radio programs were produced as long-running series, scheduled at the same day and time each week, substituting predictability for tangibility, repetition for materiality. Music radio formats replaced seriality with the regularity of the musical clock, a cyclical schedule of constantly repeating playlists, leading listeners to the purchase of records as the material commodity of the radio form.

Early public radio, dedicated to long-form programs, struggled with this problem. If you joined your public radio station you might receive a monthly program guide which, if you could find it as you listened in your car or bathroom or office, might allow program recognition to develop. This was about the best that long-form radio could do, and it wasn't enough; non-music radio audiences grew slowly in the 1970s, reaching only about 3% of the listening audience. As radio listening became more mobile, through transistor technology and then the 1980s Sony Walkman, the immateriality problem became even more acute.[17] Radio simply could not be preserved, archived, accessed, and shared in a viable way, despite the culture of old-time radio enthusiasts who developed extensive lending libraries of audiocassette recordings during these decades. Locating and listening to long-form radio was an arduous and arcane proposition through the mid-1990s. Once missed, a program could not be heard again; titles and credits were announced once or twice and then lost to memory; complex and tightly constructed soundworks passed rapidly before the ears and vanished, never to be heard again. Under these conditions, a coherent and sustainable sound culture simply could not develop.[18]

When digital platforms emerged in the late 1990s, radio stations of all kinds were quick to see their potential. Finally, radio might acquire a material interface to present to the world, a permanent marker of its presence as well as an alternative delivery system. Internet radio streaming began in 1994, accelerated with the development of audio software in the late 1990s, then exploded in the early 2000s as broadcasters and the Recording Industry Association of America (RIAA) worked out rights and royalty issues through SoundExchange. Local radio went global. For the first time, radio stations anywhere in the world could find audiences far outside the reach of their broadcast signal; for the first time, too, stations required a web presence through which viewers could activate their stream. Radio became visible. Global listening became possible, beyond the specialized shortwave stations long hosted by governments. This went hand in hand with the increased materiality and visibility that a screen presence allowed. Previously invisible sources of sound, flowing through the ether from thousands of transmitters unknown to anyone outside the local area, now had a tangible presence and a worldwide reach on sites that aggregated them and made them accessible to a broad public.

Internet streaming had the capacity to turn virtually anyone into a virtual radio station; it challenged existing radio stations to think about the visible face they presented to the public. Very little has been written to date about the materialization of sound culture online and the various paths it took, but surely future scholars will recognize this as a turning point and trace the history of this process. Radio quickly responded to new digital possibilities in a variety of ways. Stations reproduced program schedules; described the content of individual shows; published photos of heretofore faceless radio personalities and supplied details of their lives and experience; narrated the history and mission of the station; posted advertising or underwriting announcements; linked to related sites and events; asked listeners to email the station and allowed discussion and exchange to flourish; solicited memberships and affiliations and asked for donations; showed photos of the studios and broadcasting facilities: a whole host of information and activities never before possible so easily and so comprehensively.

Radio's first wave of adaptation to the digital, then, followed the precepts of "re-mediation" as articulated by Bolter and Grusin:[19] digital platforms allowed radio stations and producers to do what they always had done, only in a different format, with more depth and permanence. The long-term consequences, however, were immense. Today, many listeners think of their favorite radio stations as online information providers as much as over-the-air broadcasters; for them, sound is just one aspect of radio across a variety of screens. National Public Radio's official name change to "NPR" in 2010 serves as a marker of this: it's not just radio anymore.

## Sound as a Screen Medium

Digital streaming brought radio stations as well as independent providers onto the web, where existing practices could be made visible and material, substituting a coherent screen-based interface for a set of prior practices that had been scattered and evanescent. Next, and more slowly, came the realization of exactly what this new convergence of sight and sound could do to alter radio completely. Radio was now a screen medium, possessing extended capabilities that posed an enormous challenge to producers used to working with sound in its traditional forms. Radio became as much a web experience—conveyed across various and shifting displays of textual and visual information—as it remained a sound experience.

And more screens were on the way. In January 2001, Apple introduced its iTunes service, the first commercially successful web-based interface for downloading audio and video files via computer screens. It also had a radio application that gave access to audio streaming sites, opening up the gates. Later that year the Apple iPod debuted, providing the first small portable screen through which music could be accessed. By early 2004, podcasting emerged on the scene, a new alternative distribution route for serially produced programming. Drawing on the ease of digital audio production, combined with syndicating software and web-based distribution, podcasting exploded in 2005 as iTunes 4.9 began podcast hosting. Millions of podcasts are produced today, hosted on a wide range of sites, distributed free or for small subscription fees.[20] Now streaming radio disaggregated, hiving off programs as podcasts from their digital archives. Live listening became one option among many others. The introduction of the iPhone and other smart phones beginning in 2007 supplied yet another screen through which audio work can be discovered and accessed, introducing the now ubiquitous "app" as an interface; not only the iPad, introduced in 2009, but other tablet and e-readers with audio capacity extend app-based soundwork onto yet another platform, along with the capacity to connect to web-based services. Today, radio happens when you access a website or activate an app, click on a "play" arrow or touch an icon, plug in your headphones and set off down the street or lean back in front of your computer. These screen interfaces are radio, as much as the audiostream itself.

Screen-based radio—this rapidly evolving combination of digital production, web-based distribution, and mobile digital reception—set off a revolution in soundwork and sound culture that has not yet been adequately assessed. I focus here primarily on the public broadcasting sector in the US, where innovation has been swift, profound, and internationally influential. Public broadcasters, with the weight of national organization and funding behind them, moved quickly into web-based operations, perceiving clearly what this new digital realm had to offer (just as they had with satellite distribution three decades earlier). US public radio experienced dramatic growth during this period, nearly doubling its audience between 1998 and 2008 and reaching a new high of 12% of the listening public.[21] NPR began distributing its archived programs online as early as 1996. Jonathan Kern, one of the few to consider the impact of the digital on radio production, still considers this the most profound change: radio now has not only a spatial presence but a temporal fixity, allowing programs and news stories that would have been almost completely inaccessible after first broadcast to be preserved both as audio and as transcribed text, retrieved, searched by keyword or topic, and used to document the past on a day-to-day basis, in a way that only magazines and newspapers could do before.[22] This archival function will have an enormous impact on the way that historians, as well as journalists, work in the future.

Besides online archiving, Kern points to several major ways that the digital screen has allowed broadcasters to enhance and extend the scope of their work. First, and most obviously, online materials can provide a *new visual dimension* to audio material, from photographs to videos to charts and graphs. The audio slide show has become an increasingly popular hybrid form, found on sound and print sites alike. Graphic display and organization of visual and audio components of a radio station's offerings make an immense difference—something traditional broadcasters are little used to dealing with. Program makers must become adept with digital cameras and video editing, and graphics editors have been added to radio station staffs. Some radio programs are also available as video productions, as with NPR's *Tiny Desk Concerts;* video clips of films and television shows can be added to reviews; footage of interviews and events can accompany the basic audio story. Indeed, it is obvious from NPR's webpage that the actual programs presented in its radio stream are only one small feature of that organization's current operations. If the main tabs at the top of a website can be used as an indication of the structural significance of activities (critical website analysis is still in its infancy), then the fact that materials disaggregated from the program flow and re-organized under the headings "News," "Arts and Life," and "Music" precede "Programs" and "Listen"—the latter two surely NPR's sole concern even a decade ago—marks a fundamental change in NPR's sense of itself and its priorities.

This also indicates the way that digital platforms can *extend and deepen* audio resources far beyond the usually limited time slots of streaming radio. The entire, unedited version of an interview, long stretches of actuality sound recorded on-location, entire speeches and public presentations, aspects of a story that get cut from the final version—all of these can find a permanent home on the web, broken down into easily accessible bits and searchable via transcription. Unlike traditional media, whether radio, print, or film, there are few length or space restrictions for digital material; no "news hole" or three-minute limit. The limitless capacity of digital media has also extended the authorial and editorial voice of radio producers, who now often preside over blogs that permit additional contributions and allow dialogue with listeners that in turn can find its way back into programs. Social media sites like Facebook, Twitter, Flickr, Tumblr, and YouTube extend radio's reach, broadening its community.

Such digital practices allow connections to be made between subjects and materials that go beyond their initial formats or presentation, another form of disaggregation. Multi-media elements can be grouped thematically, enabling a multi-dimensional exploration; they can be linked to related stories, visuals, sounds, or digital sites and materials. They can be re-contextualized, provided with new introductions and sidebars, supplemented with constantly updated resources, or linked to historical material. Finally, digital platforms present a set of *interactive* potentials of great value to producers and listeners alike. Besides audio comments and solicited contributions from listeners, which might be incorporated into programs or stories, listeners can participate in surveys, download materials, take part in online discussions, and find their own way through audio, visual, and textual materials in a unique sequence.

Digital platforms have also enabled novel forms of distribution. Digital or HD radio has been slower to roll out in the US than in the UK, where the BBC led the way in introducing a number of digital audio channels that supplement their regular service. Besides the traditional national channels, Radio 1 (pop music), Radio 2 (mixed music), Radio 3 (classical), Radio 4 (news and talk), and Radio 5 (live sports), "Extra" channels have been added: 1Xtra (R&B and hip hop), 4 Extra (arts and drama), 5 Live Sports Extra; 6 Music (alternative/ eclectic), and the BBC Asian Network (news and talk for the British Asian minority). A few US public radio stations have begun offering HD radio channels, usually as a supplement to their main service, but it has yet to become widespread and sales of HD tuners have languished.

Podcasting, on the other hand, has become a major part of most public broadcasters' offerings. By 2009 NPR boasted 14 million monthly podcast downloads, alongside 8 million Web visitors.[23] While podcasting brings new listeners to NPR programming, it also raises tensions between the network and its stations, disaggregating not only programs but audiences. Online archives and podcasts allow listeners to bypass their local public radio station as purveyor of programs and go right to the source, either through NPR, through the producing station, or via a show's own website. This has the potential to undercut public radio's local membership, which now accounts for the largest percentage of station income; it also directly conflicts with the way that NPR funds its programming—43% of NPR's income derives from local station subscriptions. As one observer states:

> If I'm running a station in Chapel Hill or Bloomington, I pay dues to NPR to get the marquee programming that brings people to my sta-tion—*All Things Considered* and *Morning Edition*. I don't care about your digital initiative, or your *All Songs Considered*—you're siphoning my dues to build your national brand. That's the essence of the conflict.[24]

The neat divisions that kept NPR in operation for decades—stations sup-ply the audience, NPR supplies the programming—break down in the era of digital distribution, when a local listener can just as easily get the main network or any other public station on his or her electronic device as the one available locally on the radio dial. NPR is working on such tensions by initiating new ways of interacting with local affiliates, such as its State Impact pilot project.

This effort, though currently with limited participation from a few stations in eight states, offers enhanced reporting and analysis of issues aimed to benefit both national and local news, and to suture the diverging missions of the national network and its local affiliates back together. But it remains a serious challenge.

New digital platforms extend the issue of national brand versus local stations and independent producers even further. When I listen to the WNYC-produced show *On the Media* via my local public radio station, whether broadcast or streamed online, I hear my station's underwriting announcements, membership drive solicitations, IDs and news updates, and other materials that enhance the bottom line of, in my case, Wisconsin Public Radio. WPR in turn pays WNYC for the show, thus supporting its production in the traditional way. When I download the *On the Media* podcast on my iPad, iPod, or phone, though a brief address to "podcast listeners" at the beginning of the recording exhorts me to contribute to WNYC, there is no good mechanism to enable me to do so, nor am I connecting with my local station. This considerably subverts NPR's existing economic system, but it has also contributed to a whole new sector of sound production that intersects with but exceeds what NPR could provide in the past. The final section of this chapter looks at a few such innovations.

## "Movies for Radio:" The Return of the Radio Feature

As Virginia Madsen points out in this volume, recent years have seen the return of the radio feature, along with renewed interest in its nearly forgotten history. This history goes back to Lance Sieveking and his fellow experimenters in the 1920s, but it became established 1936, when the BBC created a Features Department under the direction of Lawrence Gilliam. Here producers like D. G. Bridson, Nesta Pain, Louis MacNeice, and Marjorie Banks[25] developed the art of sound in a form that used an arsenal of creative techniques to represent reality convincingly within the confines of the live studio. America's answer to their experiments came with the initiation of CBS's *Columbia Workshop* also in 1936, mainly revolving around the work of Norman Corwin, celebrated in the 1940s and 50s as "radio's poet laureate." His sometimes overheated productions, especially those in the service of the war effort, combined elements of documentary realism with poetry, drama, soaring music, and hortatory address to great effect and widespread popularity; many still hail his post-war victory celebration *On a Note of Triumph* as the best single creative soundwork ever produced. In Britain and Europe generally, where national public broadcasters flourished after the war, the radio feature tradition continued and expanded. Britain's highbrow Third Programme in particular, established in 1947, weaned the feature from its war-inspired documentary emphasis and took it in a more literary and poetic direction. In the US, as radio shifted its economic and cultural base, and as the new style of documentary realism (enabled by new technologies) began to predominate in radio and television news coverage, the radio feature became a thing of the past, all but forgotten, or stripped down and compressed into eight-minute segments on *All Things Considered* or *Weekend Edition*.[26]

It took the success of Garrison Keillor's *A Prairie Home Companion*, which debuted in a small way in 1974 on Minnesota Public Radio but gradually expanded nationwide, to begin to open up US radio to new forms again. In 1983, Minnesota Public Radio joined with three other powerful centers of local public radio production—WNYC New York, WGBH Boston, and KUSC Los Angeles—to form American Public Radio, which began to provide an alternative to NPR and to produce and distribute a wider range of programs. It changed its name to Public Radio International (PRI) in 1993, but also split off a segment of its production arm which, confusingly, took the name American Public Media (APM) in 1994. Together, APM and PRI began the diversification process that revolutionized US public radio in the 90s, just as digital platforms began to emerge. NPR, APM, and PRI, along with the efforts of some visionary radio artist and producers, ushered in the era of the new radio feature, along with the programs and digital resources that sustain it.

Today's radio feature might be best exemplified by two of the most heralded programs on NPR in recent years: Ira Glass's *This American Life* and its science-based companion, *Radiolab*, created by Jad Abumrad and Robert Krulwich. Both hold tightly to their claims on factual realism and the documentary aesthetic, but both create sonic storyworlds that employ a complex palette of audio elements, including music, sound effects, intricate layering, gem-like editing, and narrative techniques ranging from the intimate confessional essay to the dramatic sound portrait. Both programs make full and creative use of the visibility and materiality that digital platforms enable. Their websites are elaborate, visually playful extensions of the soundwork of the show, providing background information, extensive archives, and various ways of interacting with the material.

*This American Life* originated in Chicago on public radio station WBEZ, after its creator Ira Glass became frustrated with the limitations that production for NPR's newsmagazines placed on his imagination. Glass envisioned a reality-based program that would draw on the immense variety of lived experience, related in the first person but incorporating an evocative use of music and materials recorded outside the studio, pulled together with a thematic emphasis that featured Glass's own distinctive voice and address in "first-person singular"—along the lines of Orson Welles's first radio experiments. The show posts its own description:

> We're not a news show or a talk show or a call-in show. We're not really formatted like other radio shows at all. Instead, we do these stories that

are like movies for radio. There are people in dramatic situations. Things happen to them. There are funny moments and emotional moments and—hopefully—moments where the people in the story say interesting, surprising things about it all. It has to be surprising. It has to be fun.[27]

And it has to be "real"—these "movies for radio" are fundamentally documentaries, even if they elaborate in dramatic ways. This was demonstrated in January 2012, when the episode "Mr. Daisey and the Apple Factory" presented an audio version of monologist Mike Daisey's theatrical exposé of working conditions in Apple's China factories that proved to be partly fictionalized. *TAL* produced an entire new episode exposing Daisey's misrepresentations and asserting its factual, journalistic credentials, later removing the original episode from its website.[28]

Yet the show frequently wanders across the lines that journalists usually observe, incorporating subjective experience, offbeat points of view, dreams, drama, and memory, along with Glass's own musings, less factual than philosophical, as its frame. As they say, "We think of the show as journalism," but add: "It's also true that the journalism we do tends to use a lot of the techniques of fiction: scenes and characters and narrative threads." Putting it even more strongly, one analyst claims, "*TAL* invites listeners to revel in a sort of postmodern opposition to mainstream journalism,"[29] much of it composed by well-known creative artists whose work crosses diverse media platforms: David Sedaris, Michael Chabon, Sarah Vowell, Nick Hornby, Mike Birbiglia, and many more. Its characteristic "themed" structure uses not topicality or urgent public affairs issues to organize each episode, but motifs that put human interest first. Show #470, "Show Me the Way," tells "stories about people in trouble, who look for help in mystifying places," while #468, "Switcheroo," is about "people pretending to be someone they're not." Others are focused on more traditionally journalistic events or issues, such as #459, "What Kind of Country," that highlights the problems facing local governments in the economic downturn, or plunge into history, like #465, "What Happened at Dos Erres," about a 1982 massacre in Guatemala long erased from the historical record, produced in cooperation with the non-profit journalism organization Pro Publica.[30]

Organizationally, *TAL*'s production structure reflects its varied focus. A team of core producers works closely with Glass, creating their own pieces and serving as story editors for other independent work brought in from all over. In this sense it is as much a showcase for a diverse range of creative soundwork, employing a wide variety of styles, as an aesthetically unified effort—though no one who listens regularly could deny the distinctiveness of its sound overall. Its success has been phenomenal: according to its website the show now reaches 1.8 million listeners over more than 500 stations weekly; its podcast is one of the most popular in the US. It has won most major awards, including three

Emmy's for its short-lived TV version (2006–08) on Showtime. This no doubt has much to do with *TAL*'s ubiquity in the new material world of radio: it can be accessed in an impressive number of ways, by broadcast, podcast, and archive, downloaded from iTunes or Amazon, streamed on iPad, iPhone, or Android, or rented from Netflix. This also demonstrates the shifting economics of public radio. Now produced in New York City by Chicago Public Radio (a non-profit venture that includes WBEZ and several other broadcasting services and nationally distributed programs) and distributed through PRI, *TAL* still relies on viewer donations even while marketing itself enthusiastically.

If *This American Life* exhibits the blurring of fact and fictional modes and the emphasis on first person expression of the traditional radio feature, another prominent show, *Radiolab,* excels in the creative experimentation with sound that also marks the genre. Created by Jad Abumrad and Robert Krulwich in 2005 on New York public radio station WNYC, *Radiolab* bills itself as "a show about curiosity. Where sound illuminates ideas, and the boundaries blur between science, philosophy, and human experience."[31] Both Krulwich and Abumrad are, like Glass, NPR-trained; they first collaborated on an episode submitted to, and rejected by, *This American Life.* In *Radiolab* the focus is on science, math, and the physical and human environment, but in place of TAL's compilation of individual stories, *Radiolab* is unified around the creative sensibilities of its two hosts and their stable of producers. Leading us into their highly varied weekly subjects—ranging from the physics of a popular toy, on "What a Slinky Knows," to an exploration of the nature of physical pain, on "Inside Ouch"—most episodes begin with the "two guys talking" frame that has become the show's trademark: an oblique, sometimes stumbling, quirky conversation between the two hosts, marked by frequent outbursts of laughter and self-reflective references to the task at hand. Here they ask the central questions that will organize that day's show, exclaiming over their own initial ignorance about the topic and surprise at their findings.

This chatty frame helps to lead the listener into topics that might otherwise be rejected as too dry or serious, but it is the show's unique and often stunning use of sound itself that persuades them to stay. *Radiolab* is crafted in the studio, creating the kind of "kaleidosonic" space[32] many listeners won't have experienced since Norman Corwin, if ever. It is made up of many elements, some of them taken from on-location interviews and actuality, but blended with strange and unusual noises, bursts of music, vocal collages, and the sonic re-creation of phenomena that may defy logic but effectively invoke understanding, like the sound of a brain under surgery, or what a bee might hear in the hive. We enter into a mental universe not our own, where abstractions take on an aural form that helps to make them real, and the unexpected, complex juxtaposition of disparate elements creates a listening experience that in itself represents the subject at hand. As one writer describes it,

> *Radiolab* is about exploring ideas—big, difficult, abstract ideas—and more than anything it achieves that through experience. Here, experience is meant in a double-sense: creating a fun, adventurous listening experience for the listener, as well as connecting, through intimacy and description, to universal thoughts and feelings that the audience will be acquainted with personally.[33]

It works; *Radiolab* is distributed by more than 300 stations and attracts a vital and communicative fan community. Its host and producer Jad Abumrad, whose sensibilities as a former composer of film music shape the show, received a MacArthur Fellow award in 2011.

*Radiolab*'s highly crafted style, where longer recorded interviews and actualities are often disaggregated and reassembled in small, heavily edited bits into the radio show, has created an opportunity for the show's digital portal to expand and re-situate some of its materials. The website features "Radiolab Blogland" where producers can extend their thoughts in print on a recent topic and provide links to additional audio, created in research but unused in the show. They can also provide news about the program and its people to the listener base, and promote upcoming appearances—like *This American Life, Radiolab* has its own highly successful touring theatrical show. Under the "Watch" tab, the producers have assembled short video clips that complement its stories. Unlike *TAL,* which uses its website not only to promote listening but also as a point of participation—encouraging listeners to submit story ideas, promoting internships, and referring would-be radio artists to a host of public radio initiatives that might help them (see below), *Radiolab* remains a singular work of genius, very much attached to its award-winning creators and to its function as a science program, supported in part by the National Science Foundation.

## The New Soundwork Infrastructure

These two nationally distributed and wildly successful programs are only the tip of the iceberg of innovations in the soundwork industry made possible by the sound's new materiality in the digital age. Digital gateways and networking organizations like Transom, Public Radio Exchange, and the Third Coast International Audio Festival provide interlinked venues for independent sound artists to display their work, offer it up for sale and distribution, receive critical commentary, and find resources to enable their efforts. Such work would have been lost in the ephemeral streaming flow of radio in years past, heard once and passed over forever, or perhaps collected in specialty catalogues of audio cassette collectors and sound enthusiasts. Now they can be enjoyed by all of us, whether or not they ever reach the air.

The two most significant organizations, Transom and Public Radio Exchange (PRX) are both spinoffs of the same public radio company, Atlantic

Public Media. All three are the brain children of radio producer Jay Allison, possibly the most influential figure in the digital soundwork field today. Allison, who started out on NPR, as most independent radio producers did in the pre-digital era, has co-produced or contributed to virtually all of the significant shows and series on radio, including *This American Life, Lost and Found Sound, The Sonic Memorial Project, Hidden Kitchens,* and currently produces the NPR series *This I Believe* and *The Moth.* In the early 1990s, he founded a non-profit company, Cape and Islands Community Public Radio (CICPR), to license and build the stations that eventually became WCAI Cape Cod, WNAN Nantucket, and WZAI Martha's Vineyard.

In 2000, with funding from the National Endowment for the Humanities and WGBH, he renamed CICPR Atlantic Public Media and, observing the opportunities that digital platforms were about to offer public radio, started up a new organization, Transom.org.[34] Both Transom and its sister site, the Public Radio Exchange (PRX), founded in 2002, were intended to actively intervene in the scattered but expanding world of digital audio production and distribution by building communities online where producers, stations, and listeners could productively converge. Both Transom and PRX have now entered their second decade of operation and have become significant facilitators of innovative soundwork, important "feeders" to the established distribution networks NPR, APM, and PIR, and valuable distributors in their own right.

Influenced by Allison's experience on the early online community network the WELL, and with seed funding from the Schuman Foundation Center for Media and Democracy, Transom was described by its co-founder, web designer Joshua Barlow, as a way to enable "citizen storytelling" through "giving people the opportunity to document using the Internet, [thereby] democratizing the media and helping to return radio to a time where you could find surprises."[35] Calling itself "a showcase and workshop for new public radio,"[36] Transom's main function is to "help ordinary people to tell their stories" by encouraging independent radio production. Allison writes,

> Transom tells you what microphone to buy and how to use it, but more than that we try to pass the baton, to attract a new generation of zealots, bred on the Internet, to bring their talents to public radio. Remarkable guests present manifestos and answer questions. We feature new work from new people. Our premise is that if we don't attract passionate talent, we wither.[37]

The website provides how-to advice on audio production tools and techniques, promotes its annual production workshops, profiles young audio artists, and makes connections between them and established producers in the field. It also showcases the work that comes out of such initiatives, aiming to attract larger audiences and to the stories it tells. In 2004, Transom won the first Peabody Award ever granted to a stand-alone website.[38] It was Jay Allison's fifth Peabody.

Transom helped provide the inspiration for the even more ambitious Public Radio Exchange, or PRX. A joint project between Allison and Jake Shapiro of Harvard University's Berkman Center for Internet and Society, PRX grew out of a discussion on Transom's active discussion boards. With the avowed mission to "help make public radio more public," PRX works as a showcase, a distribution exchange, and a rights allocator for soundwork, bringing independent sound artists together with stations primarily in the non-profit sector. As they explain it: "PRX is an open system—anyone can join, publish, license content, and earn royalties. Hundreds of public, community, college, and Low Power FM (LPFM) stations buy pieces on PRX for their local air."[39] It hosts a streaming channel to exhibit new work, called Public Radio Remix, and develops apps for public radio stations and programs. Its archiving and access system is one of the most inventive around, allowing users to search not only by topic and by format, but by tone: amusing, dark, quirky, raw, sound-rich, humorous, up-beat, and even Fresh Air-ish. Shapiro, now the executive director of PRX, explains the PRX idea: "that locally-run noncommercial radio stations can be allies in the effort to find new voices, new ideas, and new ways to connect in a diverse and complex world."[40] By 2012, PRX listed more than 50 radio series for distribution, and was running a number of projects to support independent radio production, including The Moth Radio Hour, Public Radio Remix, a streaming channel of PRX shows online and available for broadcast, and the Public Radio Accelerator, a center designed to stimulate entrepreneurial projects in public media.

The Third Coast International Audio Festival, based in Chicago, is another independent non-profit organization that promotes innovative radio work and distributes it through its website to the public and to interested stations. It does indeed host an annual festival of soundwork, but it also functions as an audio library of award-winning work. It distributes a weekly radio show, *Re:Sound* featuring radio work that extends beyond the US to producers in many other countries. Its national radio show, *The Best of the Best: The Third Coast Festival Broadcast* is carried by stations across the US once a year, featuring the festival winners. It also distributes the *Third Coast Podcast*, featuring *Re:Sound* programs and an assortment of others from the archive. One unique aspect of Third Coast is its public listening events, called "Listening Rooms," which take place not only in Chicago but in venues across the country, as well as its annual conference that attracts independent radio soundwork and artists from around the world. Unique too is its annual "Filmless Festival" that brings audiences together for a day of sitting in the dark, listening to "screenings" of work curated by well-known artists. Just like a film festival, but as they say "minus the popcorn—too noisy."[41]

## Conclusion

The new soundwork industry is alive and flourishing as never before. Sound's convergence with the digital transformed this under-studied sphere of media production, enabling new forms of creativity, distribution, funding, access, and exchange. It also places radio history in a new light, as some of the aspects of soundwork conceived as fundamental to the medium now shift and change. From the ephemerality of live radio, to the creative constraints of the analogue era, radio now embraces an enormous range of sonic forms and practices as a screen medium. In particular, the revival of the radio feature, and its extension into newly enabled digital forms and participatory models made possible by the web, has ushered in a level of creativity never before possible in the field of sound. While public service broadcasters have been among the first to embrace and extend digital innovation, commercial radio seems to have moved in the other direction, using digital distribution to consolidate and standardize formats developed in a previous era. In contrast, public radio has embraced digital populism; as John Biewen argues, "populism suits radio, a medium whose field equipment is inexpensive and, these days, practically as portable as a pencil."[42] But can this level of creative work be sustained? Radio still lurks below the level of consciousness for the culture at large, rarely reviewed in mainstream venues, cherished with almost cult-like intensity by those who appreciate its charms.

This will certainly change. Already, stage shows based on radio have attracted large audiences around the country—*This American Life*, *Radio Lab*, and *A Prairie Home Companion* were all on the road in 2012-13—and more and more scholars and appreciative enthusiasts are building up critical work, most of it, appropriately, online and often in the form of further soundwork. Radio today is building its archive as it grows, and preserving the medium's past as well. Creative soundwork functions beautifully with the way that mobile media are used today—on the move, engaged in activities that require our eyes to be free while our minds remain occupied. Among those semi-private/semi-public spaces created by new media, where we interact physically with crowds or the environment while maintaining our mental privacy, radio helps maintain a kind of attentive disengagement, an interactive solitude. This corresponds well with the kind of "despatialized simultaneity" discussed by digital media theorist Zizi Papacharissi as our current mode of civic engagement, "a technologically enabled mobile private sphere of thought, expression, and reaction" that supplements and in some ways corrects more traditional participation in the public sphere.[43] The stories told by the new soundwork resonate intimately as they circulate globally, connecting us with voices and experiences outside our everyday lives. And thanks to the new digital stuff of radio, they also form a type of archive never before possible, materializing sound on screens.

## Notes

1. I want to thank the Institute for Research in the Humanities at the University of Wisconsin-Madison for a fellowship that facilitated this project, through many lively conversations. Thanks also to the Hamel Family for funding the research that made it possible.
2. Robert W. McChesney, Robert Hilliard, and Michael Keith, *The Quieted Voice: The Rise and Demise of Localism in American Radio* (Champaign: Southern Illinois University Press, 2005).
3. I use the term "soundwork" to designate creative/constructed aural texts that employ the basic sonic elements of speech, music, and noise; this excludes the field normally encompassed by the term "music," though of course the boundaries are anything but clear. Typically speech is the dominant aspect of soundwork, with music and noise secondary.
4. Rudolf Arnheim, *Radio: An Art of Sound* (London: Faber and Faber, 1936).
5. Lance Sieveking, *The Stuff of Radio* (London: Cassell, 1934).
6. Paddy Scannell, "'The Stuff of Radio': Developments in Radio Features and Documentaries before the War," In *Documentary and the Mass Media* ed. John Corner (London: Edward Arnold, 1986), 1–26.
7. There are exceptions: The forerunner of the *Amos 'n' Andy* show, *Sam 'n' Henry*, was produced on records at WMAQ Chicago for syndication. See also Alex Russo, *Points on the Dial: Golden Age Radio Beyond the Networks* (Durham, NC: Duke University Press, 2010).
8. Shawn VanCour, "The Sounds of 'Radio': Aesthetic Formations of 1920s American Broadcasting" (PhD Dissertation, University of Wisconsin-Madison, 2008).
9. Transcription discs were 17" in diameter and had to be played on a special turntable that could handle them; many of them were grooved in such a way that the recording played back centrifugally, from the center of the record, not the outer edge. They were used to sell recorded programs to stations via syndication but were not released to the consumer market.
10. See http://www.btinternet.com/~roger.beckwith/bh/tapes/pm.htm.
11. German engineers had developed magnetic recording during World War II; American manufacturers appropriated the technology post-war.
12. However, the crime and suspense genre of radio programs, which came into prominence in the late 1940s and continued to air throughout the 1950s, though produced and broadcast live, were extensively recorded for syndication. They make up the bulk of our preserved old-time radio archive and are widely circulated online (and revived on broadcast stations) today.
13. A notable exception to this was the BBC Transcription Service, which began distributing hundreds of hours of programming, much of it drawn from the Third Programme, to broadcasters around the world from the 1950s through the 1970s. Educational radio stations in the US drew heavily on BBC transcriptions, and also recorded and shared a limited number of documentary and dramatic programs themselves.
14. This project was initiated and pushed forward by Frank Mankiewicz, head of NPR at the time—and the son of Herman Mankiewicz, Orson Welles's collaborator on *Citizen Kane*.
15. Jack Mitchell, *Listener Supported: The Culture and History of Public Radio* (Westport, CT: Praeger, 2005), 89.
16. Ibid. This had been the early BBC model, largely abandoned by the 1950s.
17. Public radio audiences more than doubled in the 1980s, thanks to a shift to block programming schedules that "served to stabilize the station's appeal [and] identity." David Giovannoni, "Radio Intelligence: A Long View of Public Radio's National Audience Growth, 1970–1983. The Service Grows Through Availability, Then Through Accessibility." *Current* 11, no. 3 (February 1992).
18. In countries with a well-established public service broadcasting tradition, as prevailed throughout much of Europe in particular, the permanence and high profile of national radio services and their supporting material practices—such as high-circulation printed program guides and a tradition of published criticism—made the invisibility of radio less acute, and diverse audio forms flourished in a way that simply was not true in the US.

19. Jay Bolter and Richard Grusin, *Remediation: Understanding New Media* (Cambridge, MA: MIT Press, 2000).
20. Podcasting is a sphere of soundwork in its own right that I wish to subsume here under the heading "radio" but whose full dimensions cannot be explored in these pages.
21. A $200 million gift from Joan Kroc, the widow of MacDonald's founder Ray Kroc, in 2003 didn't hurt, either.
22. Jonathan Kern, *Sound Reporting: The NPR Guide to Audio Journalism and Production* (Chicago: University of Chicago Press, 2008).
23. Anya Kamenetz, "Will NPR Save the News?" *Fast Company* (April 1, 2009). http://www.fastcompany.com/magazine/134/finely-tuned.html?page=0%2C0.
24. Ibid., quoting Paul Farhi of *The Washington Post*.
25. See Scannell, op. cit., for the roots of this tradition; also Hilmes, *Network Nations*, 120–132.
26. Though see Matthew Ehrlick, *Radio Utopia: Postwar Radio Documentary in the Public Interest* (Urbana: University of Illinois Press, 2011), for an excellent history of the US radio documentary during the Cold War era.
27. http://www.thisamericanlife.org/about/about-our-radio-show.
28. http://www.thisamericanlife.org/radio-archives/episode/454/mr-daisey-and-the-apple-factory.
29. Eleanor Patterson, "On Radio: Ira Glass, Radio Star," *Antenna* (April 9, 2012) http://blog.commarts.wisc.edu/2012/04/09/on-radio-ira-glass-radio-star/.
30. http://www.thisamericanlife.org/radio-archives.
31. http://www.radiolab.org/about/.
32. This term is developed by Neil Verma to indicate a sonic position untethered to a specific character or "point of audition," in *Theater of the Mind: Imagination, Aesthetics, and American Radio Drama* (Chicago: University of Chicago Press, 2012).
33. Andrew Bottomley, "On Radio: *Radiolab* and the Art of the Modern Radio Feature," *Antenna* (January 11, 2012) http://blog.commarts.wisc.edu/2012/01/11/on-radio-radiolab/.
34. http://atlantic.org/local/history.
35. Maria Villafana, "Transom.org Aims to Spread Storytelling Skills," *The Washington Post*, May 17, 2004.
36. Transom.org, http://transom.org
37. Jay Allison, "Afterword," in *Reality Radio: Telling True Stories in Sound* ed. John Biewen (Durham, NC: Duke University Press, 2010), 192.
38. http://blog.prx.org/2004/04/prx-congratulates-transomorg-on-peabody-award/
39. PRX, "About PRX: Making Public Radio More Public," Public Radio Exchange, http://www.prx.org/about-us/what-is-prx.
40. Jake Shapiro and Steve Schultze, "The Public Radio Exchange," *The Transom Review* 3, no. 8 (December 2003), 1. http://transom.org/guests/review/200312.review.prx.pdf?9d7bd4.
41. http://www.thirdcoastfestival.org/happenings/filmless-festival.
42. Biewen, op. cit., 6.
43. Zizi Paparachissi, *A Private Sphere: Democracy in the Digital Age* (Cambridge, MA: Polity Press, 2011), 136. See also Jason Loviglio's exploration of radio's public/private divide in *Radio's Intimate Public: Network Broadcasting and Mass-Mediated Democracy* (Minneapolis: University of Minnesota Press, 2005).

# 4

# THE PAST AND FUTURE OF MUSIC LISTENING

## Between Freeform DJs and Recommendation Algorithms

*Elena Razlogova*

In 2010, in response to a *New Yorker* article on Pandora Radio, an online music recommendation service, a Vermont reader objected: "All this new technology has yet to improve on the old radio model: putting yourself in the hands of independent, passionate, and deeply knowledgeable disk jockeys—the likes of which can be found at New Jersey's incomparable WFMU, for example—and following them blissfully into the world of unknown and unexpected sound."[1] This argument comes up repeatedly in online debates—in comments to a *New York Times* blog post on Pandora a reader put forward freeform radio pioneers from the late 1960s, KMPX and KSAN in California, and WNEW in NYC.[2] The unexpected freeform sound is something programmers of digital recommendation software strive for as well. As Sasha Frere-Jones noted in the *New Yorker* article, "the job" of a radio DJ "lingers as a template for much software."[3] One programmer echoed many blog posts when he called for a "serendipity revolution," arguing that the ultimate goal of a system should be to recommend "something new, non-obvious and appreciated that the user would likely not have discovered on his/her own."[4]

To be sure, WFMU is not a typical radio station. It is the longest running freeform station currently on the air, and a former college station currently unaffiliated with a college or National Public Radio, America's dominant public radio network. WFMU began broadcasting in 1958 as a station of Upsala College, New Jersey. It adopted a freeform format in 1967 and remains freeform today, with a brief 1970 to 1975 hiatus of Album Oriented Rock (AOR) format. The station executives, staff, and fans formed a non-profit organization that purchased the station license from Upsala College in the summer of 1994, a few months before the college went bankrupt. WFMU's location, first on the college campus in East Orange, and since 1998 in Jersey City, has allowed the station to reach a large and culturally privileged urban radio audience of the greater New York City area.[5]

WFMU comes up often as a superior alternative to algorithmic music services because many believe that this station provides the most unpredictable music experience for the listener today. Some WFMU DJs are obsessive record collectors with no regular jobs, others are university professors or artists. They play unpopular and, for some, unpalatable, music on purpose. As Ken Freedman, WFMU's station manager since 1985, put it, "We have an organic personality, not a market research personality."[6] The choices and opinions of WFMU DJs and listeners provide a good test case for what music "robots"—as DJs and fans derisively call algorithmic recommendation services—can and cannot do. An early and active participant in online music distribution, WFMU began broadcasting worldwide on the Internet in 1997 and has archived all of its programs for on-demand listening online since 2001. The station posts live listener comments with the show playlists, and chronicles the development of online music on its "Beware of the Blog" blog, established in 2005.[7] This online archive shows that DJs use algorithmic Internet music resources live on the air.

Histories of recommendation algorithms usually date their invention to Nicholas Negroponte's idea in his 1970 book *Architecture Machine* for an "adaptable machine" that could assist an architect in design, or even earlier, to the concept of "soft robots," made to collaborate with humans, put forth by John McCarthy in the mid-1950s and later elaborated by Oliver G. Selfridge.[8] But in the context of music history, the symbiosis of computers and DJs goes back at least a half a decade earlier. This chapter will briefly trace a genealogy of music recommendation systems back to the early popularity of the DJ in the 1940s, then forward to freeform radio and the early cybernetic art experiments in the late 1960s, and to recent, more familiar commercial services. Then, using WFMU DJs and listeners as a case study, the chapter will argue for a symbiosis between the algorithmic resources and radio DJs.[9]

Instead of the DJ–algorithm divide, this chapter argues as central the division between open-access culture and corporate uses of intellectual property. All online music distribution takes various algorithmic forms but in economic terms it divides into two kinds: on the one hand, corporate online services such as Last.fm, Spotify, iTunes, commercial ad-supported YouTube music, and for-profit Internet radio like Pandora; on the other, the non-commercial and pirate demi-monde of free online archives, podcasts, music blogs, torrent sites, non-commercial YouTube music, and nonprofit Internet radio stations like WFMU. Corporate services are inaccessible to most listeners outside of North America and Europe; non-profits and pirates distribute worldwide. This leads to yet another key tension, between cultural cosmopolitanism and narrower Western aesthetic boundaries. "The algorithmic" thus can have different political and aesthetic valences depending on the people and institutions taking it up.

The pre-history of various online music dissemination practices proposed here depends on the notion of "serendipity," a word that often comes up when recommendation system programmers describe their goals, and when music fans describe their preferred listening experience. According to the *Oxford English Dictionary*, "serendipity" means "making unexpected discoveries by chance." English nobleman and writer Horace Walpole introduced the word in a private letter in 1754, referring to an old tale about the three princes of Serendip, "who were always making discoveries by accidents and sagacity, of things they were not in quest of."[10] Historians, sociologists, and philosophers of science took up this notion to explain unexpected discoveries in science.[11] "Serendipity does exist," philosopher of science Pek Van Andel maintains, and is accessible only to humans:

> A computer program cannot foresee or operationalize the unforeseen and can thus not improvise ("imprevu")="unforeseen"). It cannot be surprised or astonished, and has no sense for humor, curiosity or oddity. Because we do not always realize all the implications of our theses, when we put them into our computer, the results can be surprising for us, whether trivial or not.[12]

Others propose a more complicated relationship between the calculated and the unexpected. The kind of "sagacity" required for serendipitous discoveries has been linked by historian Carlo Ginsburg to "conjectural" knowledge, which draws upon intuitive, circumstantial interpretation of clues, symptoms, and signs. Governments and corporations have repeatedly attempted to quantify this everyday practical knowledge in service of large-scale population management projects. Sir William Herschel invented fingerprinting in 1860 when observing Bengali peasants in his administration marking documents with fingers dipped in tar.[13] In 1882 French police officer Alphonse Bertillion proposed anthropometry and thus, by extension, contemporary biometrics. He likened his modern police methods to ancient hunters' tracking strategies.[14] Throughout its history, the radio industry, too, tried to manage music audiences by blending quantification and intuition in anticipating listener desires, aspiring to the scientific authority, yet forced to draw upon informal human judgment. Disc jockeys have been at the center of these contradictory efforts.

In the 1940s, radio began its transformation from a primarily national to a local medium. Even before regular commercial television network programming began in 1948, the U.S. radio and music industries confronted resurgent institutions unaffiliated with the national networks. In radio, the number of independent stations soared from 45 (5%) in 1945 to 916 (44%) in 1950. In the music industry, the "big three" music labels and the original performance rights organization, the American Society of Composers, Authors, and Publishers (ASCAP) were losing ground to independent labels like Savoy, National, and Chess, specialty music markets like hillbilly, bebop, and jump blues, and a new specialty artists' performance rights group, Broadcast Music Incorporated (BMI).[15] The key cultural institution of the period—the disc jockey—both demonstrated the existence of new local audiences for radio music and served as an instrument of these audiences' formation.

Taking advantage of the emergent specialized ethnic markets, disc jockeys spearheaded the production of new music genres and radio formats in collaboration with local audiences. Al Jarvis began what is considered the first disc jockey show in 1933, but DJs did not become a national phenomenon until the 1940s. Already in 1944, a survey found that teenagers knew small independent "hot jazz" labels only because of their exposure via disc jockey programs.[16] Propelled by the ASCAP recording ban of 1942 and by the reinstatement of transcription as a valid form of radio music, three thousand disc jockeys were on the air by 1947, when the networks finally lifted their ban on record shows.[17]

Disc jockeys' influence in the industry rested on their personal connection to listeners. Disc jockeys had a unique opportunity to introduce a record on the air and test its local popularity on the spot. In 1942, Capitol Records became the first studio to provide free releases for promotional purposes. Six years later, every record company, including the majors, had a budget for DJ records.[18] Music producers believed that DJs could make an individual record, and build a reputation for a record company.

Yet for every DJ who claimed to make a hit record through constant airplay, there were several who complained that their audiences did not share their sophisticated tastes. "Most of my listeners tend toward hillbilly," a jockey from Spencer, Iowa confessed. "I've been trying to educate them otherwise, but it's a long, slow process." A Pittsfield, Massachusetts spinner appealed to his colleagues to push bebop and big band jazz: "I think if more jocks would get with it there wouldn't be such an overwhelming demand for corn."[19] Not all audiences could be constructed by the music industry's publicity efforts. It was disc jockeys' ability to stumble upon emergent audiences that made their reports so valuable for the music industry.

It is at this point that computers and disc jockeys combined the algorithmic and informal aspects of the music business. In 1949, performance rights group Broadcast Music Incorporated placed a full-page ad in *Variety*, a major trade entertainment weekly. In the ad, a team of doctors examines an anthropomorphic "log" in an operating room. In such a clinical way, the ad suggested, BMI analyzed more than 32,400 daily station music logs on IBM "electronic accounting and tabulating machines." BMI promised radio station managers to diagnose the "strength of the heart of your broadcasting … according to the first scientific and automatic system of checking actual broadcast use of music." The mixed organic and technical metaphors revealed a fundamental tension in 1940s music audience research: the new powerful computer technology, programmed to increase profits, tried to learn from disc jockeys' ad hoc aesthetic choices, made to please or convert their local listeners. Today, commercial music recommendation services aspire to this "for-profit serendipity" as well.

By the late 1950s, disc jockeys lost their relative autonomy, their control over playlists decimated by payola scandals and by Top 40, a scripted format that forced DJs to play only top hits with no improvised banter. In the late 1960s, however, DJs were back as a cultural force, in a new format, freeform radio. By the early 1960s, FM radio stations proliferated and small portable transistor radios became a popular means for music listening, especially among young people. In July 1965 the Federal Communications Commission prohibited FM stations from simulcasting more than 50% of programs from their parent AM affiliates, making possible the rise of FM rock radio in general and freeform radio in particular.[20] Freeform DJ style relied on the industry's inability to count their alternative audiences, and survived beyond the pale of ratings services.

Freeform DJs broke with the fast paced, ad-dominated Top 40 format. DJs aired personal commentary on local and national events and played several tracks from the same album one after another, taking long stretches between ads. They offered psychedelic music and other rock genres unavailable on Top 40 stations. They revived the 1940s tradition of live interaction with listeners. Bob Fass, who ran *Radio Unnameable* on WBAI-FM in New York from 1965 to 1975, not only took calls from his listeners, but sometimes put several of them on the air, inviting them: "speak among yourselves."[21] In the early 1970s, radio stations returned to the commercial model and many DJs were forced out.[22]

As freeform radio emerged, the nascent computer art movement explored music, serendipity, interactivity, and programming. A pioneer computer art exhibit in London in 1968 was titled "Cybernetic Serendipity," and deliberately looked for the unexpected in the interaction between the computer, the arts—including music—and the audiences. The exhibit was extremely popular; over 45,000 visitors attended.[23] The show featured computer-programmed music as well as traditionally composed music by such composers as Iannis Xenakis and John Cage.[24]

To be sure, algorithmic music composition, based on a symbiosis of composers and computers, followed a trajectory different from algorithmic music recommendation, modeled on interactions between DJs and computers. Yet the technical aspects of exhibited algorithmic music presaged the issue of "random" algorithmic music selection tackled by contemporary music delivery algorithms such as the shuffle function in iTunes, epitomized in the iPod Shuffle, released in 2005. Famously, Apple programmers had to rewrite the algorithm to allow users to manipulate the shuffle feature, making it not truly random.[25]

Contributors to the exhibit also experimented with programmable serendipity. The press release noted that "Through the use of cybernetic devices to make graphics, film and poems, as well as other randomising machines which interact with the spectator, many happy discoveries were made."[26] The organizers' idea of interactive "randomising machines" extended to computers and their users such art experiments as William Burroughs's randomly reassembled text and sound cut-ups and much of John Cage's own works that incorporated chance sounds from devices such as radio sets.[27] Yet unlike these "analogue" experiments and like the iTunes shuffle feature, the exhibit's visual and sound effects may have seemed random, but in fact obeyed programmed software.

In some aspects, developments in freeform DJ culture and cybernetic music had different roots and goals. Cybernetic Serendipity exhibit sponsors included IBM, Boeing, General Motors, Westinghouse, Bell Telephone Labs, and the US Air Force research labs. Critics pointed out that the exhibit showcased these institutions' work without any critique of computers' role in nascent "technocratic authoritarianism" in Western societies and in the looming nuclear conflict.[28]

Yet in other ways, both freeform radio and cybernetic music provided a counter-cultural counterpoint to hyper-rational post-war scientism. As Fred Turner has shown, the earliest military projects that gave birth to the Internet may have seemed like a "closed world," but in fact rested on informal collaborations between engineers and social scientists.[29] The exhibit poster pointed to that history of informal experimentation. Continuing the theme of human-computer symbiosis introduced by the BMI ad in the 1940s, it arranged geometric lines and computer parts into a cyborg-like figure with one inquisitive eye. This image, and the exhibit as a whole, suggested democratic, participatory, and personal uses for computer programming, directed at art and everyday life rather than military or economic dominance. This alternative, although not oppositional, view of an algorithmic future echoed freeform radio's 1960s intimate and interactive practices.

One music composition at the show echoed the job of a DJ, or of a recommendation algorithm, more directly. Peter Zinovieff exhibited a computer that played variations on tunes that you whistled to it. Zinovieff recalled in 2010:

> [P]eople came along and whistled into the computer. The computer analysed the whistle and would often guess what the person was going to whistle next. I took several of the most popular tunes that people would whistle and the computer, a massive great thing, would make tunes out of the whistles.[30]

Zinovieff's robot was less like a composer creating new music then like a DJ who recommended a tune based on what users "requested" by whistling into the device. In different ways, Pandora and Spotify try to play variations on their users' chosen melodies.

Today, most algorithmic music services claim to allow users to become their own DJs, crafting their music stream according to their own tastes. But they offer competing approaches to music recommendation. Last.fm, an international online site founded in the United Kingdom in 2002, relies on genre labels and user tagging. Pandora, an online and smartphone radio service available in the US since 2005 and in a limited form in Australia and New Zealand since 2012, deliberately ignores opinions of friends or experts in favor of "music genome" descriptions created by professional musicologists. Because it relies on hand-coded data for music recommendation, Pandora Radio has a much smaller music catalogue than other music sites: one million songs against several millions on Last.fm and Spotify. Spotify, available first in Sweden, then throughout Europe, and since 2011 in the US, plays music on demand; Pandora and Last. fm do not.[31] Opponents of music services focus on how little all of them pay musicians and their privileging of algorithms over human DJs. As WFMU DJ Marty McSorley pointed out about Spotify in a typical exchange with listeners, "the artists get paid next to shit. [A]nd [it's] robots. and [I'm] scared of robots."[32]

As McSorley's comment shows, exploitation of musicians is one legacy of the 1940s music industry most evident in contemporary online music services. Spotify, in particular, has become embedded in the traditional music industry, relying on it for operation and expansion. The four major labels, Universal, Warner, Sony, and EMI, have owned 17% of Spotify since 2009.[33] The company keeps its deals with master rights holders (usually labels) secret; each is negotiated privately, and in exchange for discounts in royalties labels are offered a stake in the company. Each label pays an unknown small share to its artists. Charles Caldas, the CEO of Merlin, which represents over 10,000 indie labels in negotiations with streaming services (and owns 1% of Spotify) praised Spotify for paying 250% more to Merlin's clients in the year ending March 2012 than the previous year.[34] Yet artists who post their work on Spotify themselves via TuneCore have been getting a paltry 0.004 cents per play.[35] Spotify, and, to a lesser extent, other music services, make money for major players in the business at the expense of independent artists.[36]

At the same time, the legacy of the 1960s is evident in the ways commercial services have to band together with freeform stations to combat copyright restrictions. Tim Westergren, one of Pandora's founders, actively participated in the effort to fight high royalty rates in 2007. When online performance rights organization SoundExchange attempted to institute prohibitive per-play fees, both commercial subscription services and non-commercial stations including WFMU organized a day of blackout in protest, and led 300,000 listeners to write angry letters to Congress. After two years of negotiations, SoundExchange relented and made rates only marginally better, hurting both small stations and commercial giants like Pandora. As Ken Freedman explains, "Commercial stations have to start paying per song per listener right away, whereas non-commercial stations are given the first 230 simultaneous streams for a flat rate of $500.... [But] As soon as you start developing a significant audience, it becomes completely unaffordable."[37] Spotify, Last.fm, and similar services also have to fight for survival in the antiquated world copyright system.

The third important legacy of both the 1940s and the 1960s is the appeal of idiosyncratic music recommendations—both welcome and not—a mark of both the earliest and the later freeform disc jockey shows. In response to an Ella Fitzgerald's "Two little men in a flying saucer" heard on WFMU, a listener confessed that he in vain "tried to train a [P]andora station to play" World War II tunes like Fitzgerald's. He "wanted the feel of a radio playing in a Lockheed plant somewhere 'round '44." Unfortunately Pandora's "music genome" lacked a sense of history. "I constantly kept having to shake a can of pennies at it to not play contempo clowns covering classics done right the 1st time."[38] But such ahistorical mistakes also provide unexpected discoveries. Last.fm displayed cultural ignorance when it mixed up a jazz funk Japanese artist Kino with a 1980s Russian rock group by the same name. Some Russian fans were angry when they didn't hear the soundtrack for an iconic Perestroika-era band. Others, however, were happy to encounter a different group by the same name by chance.[39] Serendipity has become one of the key pleasures sought in the online listening experience.

Online freeform radio stations in general and WFMU in particular have become both a model for and an alternative to music recommendation software, yet their operations are more often praised than closely studied. Radio stations began to stream online in the 1990s. By 2000, shoutcast.com listed 3,615 international channels. Only a few were all online at a given time, but enough were for one observer to declare a "radio free internet" revolution.[40] In 2001, 2,000 people per day listened to WFMU's live stream or archived tracks—about 10% of the station's entire daily audience.[41] By 2008, WFMU's online public outnumbered its radio audience; by 2010, twice as many people listened to the station online as over FM.[42]

By 2007, WFMU made it possible for users to comment on the shows in real time online. By 2009 almost every playlist attracted comments from fans in the New York City area and internationally. Judging from press and online commentary, many of WFMU's most active listeners are former DJs, independent musicians, struggling writers, obsessive record collectors, and veteran music fans. Some musicians featured on WFMU are also devoted listeners. Underground sound artist Frank Pahl posted to one of the shows: "[I] was noticing a bump in my music for architecture sales"—on his personal site—"and the comments mentioned [WFMU]. [I] went to your webpage and you were playing [B]ilbao [E]ffect … [G]o figure. [Y]ou just made my day!"[43] Some DJs are active as independent musicians, sound artists, or record producers. WFMU thus blurs the line between music production and distribution.

Dubbed by one observer a station that plays "no hits, all the time," WFMU revels in promoting rare recordings.[44] WFMU plays obscure world music, unpopular cylinder recordings from the early twentieth century, 45-RPM recordings, sometimes at the wrong speed, and recordings that were never officially released. It also compiles lists of terrible music, such as the 30 tracks featured on the "Treasure Trove of Found Sound Vocal Workouts" on WFMU's blog.[45] It includes an ear-cringing karaoke cover of Queen's "Bohemian Rhapsody" by Moritz, a guest at a birthday party of a German journalist Michael Netsch, who then mixed and published the track online.[46] Not only do DJs play such tracks, they also encourage their production. While Freedman streamed the Moritz track on his show, in playlist comments another DJ, Vicki Bennett, made Netsch promise to email more mp3s for her own future broadcast.[47] At times, WFMU DJs seem focused on encouraging their listeners to explore music they ordinarily may *not* like.

At the same time, WFMU found eclectic uses for algorithms much like algorithmic music composers found serendipitous uses for military computer technology in 1968. As early as 1998, WFMU's "Accuplaylists" added the ability to list song information online in real time, reloading the playlist page every 45 seconds during the program.[48] "For the first time," remembers WFMU DJ and listener music historian David Suisman, "you could find out what some off-the-wall, indescribable recording was while it was playing—rather than waiting for the DJs mic break."[49] WFMU pioneered the streaming and archiving of its programs permanently online; was one of the first stations to add an online comments feature; and the first to add smartphone apps for listening to the station—an iPhone app in 2007.[50] WFMU has collaborated with other stations in online streaming. When New Orleans FM station WWOZ found itself homeless after hurricane Katrina, WFMU hosted *WWOZ in Exile* and helped collect support in music recordings and funds; upon returning to New Orleans, the station broadcast primarily online rather than over the air.[51]

Considering this early conversion, it shouldn't come as a surprise that WFMU online comments show that users and DJs routinely use music "robots" during broadcasts, for reference and playlist material. Listeners use Last.fm to look up pictures and schedules for bands whose songs are playing; post links to YouTube clips of songs they want to hear, and occasionally torrent links for pirated albums. With the advent of Spotify and YouTube some DJs began to search these sites in real time for a requested track.[52] Former DJ Cecile is a fan of Pandora; Richard from Venezuela keeps pushing Last.fm. WFMU has a page on Last.fm and added "scrobbling" to its latest iPhone app—a feature that allows Last.fm to use WFMU listening to improve a user's recommendations.[53] The relationship between the freeform and the algorithmic in music is more symbiosis than rivalry.

This symbiosis vastly extends the kinds of radio performances DJs can produce today. In 2012, WFMU DJ and audiovisual artist Vicki Bennett organized "Radio Boredcast, a 744-hour continuous online radio project," part of the International Festival of Art, Technology, Music, and Film in England. Bennett conceived the show as a long-playing extension of her "DO or DIY with People Like Us" show on WFMU. The broadcast, inspired by the John Cage piece "As Slow as Possible," celebrated the slow and deliberate appreciation of music, spoken word, and sound art, and featured dozens of DJs. It is now archived on the WFMU website.[54]

This collective performance of broadcasting and listening would not have been possible without the infrastructure of net servers, protocols, and apps, as well as net radio and computer art organizations. DJs submitted their original shows from various parts of the globe, from Philadelphia to Barcelona. One could listen to the broadcast via an iTunes subscription; or via the website, iPhone app, or Android app from BASIC.fm, a net radio broadcast project. The photo accompanying press reports of the show echoes both the BMI ad and the Cybernetic Serendipity exhibit poster in blending calculation and intuition. Instead of anthropomorphic and algorithmic representations favored by the two previous images, the photo represents the contingencies of human labor in a digital environment—the sticky notes precariously attached on a board, each representing a separate segment of the 744-hour online extravaganza. The freeform DJ's job has become inseparable from online and algorithmic means to recommend and distribute music.

In this common field of algorithmic online music distribution, freeform radio tradition clashes with the for-profit model represented by corporate streaming services. Unlike founders of commercial services, WFMU DJs embrace legal and pirate sites that freely share music. Vicki Bennett remembered how she herself benefited when Rick Prelinger shared his collection of educational and industrial films freely online via the Internet Archive: no longer did she have to beg national and local archives for footage to make an artwork. Listeners of Last.fm and Spotify, she argued, should be wary of leaving all music to the commercial cloud services: "this 'automatic and effortless' experience of access may be improved upon by eventually narrowing down results to only mainstream or sponsored content."[55] The eclectic aesthetic of WFMU DJs goes together with a moral economy of music, where independent artists and international audiences take precedence over excessive copyright restrictions.

The history of music blogs, a practice that peaked around 2006, is a case in point. Music bloggers take advantage of cloud storage services to democratize music recommendations previously reserved for professional music critics. They curate mp3 collections of rare and non-Western genres; some blogs eventually became advertising venues for music labels. According to Casey Ray, "Much like the FM DJs of the late 1960s and '70s, music bloggers helped define an era."[56] Many serve non-Western musicians and audiences. "A web search for an obscure artist heard on the radio will take you to a blog telling you all about them," Bennett describes the "grey culture" of listening via blogs, "sharing out-of-print material, with tags linking to related areas. An adjacent column will have links to 25 other websites and radio stations with similar interests. There then follows a wonderful odyssey into hidden and often forgotten sonic worlds."[57] WFMU's blog, too, posts YouTube clips and mp3 collections of rare music for its fans.

Currently, music blogs are under threat from federal enforcement agencies that crack down on copyright infringement. When the FBI closed Megaupload cloud storage service along with a pirate book sharing site library.nu in January 2012 and took all of its files offline, many music blogs lost their entire libraries in the action. As of mid-2012, of the three blogs WFMU listed as hit by the Megaupload shutdown, HolyWarbles no longer existed, Mutant Sounds was in hiatus but accepting re-uploads from users, and Global Groove was running as usual.[58] Users volunteered to re-upload their own files to restore libraries. As one user reported, "Mutant Sounds has helped [in] broadening my views on music, for which [I] am extremely grateful. I too would like to help you out in reuploading any item."[59] Other sounds were irretrievably lost. "The last thing I downloaded from HW [HolyWarbles]," one user remembered, "was a rare, completely out of print album by Marie Jubran, a Syrian artist who recorded mostly during the 50s."[60] When US agencies crack down on piracy, they at the same time decimate globally translocal music communities created by bloggers.

Conversely, by virtue of their business plans, online commercial streaming services stay confined within Western economic and aesthetic boundaries. WFMU, with numerically smaller audiences, reaches farther geographically than Pandora, Spotify, or even Last.fm, which is only available on the iPhone in the US, UK, and Germany. Restricted in their reach and repertoire, commercial music services cannot help but create a neo-colonial listening experience for their customers.

Take, for example, Pandora's "music genome" that describes "the relative exoticism of the melody scale." As the *New York Times* explained in 2009, during a Pandora coding session, after listening to a raga, a North Indian classic music form, one expert, a violinist, opined: "I actually put exotic at 3.5," which prompted a lecture from an Indian music expert on how one would understand "exotic" in relation to that particular melody.[61] But the very category "exoticism," a term with a long colonial history and connotations, would not make sense in the North Indian context. It does make sense, however, when we think of Pandora as the inheritor of the Western commercial "world music" marketing category invented in the 1980s and 1990s, exemplified by the Putomayo label, which sells CDs of feel-good samples of "world music" in North American retail stores.[62] Music blogs, and online playlists and comments spaces set up by WFMU and other freeform stations, provide a unique alternative to such neo-colonial projects.

Like aesthetic choices, algorithms embody particular social and political sensibilities. Recommendation services continue to "perfect" their algorithms, fixing what managers believe are errors and glitches. Yet it is precisely when the algorithm "fails" that we gain insight into the aesthetic and political judgment of Internet users. The Netflix *Napoleon Dynamite* problem is a case in point. In 2008, Netflix discovered that its algorithm failed to predict whether a user would like or hate *Napoleon Dynamite*, a film about the misadventures of an awkward high school teenager. Netflix then proposed a one-million-dollar contest for 10% improvement of the site's recommendation engine. Programmers could test their code on Netflix site in real time, and if the code helped recommend the films users already liked, their code was considered an improvement.[63]

Yet from freeform radio listeners' perspective the *Napoleon Dynamite* problem was not really a problem. WFMU DJ from 1996 to 2009, Kenny G, aka Kenneth Goldsmith, provides the best example of a DJ who invites "haters"—loudly dissatisfied listeners. In the later years, his WFMU show was called "An Hour of Pain," with the motto, "I apologize in advance—it's only an hour." Kenny G took the name of a famous smooth jazz saxophonist as his DJ pseudonym and then read on the air letters sent to him by listeners who mistook him for the musician. Goldsmith's "uncreative" books include *Day*—an entire issue of the *New York Times* for Friday, September 1, 2000, retyped in 9-point Bookman Old Style font.[64] Kenny G offered to a freeform radio listener what *Napoleon Dynamite*, before the contest, offered to a cinephile: an unpredictable element that stretched one's patience yet led one to unexpected discoveries.

Thus before its million-dollar contest, Netflix serendipitously came up with an algorithm that recommended the unexpected and the bizarre—an equivalent of what music fans have insisted makes WFMU DJs superior to apps. Then Netflix deliberately chose the code that embedded a more mainstream, predictable aesthetic—a move so far mirrored by music recommendation services.

By contrast, freeform DJs' unpredictable aesthetic comes with a politics, one especially proactive about combatting copyright. In 1996, Goldsmith created UbuWeb, an online archive of avant-garde poetry, music, and later video. "I wanted to create a warehouse for the avant-garde," Goldsmith explained, "proposing the idea that not all economies are the same." Instead of clearing sound and video files with authors beforehand, he posts them first and then waits for authors to contact him about taking them down. Very few protest, and if they do, negotiation ensues and usually Goldsmith convinces creators to leave their work available on the site.[65]

Likewise, WFMU founded and maintains several services that promote the sharing of free non-infringing music. In 2009 it launched Free Music Archive (FMA), a collection of downloadable tracks curated by freeform radio stations, independent labels, and small concert venues. All the uploaded tracks are cleared for use through a Creative Commons license or a direct agreement with the FMA. WFMU has presented its "Free Music Archive Radio app" as "Creative Commons Pandora."[66] WFMU iPhone app is streaming UbuWeb content. These intertwined freeform online algorithmic projects together acquire more cultural force than WFMU, FMA, or UbuWeb would have alone.

It remains open whether the future of online music will be defined by Spotify and its corporate shareholders, or Free Music Archive and UbuWeb. Many recent algorithmic "corrections" in commercial services—those matching listeners' music tastes, those measuring "exoticism" of world music according to Western users' expectations, and those gating music according to geographic copyright restrictions—reflect the views of the services' corporate owners. Algorithms have politics because of people and structures that create them, people either unable or unwilling to recognize the unexpected insights, political and aesthetic, that certain iterations of algorithms can provide.[67]

## Notes

1. Keith Chamberlin, "Re: You, the DJ," *New Yorker*, July 26, 2010.
2. Philip R. Olenick, comment to Claire Cain Miller, "Listening to Radio on the Web? That's So Last Year," *Bits—The New York Times*, September 10, 2009, http://bits.blogs.nytimes.com/2009/09/10/listening-to-radio-on-the-web-thats-so-last-year/.
3. Sasha Frere-Jones, "You, the DJ," *New Yorker*, June 14, 2010.
4. Steven Ruttenberg, "The Serendipity Revolution," *Universal Recommendations*, February 12, 2008, http://unirec.blogspot.com/2008/02/serendipity-revolution.html.
5. Ken Freedman, "Freeform Timeline," in *The Best of LCD: The Art and Writing of WFMU-FM 91.1 FM*, ed. Dave the Spazz (Princeton, NJ: Princeton Architectural Press, 2007), 4–5; Judy Pokras, "Is WFMU Cursed? Or Just Unlucky?" *New York Times*, March 12, 1995.
6. John Bergmayer, "Interview with WFMU's Ken Freedman," *In the Know Podcast—Public Knowledge*, August 30, 2010, https://members.publicknowledge.org/blog/pk-know-podcast-interview-wfmus-ken-freedman.
7. Freedman, "Freeform Timeline," 5.
8. Ariana Moscote Freire, "Tuning into You: Personalized Audio Streaming Services and Their Remediation of Radio" (M. A. thesis, McGill University, 2007); Asim Ansari, Skander Essegaier, and Rajeev Kohli, "Internet Recommendation Systems," *Journal of Marketing Research* 37, no. 3 (2000): 363–375; Nicholas Negroponte, *The Architecture Machine* (Cambridge, MA: MIT Press, 1970); Alan Kay, "Computer Software," *Scientific American*, 251, no. 3 (1984): 53-59.
9. I used Google site search feature to examine all WFMU playlists and comments for intersection with recommendation services Pandora, Spotify, last.fm, as well as sites where users share legal and pirated music: music blogs, YouTube, and torrent sites.
10. Walpole to Horace Mann, January 28, 1754, quoted in Theodore G. Remer, *Serendipity and the Three Princes, from the Peregrinaggio of 1557* (Norman: University of Oklahoma Press, 1965), 6
11. See Robert K. Merton, *The Travels and Adventures of Serendipity: A Study in Historical Semantics and the Sociology of Science* (Princeton, NJ: Princeton University Press, 2004).
12. Pek Van Andel, "Anatomy of the Unsought Finding. Serendipity: Origin, History, Domains, Traditions, Appearances, Patterns and Programmability," *British Journal for the Philosophy of Science* 45, no. 2 (June 1994): 631–648.
13. Carlo Ginzburg, "Morelli, Freud, and Sherlock Holmes: Clues and Scientific Method," in *Dupin, Holmes, Peirce: The Sign of Three*, ed. Umberto Eco and Thomas A. Sebeok (Bloomington: Indiana University Press, 1983), 81–118;
14. Allan Sekula, "The Body and the Archive," *October* 39 (Winter 1986): 3–64.
15. Christopher H. Sterling and John M. Kittross, *Stay Tuned: A History of American Broadcasting* (Mahwah, NJ: Lawrence Erlbaum, 2002), 830–31; Russell Sanjek and David Sanjek, *Pennies from Heaven: The American Popular Music Business in the Twentieth Century* (New York: Da Capo Press, 1996).
16. "High-School Students Label-Wise," *Billboard*, June 17, 1944.
17. Arnold Passman, *The Deejays* (New York: Macmillan, 1971).
18. Dave Dexter, "Disk Jockey: Origin of the Species, 1930–1945," *Billboard*, December 27, 1969.

19. Tim Edwards to *Billboard*, November 27, 1948, 44–45; Mac McGarry to *Billboard*, May 7, 1949, 37.
20. Susan J. Douglas, *Listening In: Radio and the American Imagination* (New York: Times Books, 1999), ch. 10; Marc Fisher, *Something in the Air: Radio, Rock, and the Revolution That Shaped a Generation* (New York: Random House, 2007); Ken Freedman, "Freeform Timeline" and "A Brief History of Freeform Radio," in *The Best of LCD*, 4–7.
21. Fisher, *Something in the Air,* 129.
22. Freedman, "Freeform Timeline," 5.
23. Quoted in Rainer Usselmann, "The Dilemma of Media Art: Cybernetic Serendipity at the ICA London," *Leonardo* 36, no. 5 (January 1, 2003), 390.
24. *Cybernetic Serendipity Exhibit Catalog* (London: Author, 1968).
25. Steven Levy, *The Perfect Thing: How the iPod Shuffles Commerce, Culture, and Coolness* (New York: Simon & Schuster, 2006).
26. *Cybernetic Serendipity Exhibit Catalog.*
27. On Burroughs and Cage, see Douglas Kahn, *Noise, Water, Meat: A History of Sound in the Arts* (Cambridge, MA: MIT Press, 1999).
28. Quoted in Usselmann, "The Dilemma of Media Art," 392.
29. Fred Turner, *From Counterculture to Cyberculture: Stewart Brand, the Whole Earth Network, and the Rise of Digital Utopianism* (Chicago: University of Chicago Press, 2006); Paul N. Edwards, *The Closed World: Computers and the Politics of Discourse in Cold War America, Inside Technology* (Cambridge, MA: MIT Press, 1996).
30. Peter Zinovieff, "The Russian-English Renaissance Man's Guide to Quadrophonic Sounds" (lecture, Red Bull Music Academy, London, 2010), http://www.redbullmusicacademy.com/lectures/dr-peter-zinovieff-the-original-tectonic-sounds?template=RBMA_Lecture%2Ftranscript.
31. Last.fm, http://www.last.fm; Pandora Radio, http://www.pandora.com; Spotify, http://www.spotify.com.
32. Marty McSorley, comment to "Playlist for Marty McSorley," *WFMU*, October 11, 2011, http://wfmu.org/playlists/shows/42234.
33. Michael Arrington, "This Is Quite Possibly the Spotify Cap Table," *TechCrunch*, August 7, 2009, http://techcrunch.com/2009/08/07/this-is-quite-possibly-the-spotify-cap-table/.
34. Charles Caldas in Eliot Van Buskirk, "David Lowery Might Be Right About Some Things, But He's Wrong About Streaming, Money, and Artists," *Evolver.fm*, June 21, 2012, http://evolver.fm/2012/06/21/david-lowery-might-be-right-about-some-things-but-hes-wrong-about-streaming-money-and-artists/.
35. "'Hey, Can You Spotify Me Some Cash?'—an Indie Artist's Perspective," *Music by Bradley James*, May 7, 2012, http://musicbybradleyjames.wordpress.com/2012/05/07/hey-can-you-spotify-me-some-cash-an-indie-artists-perspective/.
36. Steve Knopper, "The New Economics of the Music Industry," *Rolling Stone*, October 25, 2011.
37. John Bergmayer, "Interview with WFMU's Ken Freedman," *In the Know Podcast—Public Knowledge*, August 30, 2010, https://members.publicknowledge.org/blog/pk-know-podcast-interview-wfmus-ken-freedman.
38. Listener james from Westwood, comment to "Give the Drummer Some" playlist, *WFMU*, May 27, 2011.
39. "Kino—Elephant Step," Last.fm, http://www.last.fm/music/Kino/_/Elephant+Step
40. Richard Gehr, "Radio Free Internet," *Village Voice*, March 21, 2000.
41. David F. Gallagher, "Making Waves," *Interactive Week*, January 29, 2001.
42. Bergmayer, "Interview with WFMU's Ken Freedman." As a freeform station, WFMU does not have Arbitron ratings.
43. Frank Pahl, comment to "Playlist for Inner Ear Detour with David." *WFMU*, September 9, 2011. http://wfmu.org/playlists/shows/41841.
44. Jaime Wolf, "No Hits All the Time," *New York Times*, April 11, 1999.

45. Ken Freedman, "Treasure Trove of Found Sound Vocal Workouts," *Beware of the Blog*, June 20, 2005, http://blog.wfmu.org/freeform/2005/06/sing_along_with.html.

46. Michael Netsch, "Moritz Sings Bohemian Rhapsody by Queen," YouTube, http://www.youtube.com/watch?v=7vsp233gVN8

47. "Ken's Playlist," *WFMU*, March 30, 2011, http://wfmu.org/playlists/shows/39756.

48. "WFMU's Friday Afternoon Timeslot with Ken Freedman," *WFMU*, 1998, http://wfmu.org/Playlists/Ken/ken.980501.html

49. David Suisman, comments to author, September 8, 2012.

50. Mark Frauenfelder, "WFMU Streaming Radio on iPhone," *Boing Boing*, November 5, 2007, http://www.boingboing.net/2007/11/05/wfmu-streaming-radio.html.

51. Alan Stavitsky and Michael Huntsberger, "'With the Support of Listeners Like You': Lessons from U.S. Public Radio," in *The Public in Public Service Media*, ed. Gregory Ferrell Lowe (Göteborg, Sweden: Nordicom, 2009), 257–271.

52. "Playlist for Scott Williams," *WFMU*, January 23, 2012, http://wfmu.org/playlists/shows/43594.

53. "WFMU iPhone App V2.1 Is Out!," *Beware of the Blog*, July 30, 2010, http://blog.wfmu.org/freeform/2010/07/wfmu-iphone-app-v21-is-out.html.

54. Vicki Bennett, "Radio Boredcast Presents," *AV Festival*, February 19, 2012, http://www.avfestival.co.uk/blog/2012/02/19/radio-boredcast-presents.

55. Vicki Bennett, "Collateral Damage," *The Wire*, February 2, 2012, http://thewire.co.uk/articles/8439/. See also Christopher Kelty, "The Disappearing Virtual Library," AlJazeera, March 1, 2012, http://www.aljazeera.com/indepth/opinion/2012/02/2012227143813304790.html.

56. Casey Rae, "The Rise & Fall of MP3 Blogs," *Free Music Archive*, August 22, 2012, http://freemusicarchive.org/curator/FMA/blog/The_Rise__Fall_of_Music_Blogs__guest_post_by_Casey_Rae.

57. Bennett, "Collateral Damage."

58. Mutant Sounds, http://mutant-sounds.blogspot.com/2012/01/licking-wounds-and-taking-stock-after.html; Global Grooves, http://globalgroovers.blogspot.com/.

59. Jason Sigal, "Music Blogs React to Megaupload Seizure & Cyberlocker Lockdowns," *Beware of the Blog*, January 26, 2012, http://blog.wfmu.org/freeform/2012/01/music-blogs-react-to-megaupload-seizure-cyberlocker-fileserve.html#more.

60. Gary, "Guilty Until Proven Innocent?," *Bodega Pop*, January 27, 2012, http://bodegapop.blogspot.ca/2012/01/guilty-until-proven-innocent.html.

61. Rob Walker, "The Song Decoders," *New York Times*, October 18, 2009.

62. Anahid Kassabian, "Would You Like Some World Music with Your Latte? Starbucks, Putumayo, and Distributed Tourism," *Twentieth-Century Music* 1, no. 2 (2004): 209–223.

63. Clive Thompson, "If You Liked This, You're Sure to Love That," *New York Times*, November 23, 2008.

64. Kenneth Goldsmith, *Day* (New York: Figures, 2003).

65. Dave Mandl, "Interview with Kenneth Goldsmith," *The Believer*, October 2011; UbuWeb, http://www.ubu.com

66. Jason Sigal, "Free Music Archive Radio & more from Music Hack Day," *Beware of the Blog*, November 7, 2011, http://blog.wfmu.org/freeform/2011/11/free-music-archive-radio-more-from-music-hack-day.html; Free Music Archive, http://freemusicarchive.org/.

67. See Jim Johnson, "Mixing Humans and Nonhumans Together: The Sociology of a Door-Closer," *Social Problems* 35, no. 3 (June 1988): 298–310; and Langdon Winner, "Do Artifacts Have Politics?," *Daedalus* 109 (1980): 121–136.

# SECTION II

# Radio's New Sounds

# 5

# YOUTH, NEW MEDIA, AND RADIO

## Mobile Phone and Local Radio Convergence in Turkey

*Ece Algan*

Media convergence has become a widely accepted term that describes how we consume media today. While the concept is generally used to refer to the consumption of (mostly old) media using new internet and mobile platforms, it is also used to explain the current trend of media systems across the world becoming increasingly alike with regard to their products, their professional practices and cultures, and their systems of relationships with other political and social institutions.[1] This particular era of "global homogenization of media systems," as Hallin and Mancini refer to it, raises concerns over the corporate and commercial interests of big global media undermining national or community interests and highlights the urgent need to transfer power back from private to public hands.[2] However, according to Henry Jenkins, convergence is "both a top-down corporate-driven process, and a bottom-up consumer-driven process,"[3] and thus it should be viewed as more than merely a technological process; it is also a social and cultural one that can enable interactivity, cultural production, and sharing. Indeed, we have seen notable examples of enhanced user participation and agency via, e.g., YouTube,[4] through bloggers becoming new intellectuals with great cultural capital and power to move the masses,[5] and in citizen journalism where professionals end up interacting with their publics as both consumers and co-creators.[6] These examples and trends often excite scholars[7] about the possibilities that a new era of participation offers to "digital natives," where, ideally, not only can users have more input in the creative process of media production but they can also extend their networks and engage in peer-to-peer, self-directed learning. Henry Jenkins even goes so far to argue that "convergence represents a cultural shift as consumers are encouraged to seek out new information and make connections among dispersed media content."[8] There seems to be a consensus that the line between producers and users is blurred as both sides now become "participants who interact with each other."[9] Therefore, participation is assumed as the primary condition behind convergence culture with participatory culture defining the culture brought about by media convergence.

While it is important to approach media convergence from a perspective that also takes into consideration audiences' and media users' experiences, I believe it is equally important not to make sweeping generalizations about the impact of media convergence on culture. I argue that participatory culture is not always an inevitable and guaranteed outcome of media convergence, and trends toward increased participation initiated by media convergence can easily be reversed due to a new set of socio-cultural or technological circumstances. Drawing from my fieldwork in Southeast Turkey, I illustrate how, in terms of user experience and participation, media convergence enabled by the digital media systems does not necessarily indicate a new type of media experience or "a shift in the ways we think about our relations to media."[10] I argue that convergence does not necessarily transform the cultural logics that inform our use and consumption of dispersed media content, or how as consumers, audiences, and users we contribute to the reproduction of such content, or even how we interact with others through our media practices. As is true of any culture, convergence culture is context specific and thus convergence does not necessarily indicate the emergence of a brand-new participatory culture or an enhancement of an existing one.

On the contrary, due to increased commercial gains and opportunities, convergence can result in disrupting or even destroying earlier participatory cultures. In Southeast Turkey, consuming local radio via the computer while reaching the station via texting often constitutes a similar cultural practice for young people as listening to the same station on an analog transistor radio while interacting on-air via a land-line telephone. The difference, in the case of youth participation via local radio in Şanlıurfa, where I have been researching for a decade, lies in the diminished participation once the transition from analog to digital took place. Prior to 2003, when young people participated by calling-in, they had created a unique participatory youth culture, where the DJs were only seen as mediators and matchmakers and the callers and audience were the ones who had the ownership of the space created by the radio, not in reality but in terms of how they saw their roles as participants of the radio. They referred to the local radio as "our radio." They were the programming because their voices, stories, opinions, songs, and poems were shared by the whole youth community which in turn responded. After 2003, when the only access to radio stations became texting via mobile phones, the nature of participation changed drastically and with it, the involvement of the youth community with the radio.

This paper is about how underprivileged young people in Southeast Turkey adapt to new forms of media convergence in order to continue to make local radio relevant to their lives. It discusses how these new forms of convergence ended up diminishing the participatory youth culture that once was alive around local radio in the mid-1990s to early 2000s, while at the same time facilitating more one-on-one interaction and communication among marginalized Turkish teenagers, mostly living in the ghettos of the city of Şanlıurfa in the traditionally Muslim periphery of Turkey. Based on a 10-year longitudinal ethnographic study, this chapter explores the unique and changing ways that Şanlıurfa youth have appropriated the public space of radio and the socioeconomic factors behind mobile phones becoming an integral part of their interaction and dating as mediated through local radio. I examine the multiple local meanings, uses, and applications of "media convergence" created through these practices that are specific to the Southeastern Turkish case, which should help us re-think the meaning and consequences of media convergence especially as it involves radio in non-Western contexts.

## Rethinking Media Convergence and Radio in the Mobile Communication Era

In radio studies, convergence usually indicates the consumption of traditional FM radio via the new platforms on the internet and mobile phones. Websites and social media applications that allow users to become DJs and curate their own channels for their friends and followers as well as platforms that enable users to broadcast their own radio programs in the form of podcasts[11] are certainly important developments that often result in the transformation and decentralization of older forms and institutions of radio broadcasting. These examples also point to some degree of audience agency and autonomy regarding media consumption. In addition, easy distribution of music, podcasts, and radio programs via social media certainly holds out promise for the high degree of interactivity and participation, which are seen as central to convergence culture. However, when a medium like radio is considered, which still plays a crucial role in everyday life in most parts of the developing world, our assumptions regarding the impact and emergence of the so-called convergence culture need to be re-examined. As numerous studies of diasporic, indigenous, and community radio, as well as small commercial local radio stations in favelas, ghettos, and villages in various parts of the world have shown, the meanings, uses, and practices of radio are quite diverse in the South.[12] Furthermore, they are not necessarily shaped by the political economy of the convergence era driven by consumerism and commercialism as often manifest in the developed North.

Similarly, mobile phone use is quite varied in the South and carries many more important functions than to allow users to participate in a larger media synergy. Even though the research on development does not emphasize mobile phones as playing a transformative role in terms of social change in the developing world, it shows that mobile ownership contributes to broader economic development and provides significant economic and social opportunities in Africa, for instance.[13] In her study on the social implications of mobile phone usage among immigrant Jamaicans and their families, Heather Horst states that "the mobile phone has in many ways altered the perception of mobility among rural Jamaicans who may not have the economic ability or desire to participate in physical movement."[14] By creating what she calls transnational social fields, cell phones enable families to stay in touch, send each other money, monitor their kids, pursue their romantic relationships, and "express and communicate love."[15] This type of mobile communication eases worries about loved ones overseas while aiding everyday life and work. Horst's study underlines the fact that mobile phones are instrumental in maneuvering within the new global socio-economic conditions and spatial barriers immigrant families are experiencing. This is largely because "the telephone is an inherently spatial technology—its sole function is to allow communication at a distance,"[16] as Anthony Townsend has argued. Mobile phones, in particular, have modified the norms of being present and absent in social space, and citizens' relation with public space.[17] Therefore, due to their ability to transform our experience of time and space, phones have become an integral part of modern life and of both urban/rural and global/local mediations of it.

Most research on youth and mobile phone use[18] places an emphasis on the phone's role in maintaining social networks, friendships, and romantic relationships, without situating the youth in their unique environments or providing adequate context regarding their use. I agree with Crispin Thurlow and Susan McKay's observation that academic and lay writing about young people's use and understanding of new communication technologies is "often impressionistic and over-simplistic."[19] They also argue that overly homogenous, U.S. or Western-centric interpretation of youth culture "falls too easily into the trap of making unsubstantiated (and technologically deterministic) claims for the impact of new technologies."[20] Research on the use of radio and mobile phones in tandem is non-existent except in teenager media use surveys, which mention that some listen to radio on their mobile phones, keep track of radio play lists and purchase music that they hear on the radio. In these cases, mobile phones mostly function as a computer for purchasing music and tallying play lists while they can also be used as radio sets. Since more complicated spatial, economic, and social use is attributed to mobile phones in the developing world, studying the radio–mobile convergence over time can help us understand how it enhances, challenges, and disrupts an existing participatory culture.

## Marginalized Youth and the City in the Periphery: Şanlıurfa

The city of Şanlıurfa, which is inhabited mostly by people of Kurdish and Arabic descent, is located 30 miles from the Syrian border in the economically less-developed Southeastern Anatolian region of Turkey. The city, which has a population of around half a million, has undergone very rapid growth and urbanization in the last two decades due to Turkey's integration into the global economy. The government policies on the ethnic conflict in the region between Kurdish citizens and the Turkish state, rural to urban immigration prompted by the conflict, a state-sponsored development project in the region (the GAP project), and the increase of wealth due to irrigation-supported agriculture in the province all have impacted the cityscape in many different ways, but these changes left the problems of youth either unanswered or worsened. By bringing irrigation agriculture to the plains south of the city, the GAP project increased agricultural production and profit, initiated industrial development, and caused people to re-locate due to increased opportunities and the construction of a series of dams. As a result, Şanlıurfa received a large number of immigrants from the many rural villages and towns of the region. In addition, a number of other forces also contributed to a drastic change in the city's small but progressive urban character, including the increasing power of a new local government with a reactionary, conservative, and religious agenda; wider disparity in wealth; the increasing power of landlords gained through irrigation agriculture; and martial law that was in effect on and off until 2000.

The increasing power of local religious leaders and political authorities, who have adopted Islamist discourse and ideology, created numerous constraints on many aspects of social life in Şanlıurfa, especially women's participation in the public sphere. Establishments that serve alcoholic drinks as well as restaurants and movie theaters where both women and men could go were closed as a result of the social pressure that growing religious sentiment caused. Moreover, most young girls are not allowed to go to school for more than a few years, if at all, and most boys only attend elementary school. Not only do young people lack social space to experience their gender identities and sexualities, but they are also expected to obey traditional ways regarding their education, work, and marriage.

Despite these circumstances and restrictions, since their launch in the mid-1990s both national TV networks and local commercial radio channels have functioned as vitally important sites for the young people of Şanlıurfa to re-think their place among the larger Turkish youth population and to vocalize their dissatisfaction with the status quo and traditions. In the socially restrictive environment of the city, local radio and mobile communication have become crucial in working within and even renegotiating the boundaries of traditions and tribal cultural practices, which have been weakened since the 2000s. Moreover, many taboos regarding dating and sexuality, such as pre-marital sex, have been broken in the big cities of Turkey, and this has been widely discussed in the public sphere. Television series on commercial networks show dating, flirting, and messaging as new countrywide trends among teenagers and thus ease the pressure on the youth in Şanlıurfa. When I returned to Şanlıurfa in 2007 and then again in 2011, my informants kept telling me how Şanlıurfa wasn't the same place anymore and that it had changed a lot. One even suggested, "Now it's a place where every week a few young couples, who have met in chat rooms, elope!" (Personal communication, July 2007). While my informants still expressed similar frustrations in 2011 regarding lack of social space and parental and societal pressures similar to those they experienced in 2001 and 2007, the exaggerated statement above is significant for it signals the change that has been taking place. Studying young people's interactions through radio and cell phones can help us understand the larger context of socio-cultural, economic, and political change that affect youth. At the same time, it is important to examine how the local media industry benefits from youth interaction and participation, developed out of changing socio-economic conditions. There is a real danger that the local participatory culture may be hijacked in the service of profit-making activities.

## Audience Interaction on Air via SMS

In Şanlıurfa, both radio and cell phones have acquired significant roles and meanings in the lives of underprivileged youth since the beginning of the 1990s. Until 1990, Turkish broadcasting was a state monopoly with lots of cultural programming and news aimed at realizing the official ideology of westernization.[21] In 1990, pirate commercial radio and TV channels broke the state monopoly on broadcasting and enjoyed an unregulated broadcasting environment, which received an enthusiastic welcome throughout the country until the Turkish Radio-TV High Council (RTÜK) was established in 1995. During this time, many taboo subjects were discussed and the audience was called into expressing their views through phones and faxes. Soon commercial media became concentrated and big media moguls began working side-by-side with the authorities and within RTÜK guidelines.

While national radio and TV networks have changed their programming content and style drastically and focused on commercial programming since the last half of the 1990s, small local broadcasting channels, especially radio, kept their initial style of audience interaction and song requests for a variety of reasons, including having too small a budget to hire programmers and qualified staff, having to entertain continuous demands from the audience for interactive programming, and owners' being not interested in producing programming and instead wanting to keep the station to gain political and economic advantage elsewhere.[22] Therefore, radio and phones have continued to be used in tandem ever since small local, commercial radio stations emerged in Turkey. For instance, in Şanlıurfa, local radio played a matchmaker role and constituted a lively, functional, and entertaining social space for youth,[23] and it accomplished this as a result of audience interaction via phone-in programs. When I first conducted fieldwork in the city in 2001, young people were calling in to discuss arranged marriage practices, bride price, *berdel*—the cross-marriage of male and female children of two families—and other traditions that prioritize marriage among relatives, as well as restrictions on women's education. In addition, local radio functioned as a social space for them to experience various aspects of their youth identities by sharing cultural works they created, such as songs and poems, and by pursuing romantic relationships via sending songs and messages to each other.[24]

Before the 2000s, most young girls in Şanlıurfa had no access to cell phones and had limited access to land lines at home. Moreover, families who were newcomers to the city often felt concern about their daughters' reputations in a burgeoning and rapidly changing urban environment, which still embodied the semi-feudal kinship and power arrangements as well as tribal traditions of its new inhabitants. Girls, kept at home until they are married off, watch a lot of TV and listen to the radio. Boys, who are mostly sent to their fathers' workplace to help out and learn the job, also listen to the radio frequently. While local media professionals I interviewed did not want to think of their audience as predominantly consisting of teenagers, due to their belief that listeners' lack of education and maturity prevent them from pursuing "quality" programming, they continued to cater almost completely to the audience's song requests and text messages. Young people rightfully felt ownership of their favorite radio stations, calling them "ours," hailing the DJs as "one of us," sharing their own stories on air, and sending their lovers messages encoded in songs via codenames. Since young boys and girls weren't openly allowed to date, they had a chance to experience platonic relationships through this "local social field" they created over the radio.

Toward the mid-2000s, as girls were acquiring their brothers' or fathers' old cell phones and as the local radio stations shifted audience interaction from call-in participation to exclusively text messaging (SMS)—due to the extra profit it brought to the station[25]—the nature of interaction and functions once attributed to local radio changed. Boys had already had cell phones since the mid-1990s. Now with young girls owning them, they were able to send messages directly to each other without needing the radio or their close friends to carry messages back and forth. Today, young girls can give their cell phone numbers to boys in the neighborhood whom they like, via friends or sometimes directly through a note with their cell phone number written on it. So, cell phones do not necessarily allow the young people in Şanlıurfa to eliminate barriers to dating, but do allow them to experience it in privacy, even if they still cannot go out in public and walk in the parks hand-in-hand. As Anthony Townsend has asserted, mobile phones re-write spatial and temporal constraints of human communication systems.[26] And as in the Şanlıurfa example, they can help young people to overcome the difficulty of expressing their feelings on public airwaves, along with other constraints of radio call-in such as not being able to get through to the station, high caller traffic, DJs delivering the message inaccurately, playing the wrong song or forgetting to play it (Personal communication with DJ Mustafa Bayram from Harran FM). Since cell phone messages can be exchanged instantaneously between lovers, radio mishaps such as these can be easily remedied.

Just as local radio took over the role of friends in matchmaking—those who carried words, gifts, or letters in between lovers in rural areas—cell phones have mostly taken over the job of radio DJs, who used to act as matchmakers by playing songs that lovers wanted and giving them air time to deliver their message. Today, according to DJ Erkan Ülgen from Güneydoğu Radyo—one of the oldest radio stations predominantly catering to youth and their song requests via SMS—one continuing occurrence of young lovers treating the DJs as matchmakers occurs after a fight when the two participants are not sending each other SMS.

> Instead they send the radio station a text message like this "I am sending this song to my girlfriend who broke my heart this way...." Then the girlfriend responds [by sending a text message to the station]: "I hadn't done anything to break your heart but I will apologize anyways with this song...." This is how we end up becoming matchmakers. (Personal communication Erkan Ülgen, programmer and DJ, Güneydoğu Radyo, August 2007)

So, as Alexander Taylor and Richard Harper have suggested, "phones have provided young people with new ways to perform old rituals"[27] such as sending a text message to a third person/matchmaker or a DJ to seek reconciliation.

If cell phones remedy the constraints of communication brought about through older media and shift radio's job onto lovers to communicate with each other via their cell phones, then why do young people still send text messages to radio stations? Even though radio ceased to be the main way of pursuing a relationship for young people, sending a song for a loved one is a "gesture" as one of my informants put it, makes one "romantic" as another informant (Personal Communication, June 8, 2011) suggested, and is a "gift" as all my informants described it. In their ethnographic study, Taylor and Harper found that young people use mobile phone content and the phones themselves to participate in the practices of gift exchange or, as they refer to it, "gift-giving."[28] So, practices of sharing the content of messages sent to them by their best friends or exchanging each other's phones are gift-giving practices. While these gift-giving practices also take place in Şanlıurfa, a few others are quite unique to the area and explain why sending SMS to radio stations and requesting songs are still common. Based on my observations of the interaction on air and both my informants' and DJs' accounts, most of the song requesting that has been taking place since the wide dispersal of cell phones has the goal of showing one's love publicly and therefore aiming to cement one's relationship by acknowledging it within the public youth social network on air. Songs and text messages that accompany the songs are mostly sent to the radio for the love interest but also for friends and relatives as a gift in order to acknowledge and solidify social relations.

Sending texts and songs as gifts is an important aspect of an economy of intimacy and desire among Şanlıurfa youth. Boys are expected to provide their girlfriends with phone minutes, so dating can occur. Boys transferring minutes to their girlfriends' phones relieves girls from asking for money from their brothers or fathers, who might raise questions about who she has been chatting with so much. DJs often read text messages from girls who complain they don't have any more phone minutes left to send another song as a gift to their boyfriends, or that their boyfriends still haven't transferred minutes to their cell phones. These messages are in fact signs of relationship troubles and public displays of hurt feelings. These examples illustrate a crucial economic dimension of pursuing a relationship via cell phones, which is boys' ability to purchase minutes and send them to their girlfriends generously as gifts. Break-ups happen when boys stop sending minutes or do not send enough text messages or songs to their girlfriends. "The economy of intimacy and desire" needs to be well-balanced so that a lack of messages and song requests are not seen as lack of love.

## Radio and the Question of "Participatory Culture"

Can radio help form a participatory culture? How does the local radio and mobile phone convergence affect audience participation? As my research illustrated, the answers to these questions depend upon local context. In Şanlıurfa, between their emergence in 1993 until 2003, local radio stations functioned as a hub of youth interaction, activity, and participation, where it was possible to hear young people express their sadness over a love interest who has been married off to her cousin, play their saz (local guitar-like instrument), sing their songs, recite their poetry, voice their opinions on education and restrictive traditions, respond to each other, and send songs to those whose singing performance or opinions are valued the most. After 2003, when the radio stations only allowed sending songs, messages, and poems via SMS, interaction was reduced to DJs reading the messages verbatim and these messages were mostly song requests with some public expressions of love interests. The lively participatory culture had to be transformed into one that encouraged intimate and private communication between those who are involved in a romantic relationship but discouraged any sharing of opinions and cultural production in public.

As the local media became more converged, not only did less group participation take place but also certain groups were left out. Only girls who could obtain cell phones from their families or boyfriends could participate, for instance, and only if someone else could afford to add minutes to their phones. Similarly, boys with financial difficulties had a hard time participating and sometimes lost their girlfriends simply because they couldn't afford to spend money on both their own and their girlfriends' phones. What the case of Şanlıurfa shows us is that media convergence does not automatically encourage more participation, but rather champions types of participation that are profitable for the radio stations and phone companies. Allowing young people to interact only via texting generates enough monthly revenue for the radio stations to cover their monthly rent. Şanlıurfa youth have to come up with money in order to continue to participate and exercise their rituals of dating via songs and text messages. The fact that the convergence of media systems is enabled to serve the interests of the media industry first always guarantees increased profits, but does not necessarily cause a cultural shift that can level the playing field between consumers and producers.

I do not intend to present the participatory culture I observed in 2001 as either ideal or progressive. Youth voices were distinct and audible over the airwaves then. However, interaction was limited to the social space that was created for and by the youth for their own use and cultural sharing. Further, girls used landline phones at home to participate on air and thus did not need boys to send phone minutes to them. The advantage of mobile phones has been their ability to allow direct conversations between the unmarried and unrelated opposite sexes, which is still a taboo in Şanlıurfa and has the potential to ruin a girl's reputation. Carrying on romantic relationships via texting and local radio has enabled Şanlıurfa youth to communicate and date without any face-to-face encounters and therefore, it still continues to support young people's efforts to experience dating without upsetting the local traditions and Islamic restrictions on pre-marital relationships. On the one hand, this situation eases pressures on the youth, but on the other hand, it maintains the status quo. Thus, the case of local radio and mobile phone convergence in Şanlıurfa fails to constitute the type of ideal, progressive participatory culture that "technological evangelists" claim emerges as the cultural logic of convergence. Instead, it shows us another example of local participatory culture being hijacked in the service of profit-making convergence schemes.

## Acknowledgments

The author wishes to thank Mihaela Popescu and Michele Hilmes for their valuable comments and feedback.

## Notes

1. Dan C. Hallin and Paolo Mancini, "Americanization, Globalization and Secularization: Understanding the Convergence of Media Systems and Political Communication in the U.S. and Western Europe," in *Comparing Political Communication: Theories, Cases, and Challenges*, ed. Frank Esser and Barbara Pfetsch (Cambridge, UK: Cambridge University Press, 2004), 25.
2. The case of Google is a noteworthy example regarding the consequences of homogenization

and media convergence for creative commons and copyrights. See Siva Vaidhyanathan, *The Googlization of Everything: (And Why We Should Worry)* (Berkeley, CA: University of California Press, 2011).

3. Henry Jenkins, *Convergence Culture: Where Old and New Media Collide* (New York: New York University Press, 2006), 18.

4. Jean Burgess and Joshua Green, *YouTube: Online Video and Participatory Culture* (Cambridge, UK: Polity Press, 2009).

5. See, e.g., Antony Loewenstein, *The Blogging Revolution* (Melbourne, Australia: Melbourne University Press, 2008).

6. Mark Deuze, "Convergence Culture in the Creative Industries," *International Journal of Cultural Studies* 10 (2007): 243–263.

7. See, e.g., Mizuko Ito et al., *Hanging Out, Messing Around, and Geeking Out: Kids Living and Learning with New Media* (Cambridge, MA: MIT Press, 2009). For a call for a nuanced approach to digital natives, see Michael Thomas, "Technology, Education, and the Discourse of the Digital Native: Between Evangelists and Dissenters," in *Deconstructing Digital Natives: Young People, Technology, and the New Literacies*, ed. Michael Thomas (New York: Routledge, 2011), 1–14.

8. Jenkins, *Convergence Culture,* 3.

9. Jenkins, *Convergence Culture,* 3. For another discussion on how the current digital media environment blurs the line between media users and producers, see William Uricchio, "The Recurrent, the Recombinatory and the Ephemeral," in *Ephemeral Media: Transitory Screen Culture from Television to YouTube,* ed. Paul Grainge (London: British Film Institute, 2011), 31.

10. Jenkins, *Convergence Culture,* 22-23.

11. Richard Berry, "Will the iPod Kill the Radio Star? Profiling Podcasting as Radio," *Convergence: The International Journal of Research into New Media Technologies* 12 (2006): 143–162.

12. See e.g., Tiziano Bonini, "Crazy Radio: The Domestication of Mental Illness Over the Airwaves," *The Radio Journal: International Studies in Broadcast and Audio Media* 3 (2005): 145–153; Laura Kunreuther, "Technologies of the Voice: FM Radio, Telephone, and the Nepali Diaspora in Kathmandu," *Cultural Anthropology* 21 (2006): 323–353; Winston Mano, "Renegotiating Tradition on Radio Zimbabwe," *Media, Culture & Society* 26 (2004): 315–336; and Okoth F. Mudhai, "Survival of 'radio culture' in a converged networked new media environment," in *Popular Media, Democracy and Development in Africa,* ed. Herman Wasserman (London: Routledge, 2011), 253–268.

13. Jenny C. Aker and Isaac M. Mbiti, "Mobile Phones and Economic Development in Africa," *Journal of Economic Perspectives* 24 (2010): 207–232; Jonathan Donner, "The Social and Economic Implications of Mobile Telephony in Rwanda: An Ownership/Access Typology," *Knowledge, Technology, & Policy* 19 (2006): 17–28.

14. Heather A. Horst, "The Blessings and Burdens of Communication: Cell Phones In Jamaican Transnational Social Fields," *Global Networks* 6 (2006): 144.

15. Ibid.

16. Anthony M. Townsend, "Life in the Real-Time City: Mobile Telephones and Urban Metabolism," *Journal of Urban Technology* 7 (2000): 87.

17. Leopoldina Fortunati, "The Mobile Phone: Towards New Categories and Social Relations," *Information, Communication and Society* 5 (2002): 526.

18. See, e.g., Rich S. Ling, and Leslie Haddon, "Children, Youth and the Mobile," in *International Handbook of Children, Media and Culture,* ed. Kristin Drotner and Sonia Livingston (Thousand Oaks, CA: Sage, 2008): 137–151; Virpi Oksman and Jussi Turtiainen, "Mobile Communication as a Social Stage: Meanings of Mobile Communication in Everyday Life Among Teenagers In Finland," *New Media & Society* 6 (2004), 319–339; Berit Skog, "Mobiles and the Norwegian Teen: Identity, Gender and Class," in *Perpetual Contact: Mobile Communication, Private Talk, Public Performance,* ed. Elihu Katz and Mark Aakhus (Cambridge, UK: Cambridge University Press, 2002), 255–273.

19. Crispin Thurlow, and Susan McKay, "Profiling 'New' Communication Technologies In Adolescence," *Journal of Language and Social Psychology* 22 (2003): 95.
20. Ibid.
21. Ece Algan, "Privatization of media in Turkey and the question of media hegemony in the era of globalization," in *The Globalization of Corporate Media Hegemony*, edited by Lee Artz and Yahya R. Kamalipour (Albany, NY: SUNY Press, 2003), 169–192.
22. Ece Algan, "Development of Local Radio in Southeast Turkey," *Journal of Radio Studies* 11 (2004): 254–267.
23. Ece Algan, "The Role of Turkish Local Radio in the Construction of a Youth Community," *The Radio Journal: International Studies in Broadcast & Audio Media* 3 (2005): 75–92.
24. Ibid.
25. In 2003, all the local radio stations in Şanlıurfa followed the nationwide trend and eliminated audience call-ins completely. Instead, they encouraged their audiences to send their song requests and messages via SMS because the phone company paid the radio station a portion of the profit from every text that was sent. SMS revenues still bring the local radio stations between $200 and $400 per month, which is roughly equivalent to their rent.
26. Anthony M. Townsend, "Life in the Real-Time City."
27. Alexander S. Taylor and Richard Harper, "The Gift of the Gab? A Design Oriented Sociology of Young People's Use of Mobiles," *Computer Supported Cooperative Work* 12 (2003): 294.
28. Taylor and Harper, "The Gift of the Gab?"

# 6

# LISTENING TO RACE AND MIGRATION ON CONTEMPORARY U.S. SPANISH-LANGUAGE RADIO

*Dolores Inés Casillas*

Latino listeners in California's central coast area faithfully tune and call into Radio Bronco's popular mid-morning personality, Lupita Rodriguez.[1] Located on the 107.7 FM dial, Lupita hosts a local call-in show called El Bazar (meaning: marketplace or second-hand shop).[2] For a fast-paced two hours, El Bazar offers callers the opportunity to broadcast their services, sell lightly used wares, or rent out rooms or appliances.[3] For instance, a July 2010 episode featured the following on-air listings voiced by callers themselves: Ramiro sells both a refrigerator and a PlayStation PSP; Theresa offers excellent childcare on the Eastside; Fernando seeks four tires for his Dodge Ram; Jesus leases his iPhone for a month; and Clara shares a positive assessment of her "Inglés Sin Barreras" English-language learning DVD set. As the host, Lupita reminds people to repeat their phone number ("mija, despacito o no vale su llamada/slower honey or you're wasting your time"), asks clarifying questions ("… como nuevo? No me digas./… and it's like-new? Get out of here"), and makes certain that folks keep their pitch succinct ("Gracias-quien-sigue./Thanks-who's-next.").[4] On this particular morning, Lupita swiftly fielded 47 phone calls within the first 32 minutes of El Bazar before pausing for a five-minute set of commercials. With nothing valued or offered at more than $1,000 permitted, El Bazar transmutes the radio waves into a Latino-styled on-air Craigslist for a working-class listenership more accustomed to radio than the Internet, limited in shopping options within a wealthy coastal area of California, or seeking a marketplace exclusively in Spanish.

True, Lupita endears listeners with her sweet-tempered personality and skillful handling of callers. Yet listeners primarily turn to El Bazar to barter and shop for specific services and items without the interruption of jingles or musical play. Talk-centered shows like El Bazar prove that listeners-turned-callers continue to be the crux of popular radio shows, what Elena Razlogova aptly phrases as a "vernacular political economy" where ordinary people use radio for communal interests despite its corporate institutional control.[5] Listening can certainly elicit a sense of community or intimacy that later feeds into program or station loyalty.[6] In fact, radio historians argue that early local and regional radio owed much of its survival to formats that worked in collaboration with audiences.[7] In many ways, on-air dialogues between callers and radio hosts have become a hallmark element of contemporary Spanish-language radio that fosters local station loyalty precisely because the bulk of these on-air conversations rest on national and transnational matters.[8]

The most admired shows on Spanish-language radio are those that welcome callers to join them over the air, to congregate across great distances and in real-time, and most importantly, without the harsh public glare routinely given to Latinos and Latino issues. Egged on by English-language network news coverage, Latino communities within the popular U.S. imagination are seen as recently-and-illegally arrived threats to national security; perpetual abusers of social services; culprits of population growth; unsafe and unlicensed drivers; as well as secret agents in the plot to make all Americans bilingual.[9] The unpleasant publicity constructs a racialized climate of suspicion that manifests in anti-immigrant legislation where, for instance, speaking Spanish is frowned on (anti-bilingual education initiatives); standing outside Home Depot stores is discouraged (local "loitering" ordinances); or one's legal status is questioned based on phenotypic features (Arizona SB 1070). The airwaves of English-language, right-wing AM talk radio is particularly toxic with outright hate speech led by the likes of Rush Limbaugh. A recent study from UCLA researchers found a significant measure of clinical anxiety present when listeners were exposed to such broadcasts, regardless of whether or not they agreed with the show's rants.[10] Both English-language television and radio programming often malign Latinos as not quite full-fledged citizens.

Perhaps unsurprisingly, Latinos have retreated to the "safer" refuges of Spanish-language channels as evidenced by an increase in audiences across several Spanish-language media.[11] Broadcasting in Spanish itself has become increasingly politically significant given contemporary debates over English-only state mandates and proposed anti-immigrant legislation. For those unfamiliar with Spanish, the language and perceived "accent" carries racialized and classed connotations linked to the mouths and bodies of Latinos, but specifically Mexicans.[12] The post-9/11 moment, in particular, has ushered in racial and linguistic profiling under the guise of "national security."[13] On Spanish-language radio, for instance, listeners are not expected to speak English, never looked down upon for their service sector or seasonal employment, nor questioned as to their legal status. Spanish-language radio dutifully plays the role of public ally and advocate to a listenership characterized by language, race, as well as migration.

A quarter of the nation's Latino communities resides in the golden state of California; also home to the largest Mexican-origin communities and a fast growing Salvadoran population.[14] Approximately, approximately 15 percent of all California radio airs in Spanish with both the San Francisco Bay Area and Los Angeles—frequently designated as the number five and number one radio market, respectively—often reporting Spanish-language radio stations within the top five highest-rated stations.[15] This essay uses audio data recorded intermittently since 2005 from *Estereo Sol* (KSOL/San Francisco Bay Area), *Radio Bronco* (KIST/ Central Coast), and *La Raza* (KLAX/Los Angeles). California's landscape of Spanish-language radio owes its immigrant-focused character and phenomenal growth to listener-driven or talk-centered programming that candidly speaks to the political and economic realities of listeners within a diverse yet fractious border state. Ultimately, these unscripted vocal instances—morning salutations, listener requests, and song dedications—demonstrate how Latino listeners are drawn to radio for much more than musical accompaniments of homelands left behind but for guidance on how to navigate the political present.

## Listening to "Home"

> ¡Saludos a todos de Michoacán aquí en California! ¡Bue-nos días! Están listos?
>
> Greetings to those from Michoacán here in California! Good morning! Everyone ready?
>
> Morning salutation heard on Los Angeles's KLAX

Many Spanish-language radio stations reference regional townships in California in connection with specific provinces and pueblos in Mexico. Likewise, listeners fortunate enough to find themselves on the air routinely identify where they are from *and* where they are calling from. The combination of both Mexican and U.S. locations on the radio resonates with a listenership whose legal and social experiences of belonging have historically been complicated by migration. The usual reference to areas in Mexico momentarily suspends the actual 2,000 mile gap between say, Michoacán and California. The utterance of both U.S. and Mexico locales as a part of "home" evokes Pat Zavella's notion of "peripheral vision" where Latino communities maintain a bi-national perspective based on a sense of marginality experienced by those who have begrudgingly left familiar lands yet are not quite settled in newfound residences.[16] In many ways, radio genres in Spanish cater to this complicated and ambivalent sentiment of their migrant or transient listenership.

Ethnic and non-English-language media have long offered a nostalgic "window" to home countries for immigrant and migrant listening communities. For instance, during the 1920s, the Grand Ol' Opry and the National Barn Dance brought a rural nostalgic appeal to those who had migrated to urban areas.[17] Both the blues and country lyrics routinely index the train (transportation), the long road (allegorically, too), and strained relationships due to the aforementioned "long road." In short, wistfulness about "home" has long escorted migrating communities to new destinations. In fact, tapping into melancholy has been quite a lucrative practice for U.S. Spanish-language radio. Stations committed to playing music from yesteryear often identify themselves as radio recuerdo (memory) or radio romantica (romantic). Categorized under the rubric of Spanish Adult Hits, these nostalgia-laden radio stations comprise nearly 10 percent of all Spanish-language radio.[18] The rotation of mainly ranchera music—nationalist ballads about revolution, patriotism, and heartbreak, often with tequila—are prefaced with liner notes about the artists and the decade in which the song was released; a deliberate effort to jog listener memories to another time, place, and reality. For instance, Vicente Fernandez, known as the King of Rancheras and a beloved artist on recuerdo and romantica stations, sells more music and concert tickets to his Mexican base fans *within* the U.S. than in Mexico. Sold out arenas feature Fernandez in a traditional mariachi suit accompanied by a mariachi ensemble as concert participants share gritos—loud, harmonious, passionate cries—in honor of his staged and aural Mexican-ness. In essence, this tried-and-true format uses heartfelt ballads and gritos to romanticize lives and homelands left behind.

In a similar gesture, the categorization of "Mexican Regional" assigned to an astounding 44 percent of all radio stations within the top fifty Hispanic-identified U.S. radio markets also explicitly targets Mexican-identified listeners. Mexican Regional radio offers tuba-heavy bandas, accordion-laced norteños, as well as the bellows of said rancheras. Sales for Mexican Regional music account for over half of all U.S. Spanish-language record sales yet Hispanic marketers disparagingly describe the genre as "foreign, niche and old-fashioned," a distant second from to the more air play friendly salsa by the likes of non-Mexican musicians; Gloria Estefan being one.[19] Despite its industry muscle, the genre carries raced and classed undertones of its migrant, working-class, Spanish-dominant listenership.[20]

Talk-centered shows, some featuring listeners-turned-callers have routinely elbowed their way onto music-oriented Spanish-language radio stations, a reminder that listening to crooners does have its limits. Immigrant-based and ethnic communities, in general, use media for community building and advocacy across geographical boundaries. Latino listeners often turn to Spanish-language radio for public updates on key immigrant-related legislation and emergencies.[21] Listeners are familiar, for example, with on-air fundraisers hosted on behalf of home countries recovering from natural catastrophes. In 2005, for instance, Latino listeners were briefed on the aftermath of Hurricane Katrina in New Orleans as well as the devastation left by Hurricane Wilma in Cancún, Mexico. Although both garnered air-time, on-air fundraising from three Los Angeles-based radio stations sent proceeds to victims affected by Hurricane Wilma. As one caller explained to fellow San Francisco-based KSOL radio listeners: "México no tiene ningún FEMA, sino que tiene mexicanos en los EE.UU" (Mexico has no FEMA, but it does have Mexicans in the U.S.). Just as the Federal Emergency Management Agency (FEMA) was held accountable for New Orleans evacuees, Mexican listeners living in the U.S. were regarded as the financial backbone to re-building the lesser populated provinces outside of tourist-mecca Cancún. Comedian George Lopez joked post-Katrina that FEMA, indeed, would help rebuild New Orleans but that the acronym FEMA actually stood for: "Find Every Mexican Available."[22] As with both natural and bureaucratic disasters, the labor of Mexicans, as evidenced during post-hurricane radio, literally and figuratively "shoulders the transnational economy."[23]

Radio's interactive and real-time capabilities help listeners navigate newfound residences and political structures by way of radio hosts, guests, call-in shows. Each major U.S. Spanish-language radio network features a host of prominent talk-based call-in shows. Health programs, for instance, feature doctors or nutritionists who encourage listeners to advocate for bilingual health providers; pop psychologists counsel immigrant parents on the challenges of raising children in the U.S. or maintaining emotional ties to family members abroad; finance-related shows stress the benefits of setting up bank accounts on both sides of the border; and guest attorneys offer live question-and-answer sessions with listeners about the latest immigration-related news. This access to immediate legal information, culturally specific health guidance, and local resources characterize the political efficacy of talk-centered programming.[24] Specifically, these exchanges broadcast instances of listeners' migrant sensibilities and highlight the economic and racialized standings of many Latinos in the U.S.

## Spanish-Language Radio Growth

Today both urban and suburban radio listeners are bound to stumble across one of nearly 1,300 Spanish-language radio stations while surfing the dial.[25] Changes in ownership caps thanks to both the Telecommunications Act of 1996 as well as a shift in the listening practices of many older, whiter, and more affluent groups to mp3s have propelled a number of news, jazz, and alternative rock stations to switch to Spanish-language programming. This is especially true in "newfound" Latino destinations such as Tulsa, Oklahoma and Charlotte, North Carolina. Radio trade magazines credit the population growth of Latinos in the U.S. as the "cause" of Spanish-language radio's implausible growth of 110% since 2000 alone.[26] Between 2000 and 2010, Latino populations grew 43 percent to represent the largest minority group in the U.S. and now number over 50 million.[27] Surely, population growth increased potential audience numbers but the increasing anti-immigrant sentiment and state-sanctioned policies since the early 1980s has influenced the character of Spanish-language radio.[28]

Media and advertising industries point to radio as the medium of choice for U.S. Latino consumers. When given the option of eliminating either the Internet or the radio in their households, 67 percent of Latinos surveyed in the United States elected to keep radio and disconnect the Internet.[29] Even with popular Internet offerings of Latino-tailored websites, such as "iTunes Latino," and the availability of satellite dish services delivering Spanish-language television programming, Latinos continue to rely on broadcast radio as a source for news and entertainment—much more so than their English-speaking peers.[30] In fact, Latinos account for 10 percent of all U.S. radio listening, and, according to industry reports, listen to radio an average of three hours a week longer than the "general" (white, English-speaking) radio listener.[31]

Many Spanish-language radio stations target their listenership by advertising call numbers and radio personalities at public transit bus stops, metro stations, or on freeway billboards. Construction sites, hotel housekeeping carts, and restaurant kitchens are just as likely to transmit sounds of Spanish-language radio play to the surprise of passerby. The public nature of most Spanish-language radio listening found visually through prominent advertisements at bus stops and audibly at work sites, marks the listening experience as both communal and classed. This differs considerably from what I refer to as more "white collar" modes of listening—the mostly solitary practices promoted by private car commutes, personal satellite radios, iPod use, and Internet broadcasts.[32]

The volume of sound has been used before to represent disgruntled, unhappy, forms of resistance from primarily young people of color. The public display and sound of a boom box during the 1980s became emblematic of black youth "protesting" society's racial hierarchy. Both Daniel Makagon and Brenda Jo Bright both point to loud stereo systems and intricately detailed lowriders, respectively, as a means of youth calling attention to themselves; believing they're already under surveillance by police and adults.[33] In a similar gesture, Spanish-language radio listeners are turning up the volume and proudly flaunting their working-class aesthetics. Symbolically, the public practice of Spanish-language radio listening carries political significance as immigrants are chastised for their working-class labor yet make certain that radio sets boom from the back of many restaurants perhaps to remind patrons who exactly is preparing their food.

## Strength in Numbers

With an airwave presence since the 1920s, Spanish-language radio experienced its first growth spurt in the 1950s as it surpassed fellow immigrant-based shows—Polish and Yiddish broadcasting.[34] Driven by an increase in migration due to labor policies (e.g., Bracero Program), Mexican-owned broadcasting companies shifted their attention to the diaspora of Mexican listeners in the U.S. Mexican-based Spanish-language radio broadcasters attempted to deliver an "authentic" sound of Mexico through radio sets.[35]

Media and advertising industries renewed their attention towards bilingual (Spanish-English) U.S. consumers in the 1980s during the government-sponsored "Decade of the Hispanic."[36] Though just 67 Spanish-oriented radio stations existed in 1980, the number soared to 390 by 1990.[37] Many of these gains made within urban radio markets were heard on stronger, acoustically crisp FM bands rather than low-cost static-driven AM stations. The crossover from static AM to lucrative FM signaled the mainstreaming of Spanish-language radio programming in tandem, mind you, with the passage of the Immigrant Reform and Control Act (IRCA) of 1986. IRCA, referred to as the amnesty bill, provided legal permanent resident status for nearly three million persons. This parallel crossover recognized nearly three million listeners into the U.S. radio market.

By 2000, the Federal Communications Commission (FCC) identified nearly 600 Spanish-language radio stations in the U.S.[38] By then, Spanish-language radio had successfully dethroned English-language radio stations from their number one standings in many major radio markets, including Los Angeles, Houston, Miami, and New York City. By 2010, the field of Spanish-language radio featured just a handful of heavyweights—the most familiar, of course being corporate giant Univision Radio.

## Listening to Labor

> Saludos hoy a los pintores, construccionistas, todos los janitors y otros afuera trabajando abajo del solecito, pero con ganas, por el billete, pa'las cuentas, hombres, o simplemente por la remesa, ¿no?

> Greetings today to painters, construction workers, all the janitors and others working outside in the sun, but with drive, for the [dollar] bill, man, for those bills, or simply for the remittance, right? (Radio host afternoon greeting on Estéreo Sol [KSOL])

Radio sets provide a form of portable, cost-efficient companionship that attracts many working-class, immigrant Latinos. National demographic profiles of Hispanic radio listeners list their annual income as less than $25,000.[39] Elsewhere I argue that globalization's effect on labor specifically the transition from manufacturing to more service sector work has influenced Latino listening patterns.[40] Liza Catanzarite effectively calls attention to the cadre of "brown collar" occupations—low-level service sectors jobs—that are disproportionately occupied by an immigrant workforce.[41] These positions within construction, janitorial, agriculture, and manufacturing sectors consist of painters, field hands, and dishwashers. In urban centers such as Chicago, Los Angeles, New York City, and San Diego, immigrant Latinos constitute an overwhelming 40 to 70 percent of this workforce.[42] Unmistakably, the sounds of Spanish-language programming are heard from the kitchens of restaurants and outside construction sites, rendering the presence of this brown collar workforce acoustically "concrete."

In the afternoon airwave greeting quoted above, the radio host does not refer to a geographical location but rather identifies listeners through brown collar occupations: "pintores, construccionistas" (painters, construction workers). Aside from the explicit naming of multiple geographical homes, KSOL often situates listeners' U.S. locations within the contexts of labor, work, and ultimately earned income. The radio host locates her listeners discursively "afuera trabajando abajo del solecito" (outside working beneath the sun), understanding the environment in which her listeners are situated, empathizing, and recognizing the extra daily human burden that this type of labor entails.

Not only are work and workplaces frequent topics on KSOL's airwaves, particularly during the early morning hours, but "work titles" of brown collar occupations are referred to with esteem during host greetings. Morning salutations are extended to those driving taxis, washing dishes, grooming yards, or caring for other people's children—a gendered acknowledgment of Latina listeners employed as nannies and babysitters. Aware of their distinct listenership, radio hosts foreground a collective immigration and working-class experience. The added assurance that listeners—assumed to be all Latino, immigrant, and employed in positions of manual labor—toil at work "con ganas" (with drive) validates the work ethic, value, and place of immigrants.

The manner in which U.S. politicians boast about the strength of the global economy rarely accounts for the ways in which labor and immigration are intricately bound. According to Saskia Sassen, immigration constitutes a major component of the transnational economy yet its pivotal role is seldom recognized.[43] Despite the U.S. Census's 2010 figures numbering nearly 40 million in the U.S., many Latinos are often rendered as "invisible" laborers who are absent within larger discussions of U.S. politics and, as Sassen notes, global economies.[44] Yet within the mainstream English-language news media, Latinos are often framed as social welfare service predators or simply confined to stereotypic farm worker roles—both unproductive and limiting portrayals of U.S. Latinos that minimize their contributions to multiple national economies. The paradox that presents itself is that while Latinos' bodies are instrumental to the productivity of U.S. labor and its political economy, they are ridiculed in U.S. popular culture, ignored by most mass media, positioned as matters of debate for politicians, and generally isolated from U.S. public and political life.

Saskia Sassen's insistence, as noted above, that immigration be brought into the forefront of discussions on global capital reflects the tension framed by this short vignette. The radio host's focus on work is immediately followed by the acknowledgment of working: for "el billete," a distinct (Spanglish) gesture towards the U.S. dollar bill and its economic weight by comparison to Latin American currencies. Perhaps more tellingly, the casual reference to "la remesa" (remittance), or the means of wiring or sending money abroad, stresses how such transactions and their significance to national economies have become "normalized" practices that serve simultaneously as both affective and economic ties.

Economists confirm that the labor and subsequent remittances of immigrants back "home" to Mexico, Central America, and the Dominican Republic account for these countries' largest source of revenue.[45] The business of wiring money across distances has been lucrative for corporate giant (and frequent radio sponsor), Western Union.[46] Mediating the migration of money, Spanish-language radio ads entice listeners to wire additional money to an implied waiting or dependent family located miles away, asking listeners to envision "the extra room on that house" or "how pretty she'll look in that dress." Broadcast references to listeners' remesas, coupled with the prevalence of commercials that advertise sending money, accentuate further the importance of Latino and immigrant labor in the U.S. During the Mother's Day season of 2006, for instance, radio listeners were reminded of capital's deft use of affect, when assailed by the AT&T ad line: "Mexico is only seven cents away." Profiting off of families separated by both geographical and emotional distance, such radio ads help coerce immigrant listeners to become that much more emotionally invested in their jobs here; a vivid reminder of their place in the geographical U.S. and the interests of those with family located across national borders.

## Listening as Cultural Belonging

> Tengo mis dos hermanas, viven las dos in Tijuana, en mis pensamientos; ojalá que esten bien.

> I am thinking of my two sisters, they both live in Tijuana; hopefully they are both well.

> Elvira, listener-turned-caller dedication

By and large, radio allows callers to phone in, often via cell phone, with song requests, dedications, or to share the customary saludo or "shout-out." Here, both listeners and radio hosts maximize the reach of radio broadcasts to communicate messages to friends and loved ones and express opinions in a publicized sphere. While the on-air greeting is in itself a popular practice of all radio, Spanish-language radio stations send saludos over great distances in real-time. Given the limitations of technology and communications policy, on-air saludos sent across state and national lines represent more symbolic gestures, since the technological capability to link listeners across borders and thousands of miles, are not commonplace.[47] Nevertheless, the on-air citing by radio hosts or listeners of either an individual's name or hometown imparts audible public recognition. It can also send a powerful and comforting message to fellow listeners that there are others in the U.S. that hail from the same hometown. It may not ceremonially bring listeners together (à la Benedict Anderson) but it does allow listeners to "map" where other immigrants may be located.

Often, radio hosts will ask listeners to identify their calling location in an effort to boast the geographical span of their station's listener base. When listener-turned-caller Elvira above called via cell phone in the evening to dedicate "cualquier canción de Juan Gabriel" (any song by [Mexican singer] Juan Gabriel) while en route to Tijuana, she explained: "Pues, ahora vivo en Modesto... apenas pase la ciudad de Fremont ... me paré a comprar un café en McDonalds ... me esperan en Tijuana." (I live in Modesto ... I just passed Fremont ... I stopped to buy a cup of coffee at McDonalds ... my family is expecting me in Tijuana). Radio scholars Martin Montgomery and Paddy Scannell recognize the on-air mapping of listeners' locations as a strategic move to craft a more intimate on-air meeting.[48] Listeners cognitively "map" Elvira's travels vis-à-vis her descriptions. Unlike traditional notions of community building or community formation bound by and dependent on fixed parameters of space, for many Latinos, this form of on-air mapping via radio transcends official boundaries as family and friends may be scattered across great distances. On Spanish-language radio, geographical mentions include actual sites of listening and often listeners' countries of origin, as evidenced in the epigraph demonstrating KSOL's geographical coupling of the San Francisco Bay Area with "puuurrrooo MÉXICO" (despite the 700 mile distance). Here, listeners accompany Elvira on her travels from Modesto's Highway 99 and presumably across Interstate 280 to the 580 before arriving in Fremont via the 680 as she makes her trek south across the border to Tijuana. The McDonalds pit stop for coffee reminds listeners that while it may be early evening, Elvira has a long night ahead of her, warranting the companionship of Juan Gabriel.

## Politically Speaking

For Spanish-language programming, U.S. and Mexican politics are heard as two different forms of politically oriented broadcasts. In the more traditional (Anglo-U.S.) vein, Spanish-language radio invites politicians to join them over the airwaves in interactive formats that invite listener dialogue. Spanish-language programming facilitates on-air discussions by way of English-to-Spanish translators as well as by playing the role of on-air linguistic and cultural translator between political institutions and listenerships. But Spanish-language radio has also redressed conventional notions of politics by assigning local resources and service agencies prominent positions within on-air broadcasts with listeners. The latter assists listeners in more advocacy and grassroots organizing actions, activities considered paramount to legally vulnerable listeners who are trying to keep abreast of changes in immigration legislation.

In the summer of 2006, the number one rated Spanish-language radio station in the U.S., La Raza, based in Los Angeles and broadcasting nationally (via syndication), kicked off "Votos por América," an eleven-city voter registration bus tour. The tour reached out to Latinos by setting up live broadcasts outside Latino supermercados (supermarkets) in an effort to boost the number of registered Latino voters.[49] On each stop, listeners were presented with the significance of either registering to vote (if they were legally able) or investigating their next steps towards acquiring U.S. citizenship, all the while maintaining allegiances to homelands. The promotion of dual citizenship, albeit legally easier for immigrants from some Latin American countries than for others, challenges traditional notions of civic duties. In many ways, the radio tour encouraged listeners to become not just politically active at the ballot box but also politicized in terms of immigration, living wages, and so forth.

During the station's tour, listeners tuning in at home were privy to live conversations on-location. Listeners overheard the excitement, for instance, of Ricardo, a Texas listener, who had recently attained his citizenship papers, and the skepticism in María's voice as radio hosts bantered with her about her responsibility to vote both in the U.S. and Mexico. The tour ended in Washington, DC, where popular and influential radio hosts took the day to lobby specific Congress persons on behalf of "la gente Latina" (Latino peoples). The tour not only showcased how U.S. Spanish-language radio takes shows and politics "on the road," but also exemplified the public responsibility taken on by radio hosts to represent (in this case via lobbying) the political needs of their listenership.

Spanish-language radio's political role as "on-air organizer" was made most apparent in the spring of 2006 when millions of listeners attended record-breaking pro-immigrant rallies across the nation. These mass mobilizations—organized by grassroots organizations—served as powerful responses to a series of disconcerting anti-immigrant legislation.[50] Radio hosts across the nation, with the blessings of station management and network executives, used the airwaves as their public podiums in preparing listeners to join them on the streets. The slogan endorsed by a coalition of nonprofit and religious organizations and used in the numerous marches—¡Hoy marchamos, mañana votamos! (Today we march, tomorrow we vote!)—set the stage for the subsequent bus tour discussed above. Several arms of the (white) liberal, English-language media were taken by complete and unedited surprise by the record setting marches. It later dawned on many that these marches were not "spontaneous" but rather planned and advertised within Spanish-language media. The public bafflement called attention to the unique acoustic relationship between Latinos and U.S. Spanish-language radio.[51]

During campaign seasons, politicians dispatch Spanish-speaking staff or conduct on-air interviews with translators to Spanish-language morning radio shows in hopes of courting the votes of U.S. Latinos. Memorable on-air campaigning includes: New York then-mayoral candidate, Michael Bloomberg, speaking (in heavily accented Spanish) alongside salsa legend Willie Colón in staged campaign jingles; in 2008 to 2012, Mitt Romney's son politely urging Florida radio listeners (in enunciated Honduran Spanish) to "vota por mi Papá" (vote for my Dad); that same year, Democratic Presidential candidate Barack Obama's campaign pledge to Los Angeles-based host El Piolín (live and via translation) that, if President, he would, indeed, return to his morning show. Twenty-four hours later, Hilary Clinton (live and via translation) upped the ante and promised that, if President, she would welcome El Piolín to broadcast *from* the White House. Both of the latter campaign pitches were met with canned studio applause and frenzied hoots from radio hosts. In each instance, politicians or their Spanish-speaking endorsers capitalized on their experience within U.S. Latino communities (Obama, Clinton) or time spent abroad in Central or Latin America (Romney, Clinton, Bloomberg).

## Conclusion

A companion to its legion of listeners, Spanish-language radio plays an increasingly significant role precisely because the geographical and legislative realities of the border make for recurring discussion and reference over the airwaves. At a time when the language and brown bodies of Latinos are policed and surveilled through legally yet racially codified standards,[52] the sounds of spoken Spanish remind the larger public of its immigrant base of listeners.

Because Latinos and their contributions to U.S. society are persistently deemed as "foreign" and "Other," Spanish-language radio's immigrant-based, transnational character resonates with a listenership eager to keep abreast of the political and popular culture of both the U.S. and Mexico. Spanish-language radio's acoustic evocation of Mexico and its Latino listenership constructs a Spanish-language, (im)migrant, and ethnically (non-white) public sphere within the very confines of the geographical U.S.

## Acknowledgments

I thank Jason Loviglio for his generous collegiality and enthusiasm for radio; Juan Sebastian Ferrada for his exceptional research assistance; and my mother-in-law Beverly Csordas who always seems to come to the rescue.

## Notes

1. The ethnic labels "U.S. Latino" and "Latino" refer to persons of any Latin American origin living within the geographic boundaries of the United States. Given that this essay focuses

on radio programming from three California-based radio stations, these terms refer to Mexican and Central American listeners.

2. This essay focuses on Mexican-dominant radio listeners in, and radio excerpts from, the Pacific Northwest, yet Caribbean-directed radio functions similarly with shows that feature steadfast engagement with callers.

3. This practice of using radio as a "community bulletin" is not limited to Spanish-language radio. William Barlow discusses this in his stunning text, *Voice Over: The Making of Black Radio* (Philadelphia, PA: Temple University Press, 1998).

4. Within English-language print, words and phrases in Spanish are often marked via italicization. Doing so, I believe sustains U.S.-based racial and linguistic hierarchies. I both privilege and applaud the bilingual reader. For an insightful discussion of language politics in relationship to Spanish, I recommend Gloria Anzaldúa, "How to Tame a Wild Tongue," in *Borderlands: The New Mestiza* (San Francisco: Spinsters/Aunt Lute, 1997), 207–43; Frances R. Aparicio, "Whose Spanish? Whose Language? Whose Power? Testifying to Differential Bilingualism," *Indiana Journal of Hispanic Literatures* 12 (1998), 5–25; and Bonnie Urciuoli, *Exposing Prejudice: Puerto Rican Experiences of Language, Race, and Class* (Boulder, CO: Westview Press, 1996).

5. Elena Razlogova, *The Listener's Voice: Early Radio and the American Public* (Philadelphia, PA: University of Pennsylvania Press, 2011).

6. Besides Razlogova's *The Listener's Voice*, several radio historians have also argued this point. For two key texts, see Michele Hilmes, *Radio Voices: American Broadcasting, 1922–1952* (Minneapolis: University of Minnesota Press, 1997) and Susan J. Douglas, *Listening In: Radio and the American Imagination* (Minneapolis: University of Minnesota Press, 2004).

7. Two books in particular emphasize this point see Jason Loviglio, *Radio's Intimate Public: Network Broadcasting and Mass-Mediated Democracy* (Minneapolis: University of Minnesota Press, 2005) and Elena Razlogova, *The Listener's Voice*.

8. I make this case in two other essays, "Puuurrrooo MEXICO!: Listening to Transnationalism on U.S. Spanish-Language Radio," in *Beyond el Barrio: Everyday Life in Latina/o America*, eds. Gina M. Pérez, Frank Guridy, and Adrian Burgos Jr. (New York: New York University Press, 2010), 44–62 and "Adios El Cucuy: Immigration and Laughter over the Airwaves," *Boom: A Journal of California* 1, no. 3 (2011), 44–56.

9. For three compelling texts that detail the portrayal of Latino immigrants in newsprint, see Otto Santa Ana, *Brown Tide Rising: Metaphors of Latinos in Contemporary American Public Discourse* (Austin: University of Texas Press, 2002), as well as Leo Chavez's two books, *Covering Immigration: Popular Images and the Politics of the Nation* (Berkeley: University of California Press, 2001) and *The Latino Threat: Constructing Immigrants, Citizens, and the Nation* (Stanford, CA: Stanford University Press, 2008).

10. Hermes J. Garbán, Francisco Javier Iribarren, and Chon A. Noriega, *Using Biological Markers to Measure Stress in Listeners of Commercial Talk Radio* (Los Angeles: UCLA, Chicano Studies Research Center, August 2012).

11. Pew Research Center's Project for Excellence in Journalism, "The State of the News Media 2012," accessed January 10, 2012, http://stateofthemedia.org/. That's not to say, however, that homophobic rants in Spanish do not exist, see Horacio Roque Ramirez, *A Language of (In)Visibility: Latina and Latino LGBT Images in Spanish-Language Television and Print News Media* (New York: GLAAD Center for the Study of Media & Society, 2003).

12. Jane Hill, "Covert Racist Discourse: Metaphors, Mocking, and the Racialization of Historically Spanish-Speaking Populations in the United States," in *The Everyday Language of White Racism* (Malden, MA: Blackwell, 2008), 119–57. Equally significant, this form of racialization takes place with Puerto Ricans as well; see Urciuoli's, *Exposing Prejudice*.

13. Kevin Johnson, "September 11 and Mexican Immigrants: Collateral Damage Comes Home," *DePaul Law Review* 52 (2003), 849–70; David Manuel Hernández, "Pursuant to Deportation: Latinos and Immigrant Detention," *Latino Studies* 6 (2008), 35–63.

14. United States Census, "2010 American Community Survey," accessed September 3, 2012, http://factfinder2.census.gov/faces/nav/jsf/pages/index.xhtml.

15. Arbitron, "Hispanic Radio Today: How America Listens to Radio" (2006, 2010, 2011 editions), accessed July 30, 2012, http://arbitron.com/radio_stations/home.htm.

16. Patricia Zavella, *I'm Neither Here nor There: Mexicans' Quotidian Struggles with Migration* (Durham, NC: Duke University Press, 2011).

17. Kristine M. McCusker, "Bury Me Beneath the Willow: Linda Parker and Definitions of Tradition on the National Barn Dance, 1932–1935," *Southern Folklore* 56, no. 3 (1999), 223–43.

18. At least fourteen different Spanish-language formats have flourished on the airwaves, from tejano, news/talk, and oldies to tropical, see Todd Chambers, "The State of Spanish-language Radio," *Journal of Radio Studies* 13, no.1 (2006), 34–50. For the latest tallies, see Arbitron, "Hispanic Radio Today: How America Listens to Radio" accessed July 10, 2012, http://arbitron.com/radio_stations/home.htm.

19. Luis Clemens, "The Sound That Sells," *Marketing y Medios,* December, 1, 2005.

20. Ben Quiñones, "¡Despiertese, Despiertese!" *LA Weekly,* March 25, 2005.

21. Mari Castañeda, "The Importance of Spanish-Language Radio," in *Latina/o Communication Studies Today,* ed. Angharad Valdivia (New York: Peter Lang, 2008), 51–68.

22. Vicki Ruíz, "Citizen Restaurant: American Imaginaries, American Communities," *American Quarterly,* 60, no.1 (2008), 1–21.

23. Angie Chabram-Dernersesian, "Chicana/o Latina/o Cultural Studies: Transnational and Transdisciplinary Movements," *Cultural Studies* 13, no. 2 (1999), 181.

24. Dolores Inés Casillas, "Sounds of Surveillance: U.S. Spanish-Language Radio Patrols La Migra," *American Quarterly* 63, no. 3 (2011), 807–829.

25. Arbitron, "Hispanic Radio Today: How America Listens to Radio" and Pew Hispanic Center. "Hispanic Media: Faring Better than Mainstream Media," accessed August 29, 2011, http://pewresearch.org/pubs/2093/spanish-language-media-hispanic-newspapers-television-radio-magazines-digital.

26. Federal Communications Commission, "FCC Encyclopedia," accessed September 3, 2012, http://www.fcc.gov/encyclopedia/fm-query-broadcast-station-search.

27. Pew Research Center's Project for Excellence in Journalism, "The State of the News Media 2012," http://www.pewresearch.org/2012/03/19/state-of-the-news-media-2012/

28. Dolores Inés Casillas, "Sounds of Surveillance."

29. Arbitron/Edison Media Research, "Internet and Multimedia 2006: On-Demand Media Explodes," accessed March 1, 2012, www.arbitron.com/downloads/im2006study.pdf.

30. Arbitron, "Hispanic Radio Today: How America Listens to Radio."

31. Arbitron, "Hispanic Radio Today: How America Listens to Radio."

32. Dolores Inés Casillas, "Sounds of Belonging: A Cultural History of Spanish-Language Radio in the United States, 1922–2004" (PhD diss., University of Michigan, Ann Arbor, 2006).

33. Brenda Jo Bright, *Looking High and Low: Art and Cultural Identity* (Tucson: University of Arizona Press, 1995).

34. Ari Y. Kelman, "The Acoustic Culture of Yiddish," *Shofar: An Interdisciplinary Journal of Jewish Studies* 25, no. 1 (2006), 127–151.

35. Felix Gutiérrez and Jorge Reina Schement, *Spanish-Language Radio in the Southwestern United States* (Austin: Center of Mexican American Studies, University of Texas at Austin, 1979).

36. Arlene Dávila, *Latinos Inc.: The Marketing and Making of a People* (Berkeley: University of California, 2001).

37. Reports on the growth saturated broadcasting and mainstream news, for instance, see Susan Warren, "Stations Change Tune to Woo Hispanics," *Wall Street Journal,* January 25, 1995; Donna Petrozello, "Audience Share Swells for Spanish Formats," *Broadcasting and Cable* 126, no. 4 (1996), 122; and Mari Castañeda Paredes, "The Transformation of Spanish-Language Radio," *Journal of Radio Studies* 10, no. 1 (2003), 5–15.

38. The categorization of Spanish-language radio has shifted throughout the decades, in line with the racial and immigrant politics of specific eras, from "foreign-language," "ethnic," and "Mexican," to "Spanish"; Dolores Inés Casillas, *Sounds of Belonging.*

39. Arbitron, "Hispanic Radio Today: How America Listens to Radio."

40. Dolores Inés Casillas, "Sounds of Belonging."

41. Liza Catanzarite, "Wage Penalties in Brown-Collar Occupations," *Latino Policy and Issues Brief* 8 (2003), 1-4.

42. Liza Catanzarite, "Wage Penalties in Brown-Collar Occupations."

43. Saskia Sassen, *Globalization and Its Discontents: Essays on the New Mobility of People and Money* (New York: The New Press, 1998.)

44. Two compelling accounts of how gender and immigration renders laborers invisible are offered in Grace Chang, *Disposable Domestics: Immigrant Women Workers in the Global Economy* (Cambridge, MA: South End Press, 2000) and Alejandra Marchevsky and Jeanne Theoharis, *Not Working: Latina Immigrants, Low-Wage Jobs, and the Failure of Welfare Reform* (New York: New York University Press, 2006).

45. Elisabeth Malkin, "Mexicans Barely Increased Remittances in '07," *New York Times*, February 26, 2008, accessed September 12, 2012, http://www.nytimes.com/2008/02/26/business/worldbusiness/26mexico.html?ref=worldbusiness&_r=0

46. Julie Rawe, "The Fastest Way to Make Money," *Time*, June 23, 2003; and Linda Singer, "Make Regular Remittance a Creditworthy Activity," *American Banker*, April 30, 2004.

47. An exception is Fresno-based community radio station Radio Bilingüe, which hosts a daily talk-based public affairs program that broadcasts nationally and, as of 1992, transnationally to sister radio stations in Puerto Rico and Mexico.

48. Martin Montgomery, "DJ Talk," in *Media, Mobility, and Identity* (New York: Routledge, 1986); and Paddy Scannell, *Radio, Television, and Modern Life* (Cambridge, MA: Blackwell, 1996).

49. Tyche Hendricks, "Popular DJ Takes Registration Drive to Latino Voters," *San Francisco Chronicle*, August 1, 2006.

50. Two controversial pieces of legislation were passed in December 2005 (U.S. House of Representatives) and May 2006 (U.S. Senate). HR4437: the former, known as "The Border Protection, Anti-Terrorism, and Illegal Immigration Control Act," asked, among other things: (a) that a 700-mile wall be constructed along the U.S.-Mexico border; (b) that state and local enforcement be authorized to enforce federal immigration law; (c) for changes in law so that individuals, organizations, and religious factions could be penalized criminally for assisting undocumented immigrants; and (d) that felon penalties be imposed on immigrants for residing in the U.S. as undocumented. The latter, S2611, was largely a modified version of HR4437. For a detailed trajectory of the bill's route to passage, see http://www.govtrack.us/congress/bill.xpd?bill=h109-4437, accessed 1 November 2006.

51. Joel Stein, "500,000 and No One Invite Me?" *Time*, March 28, 2006.

52. Jonathan X. Inda, *Targeting Immigrants: Government, Technology, and Ethics* (Malden, MA: Blackwell, 2004).

# 7

# VOICES MADE FOR PRINT

## Crip Voices on the Radio[1]

*Bill Kirkpatrick*

Winner of the "Best Picture" Academy Award for 2010, *The King's Speech* dramatizes the struggles of Britain's King George VI (Colin Firth), a rather private man who had suffered with a speech impediment since his youth. When George suddenly finds himself elevated to the throne and called upon to reassure and guide the nation through World War II, his stammer becomes a particular liability: how can he be the symbolic voice of the nation if he cannot even control his own physical voice? The stakes couldn't be higher, with nothing less than the fate of the nation resting on the king's ability to produce "normal" speech for radio.[2] Fortunately, with the help of an unconventional speech therapist, the king learns to conquer his stammer enough to address his subjects on BBC radio, thereby fulfilling his duty as the emblem of England's character at a time of extreme crisis.[3]

*The King's Speech* follows Hollywood's typical triumph-over-adversity template for movies about disability (albeit with more integrity than most: although some complained that the film industry had, as usual, cast a non-disabled actor to play a disabled character, groups like The Stuttering Foundation applauded Firth's portrayal as authentic to the experience of individuals with this impediment).[4] But despite the predictable narrative of "overcoming," it is worth considering exactly what the king did and did not overcome. Although his stammer could be tamed, radio itself could not. Its norms and practices remained an unyielding force that refused to bow—even a little bit—before the monarch. In other words, the narrative logic of the film demands that George must adjust to radio, not vice versa, and it is the king's speech that must be repaired. Meanwhile, the cultural institution of broadcasting, symbolized visually by a cold steel microphone looming implacably in front of him, as menacing and merciless as the T-1000 liquid metal assassin in *Terminator 2*, enjoys the ultimate triumph.

To the extent that viewers saw George's stutter, rather than radio, as his primary foe (and an informal review of online reactions suggests that was overwhelmingly the case), the film illustrates how naturalized and necessary "good" voices have become to our understanding of radio as both a technology and a cultural form. And that makes perfect sense: of course the voice emerging from your radio speaker should be comprehensible, intelligible, and "listenable." Of course it should be easy on the ears and easy to understand. It is a self-evident rule reinforced by a near-total absence of exceptions. Quick: name a prominent radio personality with a significant speech impairment. In the U.S. there's Diane Rehm, a nationally syndicated public radio talk show host who suffers from spasmodic dysphonia, and then there's … normative voices pretty much everywhere you listen. At least on American radio, the number of prominent voices that "sound disabled" can, for all intents and purposes, be counted on one finger.[5] Variations and degrees of "able-voicedness" occur, of course, but the overwhelming evidence suggests that radio—as a technology, as a cultural phenomenon, as a structuring force of social relations—will brook no deviation from certain standards of what counts as "a voice made for radio." If disability is a form of subalternity, then the absence of disabled or "Crip"[6] voices in contemporary sound media suggests yet another wrinkle to the question of whether the subaltern can speak.[7]

In those rare instances when someone with a speech impediment does make it onto the radio, the reaction can be cruel. As a poster to one of several Internet threads devoted to Diane Rehm's voice wrote, "I know she has a medical condition and I have great sympathy for her but aarrghh! Her voice is awful. Someone please take the microphone away from her." Added another, "To me this is like keeping a player on the [Washington] Wizards [basketball team] who's lost a leg. I don't get it."[8] A similar thread on a different forum brought out the same complaints: "Sorry if I'm violating the ADA[Americans with Disabilities Act] or being prejudiced [sic] here, but I have no idea how a woman who speaks like that gets a job in radio."[9] Then there is the "Get Diane Rehm Off the Radio" Facebook group with comments such as "[I]t's like listening to someone get run over by a car every time she talks."[10] Other radio hosts with significantly less noticeable speech variances than Rehm's come in for similarly harsh treatment. In a thread on "Most Annoying NPR Voice," commenters nominated WNYC's Lorraine Mattox, who supposedly "has [a] problem with t's in final syllables"; "the lispy health/medical reporter" Joanne Silberner with her "Thindy [Cindy] Brady sibilance," and Louisa Lim, the Beijing-based correspondent, who was described as "a Baba Wawa Elmer Fudd mashup" (a reference to iconic U.S. journalist Barbara Walters, whose soft r's were famously mocked by comedienne Gilda Radner in her "Baba Wawa" impersonations on *Saturday Night Live* in the 1970s).[11] To be fair, several posters chimed in on these threads to defend Rehm and the others, but the fact remains that a powerful proscription on non-normative voices on the radio is widely enforced, not just by the professional broadcast industry but also by many listeners.

This proscription, perhaps precisely because it appears so self-evident, has not been sufficiently investigated by scholars in either disability studies or radio studies. Much work has been done on visual representations of disability, but studies of the aural representation of disability (or its absence), and the complex dynamics of normalization in sonic media, remain a significant gap in the literature. Therefore, this chapter seeks to denaturalize the hegemony of aural able-bodiedness that has long appeared so obvious, investigating the ideological operations that might contribute to the absence of Crip voices on the radio. Doing so reveals the overwhelming ocularcentricity of present scholarship on disability and representation, but more importantly it reveals much about both radio sound and social constructions of disability. In the intersection of radio and disability, then, we can learn more about the cultural meanings of both. Specifically I argue that the confluence of three ideological threads—the sight/sound dichotomy, the dominant understanding of radio as an "intimate" medium, and our enculturated responses to disability—make the aural (more so than the visual) representation of disability a particularly fraught process that results in extraordinarily restrictive norms for the voices that may speak on the radio. Adding these ideological operations of sound, radio, and disability to the political-economic underpinnings of the radio industry, we can see that the "compulsory able-voicedness"[12] of contemporary radio is effectively over-determined. Nonetheless, while it is probably unreasonable to expect that people with vocal disabilities will be welcomed into professional radio anytime soon, I argue that the promise of new distribution models creates the potential for more Crip voices to be heard, even if their ability to actually get a hearing depends ultimately on questions of communicative ethics.

## Good Voices, Good Bodies

From the beginnings of voice broadcasting, radio practitioners have been preoccupied with vocal quality. These concerns emerged, as Shawn VanCour has discussed, within a broader "voice culture" in the early twentieth century in which a wide range of experts offered guidance on how to maximize the effectiveness of one's speaking voice. This training usually emphasized the proper discipline of one's body (breath control, enunciation, volume, etc.), establishing early the connection between vocal normativity and able-bodiedness. A good voice, it was widely maintained, was one that signified a healthy body, and it was incumbent upon the speaker to eradicate any trace of infirmity including "undue digestive disturbance," "muscular twitchings," "fatigability," "long bones," or "sagging stomach."[13] In an era preoccupied with vigor and vitality, one had to learn to avoid sounding even minimally disabled.

As VanCour explains, radio introduced important new complications into this voice culture, since the electronic mediation of the voice, not to mention the cultural shifts engendered by new sound technologies, rendered many previously held notions of the "good voice" newly problematic. No longer was the ability to project a strong and robust voice paramount; instead, radio demanded that the speaker maintain a steady volume and learn to trade oratorical flourishes for intimacy. These strategies for voice broadcasting (also illustrated in *The King's Speech* when a BBC announcer goes through an elaborate routine of gargling, misting his throat, etc.) were still rooted in the proper discipline of the body, but now it was in the service of successfully adapting to the technology:

> Radio speakers throughout this decade were not only cautioned to guard against casual drops in volume that could prove as damaging as the acoustic excesses of traditional oratory, but were also warned that broadcasting required far greater attention to enunciation and a much slower speaking rate than that used in normal conversation. Achieving the "natural" style, in other words, required disciplined effort and special care.[14]

Scholars have examined various aspects of the shift from unmediated to mediated uses of the good voice. Allison McCracken, for example, has focused on changes in singing technique (as the microphone ushered in the age of crooning), while Emily Thompson has described the importance of constant volume to effective radio speaking.[15] Speakers who failed to adapt to this new vocal style were frequently described using the language of moral character flaws, with references to those who had developed "bad habits" or who were simply "lip-lazy." This, too, was part of the broader voice culture in which it was widely believed that "speech is a revelation of personality," as one speech expert put it in 1920, and that a problematic voice indicated a problematic character.[16]

In discussing these transformations, it is common to argue that technology has increasingly separated the body from the voice, with the trope of "disembodiment" looming large. In a key early work on radio, Rudolf Arnheim wrote eloquently of "voices without bodies"[17] and this theme has remained constant ever since; e.g., as Anne Karpf has written, the telephone was "the first technology to disembody the voice—to transport someone's voice without the accompaniment of their body."[18] However, while it is obviously true in a simple sense that radio transmits disembodied voices, this habit of thinking about radio masks the important ways that voices continue to reference and produce bodies, even as the body-voice relationship grows more complicated through mediation. As scholars of the Internet are currently (re)discovering, the visual absence of a body does not result in meaningful "disembodiment" but instead produces a body through signifiers other than the visual.[19] Written, heard, pictured, or imagined bodily markers such as race, gender, class, region, age, and sexuality signify certain kinds of bodies; the absence of such markers tends to produce the "normal" body, which in contemporary Western societies is usually understood to default to such entities as whiteness, masculinity, heterosexuality, and middle-classness.

Radio studies has been especially effective in tracing how the voice has produced different kinds of bodies for performing different kinds of cultural work. In the case of race and ethnicity in early radio, for example, Michele Hilmes demonstrates the centrality of the aural signification of blackness to the construction of a hegemonically white American national identity. Early radio programs frequently invoked race using established sonically transmittable stereotypes—accents, speech patterns, distinctive vocabularies, and routinized themes—borrowed from vaudeville and other cultural forms. Writes Hilmes, "Here is blackness on radio: marked by minstrel dialect, second-class citizen traits, cultural incompetence." Noting that radio's "blindness" did not prevent broadcasters from evoking non-white bodies in order to shore up norms of white cultural privilege, Hilmes argues, "[B]y setting up only this category of representation as 'black,' radio engineered its freedom to categorize all other representations as white."[20] Furthermore, the disconnect between the body signified by the voice and the "real" body of the speaker introduced new instabilities into the use of the voice as an index of a person's body, not to mention their character; Elana Razlogova has used the term "racial ventriloquism" to describe this phenomenon.[21] As Jason Loviglio writes, "White men who 'sounded black,' straight men who 'sounded queer,' Americans who 'sounded foreign,' and men and women, boys and girls, who sounded like each other— all these performances evoked intense pleasure and anxiety precisely because they seemed to put fixed social identities into play in highly public ways."[22]

Taken as a whole, this scholarship demonstrates the problems with imagining that radio is a medium for channeling "disembodied" voices, as if it could fail to produce bodies or could somehow produce "identity-neutral" bodies. To take Hilmes's key example, the white actors of the immensely popular *Amos 'n' Andy* might not have been primarily signifying their own bodies, but that does not make the resulting sounds "disembodied." Instead, their voices were inescapably attached to bodies; the twist is simply that those bodies were, among other things, black and working-class. In other words, semiotics supplies the bodies that the technology renders invisible. Hilmes makes one error, however, in claiming that "[r]adio might have developed as a medium in which race was simply absent,"[23] since the absence of overt markers of racial identity would not actually have absented race or produced some kind of race-neutrality. Instead, in the racially over-determined American context, radio simply would have produced—and in fact usually did produce—a default whiteness, even without the explicit production of blackness as its Other.[24] Despite the commonsense notion of disembodiment, radio cannot *not* signify racially marked bodies.

If examining race on the radio illustrates the problems of positing voices without bodies, examining gender helps reveal which embodied voices are allowed to speak and with which kinds of cultural authority. Early discussions of women's voices on the radio often sought to exclude them on the basis of intelligibility, with several studies claiming to empirically prove that women's voices could not be deciphered as easily as men's. One such study, from 1927, asserted, "Women's higher fundamental tone ... produces only one-half as many audible overtones as a man's voice.... It thus appears that nature has so designed woman's speech that it is always most effective when it is of soft and well-modulated tone."[25] Informal (and perhaps less than entirely scientific) polls of listeners seemed to confirm the greater suitability of men's voices for radio, such as a 1926 survey by New York NBC station WJZ that showed an overwhelming 100-to-1 split in favor of male announcers.[26] Again, such preferences were widely understood as an inevitable technological bias of radio itself, rather than the imposition of cultural norms; as *Radio Broadcast* explained, "[M]ost receiving sets do not reproduce perfectly the higher notes. A man's voice 'takes' better. It has more volume.... Men are naturally better fitted for the average assignment of the broadcast announcer."[27] From our contemporary vantage point, such explanations are self-evidently problematic. As Anne McKay points out, vocal characteristics such as pitch and volume are themselves enculturated, and it is easy to see the preference for "soft and well-modulated" female voices as reflecting social attitudes about appropriate roles for women more generally.[28] Similarly, Michele Hilmes and others have explored the ease with which anxieties about women's figurative voices in the public sphere gave rise to conventional wisdom about the undesirability of women's literal voices on the radio.[29] In other words, vocal qualities of transmitability, intelligibility, and listenability all function in dialog with—even as proxies for—the cultural value of the gendered bodies for which any given voice is an indexical signifier.

The foregoing demonstrates the degree to which ideas about what constitutes a "voice made for radio" were, from the beginning, inseparable from the cultural politics of race, gender, class, and other axes of social difference. Moreover, in studies of visual culture, this co-articulation of representations of bodies and the cultural work those bodies perform is, at this point, already well established. Yet too often the trope of disembodiment masks analogous operations in the realm of sound culture. For the purposes of this study, one particular axis of social difference is particularly salient: for nearly a century, ideas about the good radio voice have produced a default able-bodiedness on the airwaves that works to render disability inaudible—and thus invisible. Just as radio cannot not signify race but can only silence racial alterity in its production of unmarked (read: white) bodies, so too radio cannot *not* signify dis/ability: the absence of markers of disability does not produce non-bodies, but instead produces non-disabled bodies even in the near total absence of disabled Others.

This power of the "normal" voice to produce a "normal" body is illustrated by a regular feature on the BBC's *Ouch!* podcast, a monthly talk show focusing, appropriately enough, on disability issues. The feature is called "Vegetable, Vegetable, or Vegetable," a variation on the game "Animal, Vegetable, or Mineral" (better known in the U.S. as "Twenty Questions"). In each episode, a listener with a different condition (e.g., multiple sclerosis, dwarfism, paraplegia) calls in, and the show's hosts ask yes-or-no questions in order to guess what that condition might be. The name of the game, by (self-)mocking people with disabilities as "vegetables," indicates the podcast's playful and irreverent tone, but what is interesting here is the way that the game is premised entirely on the absence of sonic indicators of disability: if the nature of the caller's disability could be detected in their voice (e.g., the dysarthria common to cerebral palsy, the speech delay common to Down syndrome), then the game wouldn't really work. Instead, the performance of vocal normativity is required to produce a non-disabled body that will then become semantically (rather than sonically) marked as "disabled." This happens quite literally since, as part of the ritual reading of the rules during each episode, callers must affirmatively identify themselves as disabled before the questioning can proceed: "To take part in this intrusive and unpleasant game, the rules clearly state that you have to be disabled. [Caller's name], are you disabled?" As soon as the caller says "yes," a disconnect is established between the unmarked (i.e., normal) radio body produced by the voice and the abnormal physical body of the speaker, enabling the hosts to begin solving the mystery of this person who sounds normal but is in fact disabled.

## Aesthetics, Power, and Intimacy

To summarize my argument thus far, despite the trope of "disembodiment," voices, bodies, and identities all travel together through the ether, perhaps unmoored from and only loosely correlated with the speaker's "actual" body and identity, but nonetheless entering the world of representation and therefore, importantly, the world of political effectivity. The question then arises: why is it that so few of those sonically represented bodies on the radio—regardless of the ways that they signify race, gender, class, or region—happen to also signify disability?

As mentioned above, there is no shortage of self-evident reasons why non-disabled voices thoroughly dominate radio, not least of which is the commercial imperative: broadcasters want listeners to stay tuned, therefore they find speakers and speaking styles that audiences are willing to listen to, with voices that listeners can easily understand and find pleasing to the ear. While undoubtedly sensible as a matter of capitalist logic, however, we need to question the aesthetic reasoning at the root of this supposedly listener-centered approach to speaker selection as well as the idea that "pleasing to the ear" is somehow a sufficient explanation for the absence of disabled voices on the radio. The key problem is that, as Lawrence Grossberg has pointed out (and as the earlier discussion of female broadcasters illustrates), aesthetics and affect are not easily disentangled from the larger ideological context within which they emerge; instead, "affect always demands that ideology legitimate the fact that [some] differences and not others matter."[30] Shawn VanCour suggests that the affective character of radio voices "might be perhaps more productively viewed not as unraveling operations of discourse but instead forming their explicit target, as that aspect of voice which ideology works to legitimize and imbue with special cultural meaning or value."[31] The target here, it seems clear, is the ideology of "compulsory able-bodiedness" and the rejection of disability identities. Tobin Siebers writes that, "The ideology of ability stands ready to attack any desire to know and to accept the disabled body in its current state."[32] We cannot begin to expand the range of permitted voices on radio without simultaneously undermining the ideologies of ability and disability that disqualify those voices in the first place.

The aesthetic argument against disabled voices runs into further difficulty when we consider how the normative limits of aural culture are at such marked variance with the thirst for bodily non-normativity we find in visual culture: from Victorian-era freak shows to today's film and television programs of all genres, representations of both real and fantastical non-normative bodies are in perpetual demand. This is especially true of horror and comedy but can also be routinely observed in drama, reality television, and other genres (e.g., Dr. Weaver's hip dysplasia on *ER*, wheelchair-user Artie Abrams on *Glee*, Gregory House on *House, M.D.*, the entirety of shows like *The Biggest Loser* or *Rollin' With Zach*; the list is endless). Furthermore, the difference between the relative frequency of visual representations and the relative paucity of aural representations of non-normative bodies also extends to the soundtrack: except in the realm of comedy (e.g., the variety of disabled misfits on *South Park*), surprisingly few characters have speech impediments, strong aural correlates to their physical disability, or impairments that produce vocal difference: they are disproportionately Crips without Crip voices. In other words, disabled and other non-normative bodies are everywhere you look, but almost nowhere you listen.[33] The decline of fictional radio obviously accounts for much of the narrowness of U.S. sound culture,[34] but this does not in itself explain the popular fascination with (or tolerance for) visual representations of disability as compared to aural representations.

Visual representations of disability have received a great deal of scholarly attention in recent years, with the work of Rosemarie Garland-Thomson especially influential. In a widely cited essay, Garland-Thomson presents a taxonomy of how persons with disabilities are routinely depicted: the *wondrous* mode that seeks to inspire awe at the accomplishments of persons with disabilities, the *sentimental* mode that invites pity at their plight, the *exotic* mode that sensationalizes or eroticizes physical difference, and the *realistic* mode that normalizes and regularizes the disabled figure.[35] These representational strategies have, according to Garland-Thomson, a common quality: "In representing disability, the visualization of impairment, never the functional experience of it, defines the category of disability."[36] Additionally, such visual representations provide the viewer with a critical distance on physical abnormality and a safe space from which to observe it: "In this sense, disability exists for the viewer to recognize and contemplate, not to express the effect it has on the person with a disability."[37]

Central to this analysis is Garland-Thomson's understanding of the power relations that inform the act of staring, which she defines as "an intense form of looking that enacts a relationship of spectator and spectacle between two people."[38] This asymmetry between (normalized) viewer and (abnormalized) viewee is deeply enculturated and remains the dominant mode of looking at disability in Western culture: "Even children learn very early that disability is a potent form of embodied difference that warrants looking.... Staring is the social relationship that constitutes disability identity and gives meaning to impairment by marking it as aberrant."[39] At the same time, however, staring is "a form of inappropriate looking in modernity" and currently considered rude at best—the public display of "freaks" that was common in the Victorian era seems barbaric and dehumanizing today—which makes the disabled body "a visual paradox: it is at once to-be-looked-at and not-to-be-looked-at."[40]

It is, of course, a mark of some degree of progressive social change that older norms of interpersonal interactions with persons with disabilities—interactions predicated on the unquestioned right of the "normal" to openly objectify the "abnormal"—have become more problematic in contemporary society. However, such power relations live on through mediated encounters with disability such as photography, film, and television, sites where disability can be observed and contemplated without stigma or rebuke, where normalcy can be constructed in its difference from the to-be-looked-at bodies of persons with disabilities. Our relations to disability thus continue to be characterized by the impermeable logic of normalization: we are made "normal" in and through our communicative relation to the "abnormal" body. In this sense, visual representations of disability perpetuate "a system that produces subjects by differentiating and marking bodies" in order to imbue some of those bodies—those marked as normal—with greater social and cultural power.[41] Related to the theory of the male gaze, which proposes that conventions of representing gendered bodies put the viewer into a relatively empowered masculine subject position predicated on norms of male desire, Garland-Thomson argues that conventions of depicting disability empower viewers by inviting them—through the process of destigmatized staring at physical abnormality—into an able-bodied subject position that structurally secures the starer's empowered normalcy and the staree's disempowered deviance and abjection.

The work of Steven Connor supplies another perspective on this process in his analysis of the construction of the modern self, particularly with regard to sight versus sound. Drawing on Heidegger, Martin Jay, and others, Connor argues that the privileging of vision is integral to a modernist understanding of the self:

> Visualism signifies distance, differentiation and domination; the control which modernity exercises over nature depends upon that experience of the world as separate from myself, and my self-definition in the act of separation, which vision seems to promote. Where knowing is associated so overwhelmingly with seeing, then the will-to-self-knowing of the epistemized self has unavoidably taken a scopic form.[42]

In contrast to this condition of modernity in which knowing equals seeing, the condition of post-modernity is one in which increasing suspicion of the visual (e.g., Foucault's critique of surveillance) and the rise of man-made "noise" (including technologies of sound reproduction such as the telephone, phonograph, and radio) undermine the ocularcentrism of modernity in favor of subjective experiences "formed around the auditory rather than the visual, or at least formed in a certain contest between the two."[43] The problem that Connor identifies in this production of a post-modern self is that sound alone is too disorganized and too dependent on the other senses to provide a stable basis for self-knowledge in the way that sight once could under conditions of modernity. Drawing on Michael Chion, Connor notes that sound—perhaps for historical reasons—is perceived as insufficient in itself, always requiring completion and confirmation by sight and the other senses.[44] This insufficiency makes the auditory importantly different from the visual: "We ask of a sound, 'What was that?', meaning 'Who was that?', or 'Where did that come from?' We do not naturally ask of an image 'What sound does this make?'"[45] Additionally, sound's particular ability to dissolve boundaries—"to pervade and to integrate objects and entities that the eye kept separate"[46]—problematizes the relations of separation between self and other that the modern "I/eye" had so assiduously constructed. Together, the insufficiency and pervasiveness of sound mean that the auditory, to a greater degree than the visual, is capable of threatening and even destabilizing the self unless it can be meaningfully captured, organized, and socially ordered.

Importantly, this organization of auditory information is inseparable from questions of social power, since the resources available for making sense of sound are not just psychic but also social and cultural. Connor uses the example of Kaja Silverman's work on sound in film,[47] which demonstrates that male voices are relatively more self-sufficient and less dependent on the visual than female voices: male voices can speak outside the frame of the film as the narrator or as a controlling voiceover, while female voices are required to be made visible on screen.[48] In other words, the relative sufficiency of sound as a basis for understanding the world—and thus the self—is never independent of the meaning-making processes through which it can be organized, and thus never independent of questions of social and cultural power. Writes Connor, "[I]t is in the passage [from disorganized to organized sound] that the self is formed, in a process in which power and pleasure are intricately interwoven."[49]

To bring this back to the question of Crip voices on the radio, it is important to note that, like gender and race, dis/ability is one of the modes of social power through which we organize sound and thus the self. This insight alone goes a long way toward understanding the differences between visual and aural representations of disability: sound complicates the processes of distanciation and self-other separation that characterize our relations to persons with disabilities in the visual realm. But I want to argue further that radio sound in particular challenges our cultural strategies for relating to disabled Others, that radio itself—not just as pure aural stimulus but also as a culturally and historically specific institution—must be considered an important constitutive element in how we organize sound and integrate the auditory world into our sense of self. Voices on the radio, that is to say, are not merely encountered as "voices," but also as "on the radio," and thus the meanings of what radio is, its proper and legitimate position in our lives, and our relation to it as a medium for knowing the world and ourselves are integral to the ways in which radio sound and social power interrelate.

In this regard, the most salient aspect of radio as a cultural institution for issues of vocal alterity is not its commercialism, nor its nationalism, nor its status as a state-regulated public good, but rather its "intimacy." For nearly a century, radio has been constructed as the "intimate" medium, the communications technology that feels most personal and through which we establish the closest, most intimate, most emotional bonds. Marshall McLuhan put it this way: "Radio affects most intimately, person-to-person, offering a world of unspoken communication between writer-speaker and the listener. That is the immediate aspect of radio. A private experience."[50] Multiple features of radio and various byproducts of the affordances of the technology help underwrite these feelings of intimacy: the ability of radio waves to cross boundaries in order to enter the privacy of the home, the amplification technology that allows more conversational speaking styles or intimate singing styles that mimic interpersonal communication, the pervasiveness of sound itself as an omnipresent and inescapable form of sensory input. But radio's intimacy was also a deliberate creation: from the earliest days of broadcasting, radio practitioners have actively sought to cultivate "a sense of spontaneity and sincerity, enabling listeners to enjoy an illusion of direct and intimate conversation that transcended radio's limitations as a medium of one-way mass delivery"[51] Successful announcers and DJs "sought to sound familiar, intimate"[52] in order to reach people at a remarkably personal level, while crooning "helped create and maintain an illusion that listeners' relationships to singers and other broadcasting individuals were unmediated, personal."[53] From the audience's perspective, they often succeeded: as Susan Douglas writes in her history of radio listening, "Maybe it was the darkness, the solitude, or being in bed, but the intimacy of this experience remains vivid; listeners had a deeply private, personal bond with radio."[54]

Unsurprisingly, this production of intimacy was complicated, not least because these close interpersonal bonds were potentially felt by millions simultaneously; as Jason Loviglio points out, radio's address was both private and public, "peculiarly intimate and national."[55] Additionally, John Durham Peters notes that the "yearning for contact" that helps structure radio listening must forever be frustrated, since the human condition is one of always incomplete communication.[56] Finally, as Paddy Scannell points out, other media forms would also have strong claims on the discourse of intimacy; he mentions that the cinematic close-up and the hand-written letter are potentially as "intimate" as radio.[57] This suggests that radio's privileged reputation as the intimate medium is not inherent in the technology itself or the phenomenology of sound but rather has been actively produced and asserted for so long and with such success that we have subsumed them into our listening practices: expectations of intimacy are integral to how we encounter and relate to radio. Although the industry has undergone significant transformations in the twenty-first century, radio's construction as intimate and personal remains potent today and a hallmark of the medium's distinctiveness in the landscape of communications technologies.

While it is beyond the scope of this essay to join a broader philosophical or psychological discussion of what might be meant by intimacy, the concept clearly has to do with inter-subjective relations—sociologist Niklas Luhmann suggests the phrase "interpersonal interpenetration"[58]—with connotations of privacy, personal space, dialogue, privileged self-revelation, affinity, and domesticity, not to mention love, passion, and sexuality. In writings on radio and intimacy, it is clear that authors usually have in mind the bond that the listener feels with the speaker on the radio, a connection that produces the illusion of an unmediated, one-on-one experience. However, the intimacy that results from the speaker-listener bond is not necessarily a relationship between equals: aside from simple star power or the gendered norms that could structure the relationship between masculinized/male broadcasters and feminized/female listeners, the radio host often functioned as a more knowledgeable compatriot, a trusted guide leading the listener into mysterious worlds, unfamiliar music, and exotic cultures.[59] Even the commonsense understanding of speaking as "active" and listening as "passive" structurally positions the broadcaster as dominant. In other words, radio's intimacy is rooted in multiple overlapping asymmetrical relationships that tendentially privilege and empower the speaker.

The construction of radio as intimate has two implications for the listener encountering vocal non-normativity. First, it reinforces the structural subordination of the listener to the speaker, which inverts the culturally conditioned relations of dominance and subordination in the starer–staree relationship characteristic of disability in visual culture. Whereas vision and the politics of staring allow the viewer to adopt a distanced position of normalcy vis-à-vis an abnormal other, radio sound offers no such subject position from which the listener can achieve empowerment, distance, or psychic separation from the disabled body. Second, the expectation of intimacy conditions listening practices based on the illusion of disintermediation and interpenetration of self and other, and this mimicry of interpersonal communication troubles the processes of normalization by which we typically separate our "normal" selves from "abnormal" others. As Connor argues, sound in general makes us particularly vulnerable to alterity[60]; since radio sound in particular gets filtered through listening practices of interpersonal intimacy, that vulnerability is heightened and intensified, making the alterity of disability too close, too pervasive. Our strategies of distanciation and objectification that, in the visual and interpersonal realms, permit us to reassure ourselves of the boundaries of self and other, normalcy and abnormalcy, are destabilized by sound in general and our particular expectations of the medium of radio and its role in our lives. In this way, the social production of radio intimacy is inseparable from the compulsory able-voicedness that dominates it. The structural relations of empowerment and disempowerment that allow us to keep non-normative bodies at arm's length in the visual realm are inverted in the auditory realm, making the Crip voice with its significations of a Crip body inseparable from a self that demands its exclusion. The radio listener, unable to maintain a safe distance from the sound of disability, instead refuses to listen at all.

## On the Political Economy of Crip Voices

If vocal non-normativity in radio sound challenges or even threatens audiences and enculturated listening practices, what conditions or institutions might we identify as potential fulcrums for progressive change toward a less restrictive voice culture? The unfortunate answer is that, both on the basis of the analysis above and on the evidence of radio today, this is not primarily a political economic question that can be easily addressed through changes in funding or regulatory structures.

The primary argument for a political economic explanation for pervasive able-voicedness is the simple fact of commercial radio itself as it currently exists: with the exception of comic foils for "morning-zoo" type radio shows, people with vocal disabilities are unlikely to enjoy a hiring boom in commercial radio any time soon. Professional practice, advertiser demands, and audience expectations all conspire against experimentation with non-normative voices. In contrast, public radio and alternative distribution methods such as podcasting offer somewhat more promise. Jason Loviglio has analyzed National Public Radio as a site where one can find a wider range of permitted voices, including atypically masculine-sounding female voices such as Susan Stamberg, queer voices such as David Sedaris, anomalous voices such as the "rubber-duck-voiced

Sarah Vowell," and other speakers whose vocal qualities would be unwelcome on most commercial stations.[61] Loviglio persuasively argues that these voices are an important part of the cultural work that NPR performs, but they are also reflective of an economic model that benefits in multiple ways from public radio sounding different than commercial radio. After all, this is the institution that kept Diane Rehm on the air—even took her show to national distribution—even as her spasmodic dysphonia was intensifying.[62] In this light, the Internet thread that I referenced above as evidence of listener intolerance for non-normative voices ("Most Annoying NPR Voice") is at the same time indicative of public radio's openness to putting these speakers on the air in the first place.

Nonetheless, Rehm remains—even in the universe of public radio—almost unique in her ability to maintain a career on radio with an overtly Crip voice. Other non-commercial and public interest broadcasting outlets are similarly constrained by vocal norms. For example, Mary Pat O'Malley has analyzed the program *Outside the Box*, a show for and about persons with disabilities on the Irish public service broadcaster RTÉ. She found that, in two years of the program, only one episode featured communication impairment as a topic, and in the fifteen episodes on a wide range of topics that she analyzed in depth, not a single guest with a speech impairment was interviewed.[63] In contrast, *Ouch!*, the BBC's disability-themed show, is significantly better at including non-normative voices; although the main hosts—all persons with disabilities themselves—have quite "good" radio voices, the show occasionally thematizes vocal disabilities and not infrequently features guests with speech impediments. Notably, however, the show has been "demoted" from on-air broadcast to Internet-only podcast, suggesting that the BBC's commitment to disability issues and disabled voices is far from secure. Unfortunately, then, the few public service institutions and programs that have demonstrated awareness of and sensitivity to disability issues are still far from expanding the voice culture of radio in any sustained and significant way.

Finally, it is already a truism that Internet distribution has opened up radio production to a wider range of voices and topics, and there is no shortage of disability-related radio documentaries and podcasts. This suggests that amateur and cottage production might step up and fill the gap left by professional broadcasters, although an informal sampling of the current podcast offerings on iTunes reveals that most of these programs are hosted by normatively voiced individuals and overwhelmingly feature normatively voiced guests. Even if that were to change, the more important problem with investing our hopes in amateur and DIY Internet distribution is that it allows Crip voices to remain marginalized within the radio ecosystem. Many of the disability podcasts available appear to have ceased production after a handful of episodes, suggesting that—like many short-lived attempts at podcasting on any topic—the absence of secure funding sources is a major stumbling block to sustained production.

Disability-themed shows face an additional hurdle in that, insofar as hosts and guests are themselves disabled, the practical challenges of maintaining a regular schedule of audio production can often be multiplied exponentially. It will be an extraordinary moment if a cottage-produced podcast brings greater vocal non-normativity with any regularity to more than the smallest of audiences. In short, the progressively greater inclusion of Crip voices in radio is unlikely to result from tinkering with the funding or distribution models currently available.

## Conclusion: Crip Voices and the Implications for Communication Ethics

> [L]istening is the invisible and inaudible enactment of the ethical relation itself; on it, everything depends.[64]

I have argued in this essay that the problem of Crip voices on radio is primarily one of inadequate distance to alterity: sound, especially as filtered through "the intimate medium," disturbs and frustrates our cultural strategies for relating to disability. Our enculturated engagement with radio sound allows no position from which to normalize the listener through separation from the abnormal/disabled speaker, inverting the processes that dominate our encounter with disability in visual culture. We have no place to stand, so to speak, from which to allow the non-normative voice to reassure us of our own normalcy. Furthermore, I have made the pessimistic claim that we cannot expect changes in the political economy of radio production and consumption to meaningfully address this disabling character of our social construction of radio. Perhaps the slow, difficult process of ideological struggle will continue to chip away at the subalternity of disability and reshape social meanings of impairment for the better, ultimately resulting in a diminishment of compulsory able-voicedness. Even this more optimistic position, however, must measure progressive change in decades.

If a more immediate change is to occur, it will have to emerge first and foremost from a recalibration of our communicative ethics. A brief anecdote should illustrate the issue: I once heard a student complain about one of his teachers, a South Asian woman with the British-influenced accent common on the Indian subcontinent, "I can't understand a word she's saying." Since the teacher's English was impeccable, it was obvious that the problem was not in *her* speaking, but in *his* hearing: all he could see was racial and gender difference, and thus all he could hear was unintelligibility. To understand her—and therefore to learn from her—what he really needed to do was adjust his listening.

The absence of Crip voices on the radio, similarly, is not primarily a technological problem, an aesthetic problem, or even a political economic problem. It is a social problem and derives above all from deeply rooted processes of normalization and ideologies of ability that marginalize and subordinate persons with disabilities. Clearly, no approach that fails to address social and cultural inequality along the lines of dis/ability can claim to offer a "solution" that will enable the disabled subaltern voice to speak. Nonetheless, the realm of communication ethics does offer insights into, at the very least, an individualized response to Crip voices, one particularly suited to the affordances of radio itself and the centrality of listening to its operations. As Lisbeth Lipari has argued, "[T]he relation with alterity in communication ethics is enacted primarily through the process of listening, rather than speaking. What interrupts our dialogic engagement is not speaking, but the failure to listen for the other's alterity."[65] According to Lipari, what differentiates listening from hearing is the act of opening oneself to let the other in, "an enactment of responsibility made manifest through our posture of receptivity."[66] Lipari points out that, despite the pervasive understanding of listening as a passive activity subordinate to speaking, one that is supposed to be transparent, uncomplicated, and even "easy," listening—especially ethical listening that is open to the voice and experience of the other—is a challenging and often difficult act but one that in fact *enables* speech.[67]

Kate Lacey, although not writing from the perspective of communication ethics, has discussed the historical specificity of listening practices and has called for greater attention to the plurality of possible listening positions.[68] By reconstituting the absence of Crip voices as a problem of listening, rather than speaking, we might be able to begin redefining our enculturated responses to sound, radio, and difference that, as argued above, make sonic representations of disability so fraught. For, whatever else it might be, the absence of Crip voices on the radio represents a refusal to listen to difference and a failure to engage humanistically with persons with disabilities. Re-thinking the relations between speaker and listener from the perspective of the contingency of listening practices, then, suggests that a hegemonic able-bodied listening position is not the only one available to us, and that alternative modes of organizing sound in the constitution of self-other relations is possible. And we *know* it is possible. After all, amid all the complaints online about Diane Rehm—the creatively cruel metaphors for her voice and the wiseass Facebook pages calling for her dismissal—you will also find comments like this one: "A melodious voice is NOT a requirement. A mind is. She's got one. I actually like that she speaks slowly, she makes everyone slow down and think. It's quite a concept."[69]

## Notes

1. I would like to thank Amanda Gunn, Kate Lacey, Lisbeth Lipari, Jason Mittell, Anna Nekola, and Shawn VanCour for their contributions to this essay. The title borrows a phrase I heard in a lecture in Madison, Wisconsin by National Public Radio correspondent Susan Stamberg, who joked that she had "a face made for radio and a voice made for print." For discussion of my use of the term "Crip," see note 6 below.
2. This theme is not uncommon. For example, Lennard J. Davis has argued that the production

of the ideal body (as measured against the disabled Other) is necessary to the emergence of nationalism, while Robert J. Scholnick has identified the ways in which Walt Whitman's work "promot[ed] physical health as a means of fostering national stability, control, and improvement" (249). The connection between physical health and a healthy nation is also central to the twentieth-century voice culture discussed later in this essay. Lennard J. Davis, "Bodies of Difference: Politics, Disability, and Representation," in *Disability Studies: Enabling the Humanities,* ed. Sharon L Snyder, Brenda Jo Brueggemann, and Rosemarie Garland-Thomson (New York: Modern Language Association of America, 2002), 100–108; Robert J. Scholnick, "'How Dare a Sick Man or an Obedient Man Write Poems?' Whitman and the Dis-ease of the Perfect Body," in *Disability Studies: Enabling the Humanities,* ed. Sharon L Snyder, Brenda Jo Brueggemann, and Rosemarie Garland-Thomson (New York: Modern Language Association of America, 2002), 248–259.

3. Tom Hooper, *The King's Speech* (Troy, MI: Anchor Bay Entertainment, 2011).
4. Rosie Mestel, "'The King's Speech'—A Once-in-a-Lifetime Moment for the Stuttering Foundation," *Los Angeles Times Articles,* February 11, 2011, accessed September 12, 2012, http://articles.latimes.com/2011/feb/11/news/lat-heb-the-kings-speech-a-onceinalifetime-moment-for-the-stuttering-foundation-of-america-20110211.
5. This is a slight exaggeration, but only slight. For example, John "the Stutterer" Melendez was a longtime member of *The Howard Stern Show,* but his speech impediment was part of the comedy, with Melendez taking his place alongside "Gary the Retard" and "Eric the Midget" in Stern's carnivalesque "Wack Pack." By highlighting the freakery of these performers, such examples reinforce rather than challenge aural norms. In a less transgressive vein, some radio personalities such as National Public Radio reporter Louisa Lim and British comedian Jonathan Ross have minor speech impediments such as slight lisps and rhotacism, the inability to clearly pronounce r's. But individuals who have more significant vocal abnormalities—much less those who have other serious impairments that can be detected in their voices, such as muscular dystrophy or lateral sclerosis—are exceedingly rare on radio. Doubtless some readers will know of exceptions—and the author would appreciate learning of them—but the widespread enforcement of vocal normativity certainly holds.
6. The term "Crip," analogous to the term "Queer" in queer theory and queer studies, is increasingly finding purchase in disability studies as a way to express a critical disabled subject position and oppositional political identity for people with disabilities. Like "Queer" before it, "Crip" signifies a desire to "challenge oppressive norms, build community, and maintain the practitioners' self-worth" (Carrie Sandahl, "Queering the Crip or Cripping the Queer?: Intersections of Queer and Crip Identities in Solo Autobiographical Performance," *GLQ: A Journal of Lesbian and Gay Studies* 9, no. 1 [2002]: 25–56, 38). Writes Sandahl, "Both queering and cripping expose the arbitrary delineation between normal and defective and the negative social ramifications of attempts to homogenize humanity, and both disarm what is painful with wicked humor" (37). As Robert McRuer discusses in *Crip Theory: Cultural Signs of Queerness and Disability* (New York: New York University Press, 2006), 35–37, the analogy only goes so far, since the voluntary adoption of a "Crip" identity by able-bodied-identified persons, in the way that straight-identified persons can and do adopt "Queer," is both rare and inherently problematic. Nonetheless, the term performs important political work in establishing and signaling a critical stance for disability identities vis-à-vis normate culture, and it is in that sense that I use it in this essay.
7. Routine discrimination against people with disabilities has long been an obvious fact of existence in most industrialized societies, but this refers as well to the social and cultural subalternity of "disability identities," which has become a well-established tenet of critical disability studies. In this sense, the subordination of people with disabilities extends well beyond routine political discrimination and silencing, not to mention the normalization of able-bodiedness that produces a ubiquitously disabling built environment, to the shaping of subjectivity itself. As Alison Kafer writes, "[U]nder a system of compulsory able-bodiedness...a disability identity is to be avoided at all costs" (80). Alison Kafer, "Compulsory Bodies: Reflections on Heterosexuality and Able-bodiedness," *Journal of*

*Women's History* 15, no. 3 (2003), 77–89. For more on the subalternity of disability, see Lauri Umansky and Paul K. Longmore, "Introduction: Disability History: From the Margins to the Mainstream," in *The New Disability History: American Perspectives,* ed. Lauri Umansky and Paul K. Longmore (New York: New York University Press, 2001), 33–57. The question of "can the subaltern speak" is, of course, from Gayatri Chakravorty Spivak, "Can the Subaltern Speak?" in *Marxism and the Interpretation of Culture,* ed. Cary Nelson and Lawrence Grossberg (Urbana, IL: University of Illinois Press, 1988), 271–313.

8. "Diane Rehm's Voice," Web Forum, DC Urban Moms and Dads, accessed September 12, 2012, http://www.dcurbanmom.com/jforum/posts/list/60/129230.page.

9. "Keeping It in 'The Family,'" Web Forum, MetaFilter, June 24, 2008, accessed September 12, 2012, http://www.metafilter.com/72761/Keeping-it-in-The-Family.

10. "Get Diane Rehm Off the Radio," Facebook Page, Facebook, January 26, 2011, accessed September 12, 2012, http://www.facebook.com/pages/Get-Diane-Rehm-Off-The-Radio/155613797822938.

11. "Most Annoying NPR Voice," Web Forum, The Data Lounge, May 2010, accessed September 12, 2012, http://www.datalounge.com/cgi-bin/iowa/ajax.html?t=9224876#page:showThread,9224876.

12. I adapted this term from Robert McRuer's "compulsory able-bodiedness," which itself is an adaptation of Adrienne Rich's idea of "compulsory heterosexuality." See McRuer, *Crip Theory;* Adrienne Rich, "Compulsory Heterosexuality and Lesbian Existence," *Signs* 5, no. 4 (Summer, 1980): 631–660.

13. Shawn Gary VanCour, "The Sounds of 'Radio': Aesthetic Formations of 1920s American Broadcasting" (PhD diss., University of Wisconsin—Madison, 2008), 120.

14. Vancour, "The Sounds of 'Radio,'" 390.

15. Allison McCracken, "'God's Gift to Us Girls': Crooning, Gender, and the Re-Creation of American Popular Song, 1928-1933," *American Music* 17, no. 4 (December 1, 1999): 365–395; Emily Ann Thompson, *The Soundscape of Modernity: Architectural Acoustics and the Culture of Listening in America, 1900–1933* (Cambridge, MA: MIT Press, 2002). See also VanCour, "The Sounds of 'Radio,'" and Donald Crafton, *The Talkies: American Cinema's Transition to Sound, 1926–1931* (History of the American Cinema 4) (New York: Charles Scribner's Sons, 1997).

16. Quoted in VanCour, "The Sounds of 'Radio,'" 408. It is important to note that, in addition to being a time of particular hostility to immigrants, racial and ethnic Others, political dissidents, and so on, this was also the era of the "ugly laws" restricting the rights and freedoms of persons with disabilities. In other words, the enforcement of normative ideas about the voice-body-character connection fell particularly hard on people with non-normative bodies. See Susan Schweik, *The Ugly Laws: Disability in Public* (New York: New York University Press, 2009).

17. Rudolf Arnheim, *Radio* (London: Faber & Faber, 1936).

18. Anne Karpf, *The Human Voice: How This Extraordinary Instrument Reveals Essential Clues About Who We Are* (Bloomsbury USA, 2006), 234–235.

19. See, for example, Cameron Bailey, "Virtual Skin: Articulating Race in Cyberspace," in *Reading Digital Culture,* ed. David Trend (Keyworks in Cultural Studies 4) (Malden, MA: Blackwell, 2001), 334–346; Michael Warner, "The Mass Public and the Mass Subject," in *Habermas and the Public Sphere,* ed. Craig Calhoun (Cambridge, MA: MIT Press, 1992), 377–401.

20. Michele Hilmes, *Radio Voices: American Broadcasting, 1922–1952* (Minneapolis: University of Minnesota Press, 1997), 93.

21. Elena Razlogova, *The Listener's Voice: Early Radio and the American Public* (Philadelphia: University of Pennsylvania Press, 2011).

22. Jason Loviglio, *Radio's Intimate Public: Network Broadcasting and Mass-Mediated Democracy* (Minneapolis: University Of Minnesota Press, 2005), xviii.

23. Hilmes, *Radio Voices,* 93.

24. For more on the discursive production of whiteness, see Ruth Frankenberg, *White Women,*

*Race Matters: The Social Construction of Whiteness* (Minneapolis: University of Minnesota Press, 1993).

25. Quoted in Anne McKay, "Speaking Up: Voice Amplification and Women's Struggle for Public Expression," in *Technology and Women's Voices: Keeping in Touch*, ed. Cheris Kramarae (New York: Routledge, 1988), 192.

26. John Wallace, "The Listeners' Point of View: Who and Where the Infants Really Are in Radio," *Radio Broadcast* 10, no. 1 (November 1926): 44.

27. Wallace, "The Listeners' Point of View," 45.

28. McKay, "Speaking Up."

29. Hilmes, *Radio Voices*, especially 130–50.

30. Lawrence Grossberg, *We Gotta Get Out of This Place: Popular Conservatism and Postmodern Culture* (New York: Routledge, 1992), 82.

31. VanCour, "The Sounds of 'Radio,'" 491.

32. Tobin Anthony Siebers, *Disability Aesthetics* (Ann Arbor: University of Michigan Press, 2010), 26.

33. Noteworthy among the rare exceptions to this rule are characters on *Deadwood* and *Breaking Bad* with cerebral palsy, played by actors who have CP in real life (Geri Jewell and RJ Mitte, respectively). Interestingly, Mitte plays the character with a more pronounced dysarthria than he himself speaks with off-screen, suggesting a conscious effort to use vocal non-normativity to emphasize the character's disability. The other major exception, characters with Down syndrome (a condition that often includes among its symptoms alalia, or speech delay), are usually played by actors with Down syndrome, including such prominent actors as Andrea Friedman (*Saving Grace, Law & Order, ER, Life Goes On*, and voice work for *Family Guy*), Chris Burke (the Golden-Globe nominated actor who, in *Life Goes On*, played the first major television character with Down syndrome), and Lauren Potter, who plays a cheerleader on *Glee*. I thank Jason Mittell for pointing me to these exceptions in an email exchange.

34. Like accent and timbre, vocal disability was a convenient and widely used tool for quickly and easily conveying specificities of character to radio audiences. As such, the so-called golden age of radio might also have witnessed the greatest number of voices on the airwaves that "sounded disabled," at least in the U.S. Once again, however, such representations could hardly be considered consistently progressive blows for inclusivity and tolerance. Many, such as the creative range of lisps and stutters employed by Mel Blanc, were standard targets of comedic ridicule, while in dramatic radio the use of non-normative voices could be equally problematic: the broken voice as indexical of a broken soul. As with physical deformities on stage and screen going back at least to *Richard III*, vocal impairment in radio drama routinely signaled moral degeneracy and spiritual defectiveness: "slow talking" suggested stupidity, lisps (say, as used by Peter Lorre) indicated villainy, and so on. The other great use for lisps, of course, was as a signifier of homosexuality, itself widely seen as a form of mental disability and perversion. In other words, even in the broader vocal culture of fictional radio, the meanings of vocal non-normativity overwhelmingly perpetuated the subalternity of persons with disabilities. See also Robin Larsen and Beth Haller, "The Case of *Freaks*: Public Reception of Real Disability," *Journal of Popular Film and Television* 29, no. 4 (Winter 2002): 164–172; Matthew Murray, "'The Tendency to Deprave and Corrupt Morals': Regulation and Irregular Sexuality in Golden Age Radio Comedy," in *Radio Reader: Essays in the Cultural History of Radio,* ed. Michele Hilmes and Jason Loviglio (New York: Routledge, 2002), 135–156. My thanks to Jason Loviglio for this insight.

35. Rosemarie Garland-Thomson, "Seeing the Disabled: Visual Rhetorics of Disability in Popular Photography," in *The New Disability History: American Perspectives*, ed. Lauri Umansky and Paul K. Longmore (New York: New York University Press, 2001), 338–346.

36. Garland-Thomson, "Seeing the Disabled," 346.

37. Garland-Thomson, "Seeing the Disabled," 346.

38. Garland-Thomson, "Seeing the Disabled," 346.

39. Garland-Thomson, "Seeing the Disabled," 346–47.

40. Garland-Thomson, "Seeing the Disabled," 347.

41. Garland-Thomson, "Seeing the Disabled," 348.

42. Steven Connor, "The Modern Auditory I," in *Rewriting the Self: Histories from the Middle Ages to the Present*, ed. Roy Porter (New York: Routledge, 1996), 203–204.

43. Connor, "The Modern Auditory I," 205.

44. Connor, "The Modern Auditory I," 220.

45. Connor, "The Modern Auditory I," 213.

46. Connor, "The Modern Auditory I," 207.

47. Kaja Silverman, *The Acoustic Mirror: The Female Voice in Psychoanalysis and Cinema* (Bloomington, IN: Indiana University Press, 1988).

48. Connor, "The Modern Auditory I," 219.

49. Connor, "The Modern Auditory I," 215.

50. Marshall McLuhan, *Understanding Media: The Extensions of Man* (Cambridge, MA: MIT Press, 1994), 299. See also Timothy D. Taylor, "Music and the Rise of Radio in 1920s America: Technological Imperialism, Socialization, and the Transformation of Intimacy," *Historical Journal of Film, Radio & Television* 22, no. 4 (October 2002): 425–443; Susan J. Douglas, *Listening In: Radio and the American Imagination* (Minneapolis: University of Minnesota Press, 2004); VanCour, "The Sounds of 'Radio'"; Loviglio, *Radio's Intimate Public*; Paddy Scannell, *Radio, Television and Modern Life* (Hoboken, NJ: Wiley-Blackwell, 1996).

51. VanCour, "The Sounds of 'Radio,'" 383.

52. Douglas, *Listening In*, 31.

53. Taylor, "Music and the Rise of Radio," 437.

54. Douglas, *Listening In*, 5.

55. Loviglio, *Radio's Intimate Public*, xxv (emphasis added).

56. John Durham Peters, *Speaking into the Air: A History of the Idea of Communication* (Chicago: University of Chicago Press, 1999), 212.

57. Scannell, *Radio, Television and Modern Life*, 64, 70.

58. Niklas Luhmann, *Love as Passion: The Codification of Intimacy* (Cambridge, MA: Harvard University Press, 1986), 161.

59. Hilmes, *Radio Voices*, 62; Douglas, *Listening In*, Chapter 9.

60. Connor, "The Modern Auditory I," 209.

61. Jason Loviglio, "Sound Effects: Gender, Voice and the Cultural Work of NPR," *Radio Journal: International Studies in Broadcast & Audio Media* 5, no. 2 & 3 (2007): 76.

62. Diane Rehm, *Finding My Voice* (New York: Knopf, 1999), 189–201.

63. Mary Pat O'Malley, "Voices of Disability on the Radio," *International Journal of Language & Communication Disorders* 43, no. 1 (May-June 2008): 18–29.

64. Lisbeth Lipari, "Rhetoric's Other: Levinas, Listening, and the Ethical Response," *Philosophy and Rhetoric* 45, no. 3 (2012): 242.

65. Lipari, "Listening for the Other: Ethical Implications of the Buber-Levinas Encounter," *Communication Theory* 14, no. 2 (2004): 137.

66. Lipari, "Listening for the Other."

67. Lipari, "Rhetoric's Other." See also Lisbeth Lipari, "Listening Otherwise: The Voice of Ethics," *International Journal of Listening* 23 (2009): 44-59. Additionally, Amanda Gunn has proposed the term "invitational listening," an adaptation of Foss and Griffin's "invitational rhetoric," as a way to capture the ethical relations inherent in the act of listening and the primacy of listening in communicating across difference. Amanda Gunn, conversations with the author, 2012; Sonja K. Foss and Cynthia L. Griffin, "Beyond Persuasion: A Proposal for an Invitational Rhetoric," *Communication Monographs* 62 (March 1995): 1–18.

68. Kate Lacey, "Towards a Periodization of Listening: Radio and Modern Life," *International Journal of Cultural Studies* 3, no. 2 (2000): 279–288.

69. "Diane Rehm's Voice."

# 8

# "YOUR EARS ARE A PORTAL TO ANOTHER WORLD"

## The New Radio Documentary Imagination and the Digital Domain

*Virginia Madsen*

> The programmes "on the air" of the future will surely be partly only audible, partly only visible, and partly audi-visible, according to their content and destination.
>
> Lance Sieveking, 1934[1]

> The advantage of radio over cinema: the screen is larger.[2]
>
> Arte Radio, 2008, attributed to Orson Welles

It is almost impossible to approach the subject of the documentary in radio today without invoking an earlier time when the radio documentary field was born, appeared to wear itself out, and then found itself in the midst of a new wave. Prior to the most recent pronouncements of the death of radio via digital convergence, it was television that threatened to eclipse sound broadcasting. Many in the industry believed this even before the 1950s came to an end, as television spread and radio audiences dwindled, especially for once popular radio genres. This was the era when radio, still so young in reality, began to take on a patina of age. In *The Radio Reader* (2002), Michele Hilmes wrote: "[B]y 1955 the vast bulk of radio's established programming capital was hard at work bringing in profits for television.... Radio, gutted and demoralized, struggled to adapt.... Meantime, as so often happens in history, to the victor went the spoils of memory."[3] Hilmes is referring to the American context here, but nevertheless strong evidence elsewhere supports the view that a crisis situation existed for radio across commercial and public models internationally by the mid- to late 1960s, even as European, Australian, and Canadian public broadcasting institutions continued to support and innovate "older" traditions and formats which featured classic "built programming" styles.

Perhaps the very nature of this evanescent medium has always encouraged a sense of loss around the site of the transmission, the only trace being what remained in the memory. Until very recently, radio has excelled in forgetting its own past. It seems strange to recall now how this rich tradition of the documentary feature in radio, developed in the BBC, could almost be forgotten even in its home territory. In 1977, BBC producer Michael Bright confirmed this view; "We tended to forget about the feature. The tradition was lost. The important thing about this was that there was no school of feature-making anymore, no handing on of expertise, of knowledge…. No young writers coming up."[4] Once more the trope of radio losing its memory is there, although we know from this discussion that radio documentaries and feature making were on the cusp of a revival.

But this intensive form of radio did not die with television in the 1950s. The renaissance brought on by new portable recording technologies and magnetic tape in the 1960s laid the foundation for a whole expanded field of expressive documentary forms in radio, comparable to the renaissance we are now experiencing in the digital era. This chapter traces the aesthetic history of the radio feature, from its early years in the 1930s and 40s, to its mostly forgotten middle-era revival in the 1960s and 70s, and points to its parallels with the radio resurgence today.

## "Actualities" and "the Radio Eye": Early Development of the Radio Documentary

> [T]he documentary idea was not basically a film idea at all….
>
> John Grierson, 1942)[5]

Radio features before and after the Second World War often sounded more like radio drama than what we today consider "documentary." They were mostly written as scripts and performed by actors live. It was rare to hear unrehearsed or spontaneous voices or more than illustrative actuality before the early 1960s, excepting in some special programming made toward the later years of the Second World War and the years following, and in some other less typical instances. But we can say that both radio documentary and film documentary in these early years of development concerned themselves with "the creative treatment of actuality," as Grierson famously defined the emerging genre of documentary film in 1932.[6]

One of the earliest "features" attempted, and possibly the first British example of reportage in radio in dramatic form, was E. A. Harding's *Crisis in Spain*. This live production was broadcast on June 11, 1931 and revived for broadcast (and recorded) on March 25, 1938. "The work of E. A. Harding was instrumental in introducing statistics, facts and information into radio 'entertainments'. In three programmes broadcast on the National Programme in 1929, 1931 and 1932, Harding laid the basis of a radio montage documentary tradition."[7] In Britain, in radio and cinematic forms, we find confluences and overlaps in approaches and subject matter that have barely been acknowledged historically. W. H. Auden and Benjamin Britten worked on both radio features and film documentaries in Britain.[8] D. G. Bridson wrote of his own productions for the BBC. "Auden was writing poetry for documentary films; why shouldn't I write poems for documentary radio?"[9] Something else that unites the two fields of radio and film documentary to this day is the commitment of time: not only in the (feature length) duration of the works made, but in the time expended to make a project happen, and to think from, and *within* the medium.

In these first documentary symphonies for radio, Bridson, who worked with Auden and Britten, wrote about the making of *Coal* (1938), an "actuality" produced by a small team from BBC Northern Region Features who immersed themselves in the life of miners in Durham:

> A month's work went to making the programme … [as we] familiarised ourselves with every aspect of the miner's life. We went on shift with the men by night and morning; we helped with the hewing, loading and putting; we got the dirt ingrained into our scalps and every pore of our bodies. [One of the other producers] Joan [Littlewood] lived with a miner's family—the son had been killed in the pit—while I put up in no greater comfort at the local miners' pub. By the time that *Coal* came on the air, there wasn't a miner at the pit who didn't know us and treat us as one of themselves.[10]

There are numerous other features made during this period which could also be understood as products of such immersion; however, we are much more familiar with this approach or sensibility towards a subject in the history of documentary film. These audio programs—or let's call them now "radiophonic films"—still exist in the British Library and have been repeated on occasion over the years on the BBC itself. But beyond these broadcasts, they are barely remembered, studied, or acknowledged in the history of documentary.

According to broadcasting historian Paddy Scannell, Bridson, his co-producer Olive Shapley, and the feature team employed by the BBC in its Manchester offices had discovered that "[l]istening rather than speaking is the primary act of language."[11] Shapley was one of the first to take radio out on location, with a disc recorder inside a truck and microphones connected to a portable control desk inside the van. For the first time in radio a new type of portal could open onto another world. In this instance it was onto the streets and lives of the Manchester poor. Shapley could even imagine she was creating radio as it should be created, letting the people "speak for themselves."[12] It was the same kind of impulse we find in some of the foundational moments in cinema documentary feature film: on discovering a world outside one's own, there could be contact if one had the right approach and ethos. "I like to get very close to my subjects," Shapley recalls in a BBC interview; "I stayed a night in a doss house and a very kind clergyman came with me because he didn't think it safe, but it probably was … I would go and live in the community and find out what they wanted to say and not really rehearse them…. You had to make them feel comfortable … and talk for a good while."[13]

Bridson claims that he and Shapley were truly pioneering in that "[t]he idea of building a broadcast entirely around ordinary people was something American radio had not yet thought of doing."[14] Their programs were noticed by American producers, most notably Norman Corwin and the innovative team at the Columbia Workshop.[15] The advent of World War II brought a more urgent use of the documentary capacities of radio, with patient listening and local observation replaced by a new hybrid drama/documentary style aimed at persuasion. A number of co-productions between the BBC and American networks developed this genre, which has received more critical attention than radio documentary's other eras. Most notable in the US context was Corwin's six-part series *An American in England* (CBS), and another CBS/BBC co-production, *Transatlantic Call*, begun by Corwin but carried on by Alan Lomax as head writer/producer on the US side.[16] Lomax had already had experience, as a song hunter, in getting out into the field, recording American and Canadian folksongs on location as actuality recordings. Bridson spoke of Lomax's ability to capture ordinary people for this series which aimed to show the peoples of Britain and the United States in a time of war: "the first of his 'Transatlantic Call' programs" allowed American actuality to come alive: "he spoke the same language and sang the same songs as Americans everywhere. More to the point he was able to help them speak that language into a microphone, and to get the full flavour of their characters across. The shows that he handled came over with the same American impress as the prose of Thomas Wolfe or the poetry of Whitman."[17]

## Transition: The Post-War Feature

> We would rather indulge this idea of "shooting" an acoustical film, and not so much covering an issue, by narration, by delivering facts in old oratorical style of radio.
>
> Peter Leonhard Braun, May 7, 1984[18]

Pre-war documentary had struggled to bring reality into the studio, or to take radio into the field using the bulky, sensitive, and awkward disc recorders of the earlier era. The full impact of the magnetic tape recording technology developed in Germany during the war took a while to materialize. Norman

Corwin's 1947 radio project *One World Flight* signalled the powerful potential of new recording tools that would in time radically change the broader media-sphere, opening up new pathways for not only radio reportage, documentary, and radiophonic "films," but acting as an important catalyst and liberator for new approaches to documentary film (e.g., cinema vérité, Direct Cinema). For this 13-part series, Corwin spent months travelling more than 37,000 miles around the world, using improved wire and innovative "new" paper magnetic tape recorders,[19] to gather the hopes and dreams of people ranging from states-men to "ordinary" survivors, first person accounts of a "total war" which had left no one untouched and in some places, was still continuing.[20]

His journey took him from an interview with the Pope in Rome to a vil-lage in India, from a devastated Europe to farmers who had never left home in Australia and New Zealand. According to a report in *Hollywood Quarterly,* Corwin had in no uncertain terms "invented a new radio form." "Here is real documentary radio," wrote Jerome Lawrence, who felt Corwin had "a way of listening to the rhythms of tomorrow" adding; "more than a reporter, more than a recorder ... he is a poet."[21] Corwin recorded more than 100 hours of material, on frequently unreliable but innovative wire recorders developed by the US military for use during the war.[22] Corwin likewise, at the end of the war years, wanted to open a portal onto the world now in ruins and which was ready to be rebuilt. In this aperture he could imagine for a brief moment a new form of listening (and writing) brought about by the roving microphone's "radio eye."[23] Here one might not simply see, or shed light on a subject, but rather the other's world might be brought closer through the essential tactil-ity of the auditory dimension. Other experiments in the making of this series allowed for an even greater sense of auditory fidelity too, and in time advances in recording would lead to an increased ability to capture not only the voice as source but also its milieu or sound world.

As the capacities of the portable magnetic recorder began to make them-selves felt, a new generation of radio documentary imagination would emerge. In many ways, it was Laurence Gilliam, director of the BBC Features Depart-ment both before and after the War, who put BBC Features on the UK and international radio map. Gilliam became one of those responsible for laying the foundations for what Peter Leonhard Braun later described as a "culture of the feature."[24] Today this has become an international tradition of radio-making which in large measure we can now understand as indicating authored long format documentary styled programs made specifically for the audio medium.

The work Gilliam encouraged at the BBC Features Department cov-ered a large swathe of forms incorporating panoramas, actualities, portraits, reports, performed historical documentaries, poetic essays, and even plays—the common tie being that all features must have a pronounced connection with reality over fiction. They also often eschewed plot or story in favour of "mosaic" or musicalized forms. Poetic structures and language, at least in BBC classic feature productions, tended to create confusions between more literary-inspired output and work that displayed a closer connection to recorded reality, reportage, and the topical or news documentary. For Gilliam, loyalty to the written feature—the literary and poetic form made with pen, typewriter, and muse—perhaps made him deaf to some of these types of programs' artificiality, and to the poetry immanent "in the recorded real," which new portable tape recording technologies were making ever more accessible to the radio producer by the 1960s. However, by the 1950s new forms of actuality-styled documentaries were being attempted within the BBC, although producers, historians, and commentators at the time noted Gilliam's resistance to programs "written" more with the tape recorder than with the pen.[25]

Denis Mitchell reached the BBC Features Unit from South African radio (BBC), where he had already experimented immediately after the war with actuality features using wire recorders. Bridson, a champion of new tape recording technologies, noticed Mitchell's work and lured him back to London to join the hallowed Features Department. It turned out to be a brief period in which Mitchell would make his distinctive first *acoustic films* for radio before becoming frustrated by Gilliam's inability to see the *audio vision* contained in them. After a number of these extraordinary experiments, Mitchell transferred to BBC television where his documentary work became much better known and is remembered.

Denis Mitchell's dreamlike wanderings in the streets of Manchester in *Night in the City*, when he encountered those who slept in doorways and under bridges, was broadcast January 30, 1955;[26] it was actuality documentary meeting a new kind of radio poetics. This was an experiment, a *dérive* with the tape recorder. We catch the eerie sound of whistling drifting through reverberant streets, caught on the wind. And then a series of voices: a woman who offers, "You're walking along the streets and you see the lights on, and you wish you could get in there"; a man tries to give you an explanation, his wounds are transcribable in the way he speaks: "One Sunday arvo, my wife just passed away in my hands...." It is all like this, you hear the space, these voices of those who live the life after midnight on the streets. You feel the chill. You can almost see them as they come to the microphone, but it is something more than seeing, this audio vision. It is closer to touch. The atmosphere has a habit of remaining with you almost as if you had been there, as if it were your own experience.

In the post-war radio work of Ernst Schnabel we encounter another who opened a radio eye, a portal to a new audio vision, whose work would provide one of the foundations for a new German tradition in radio documentary. Some of these works were able to cross borders in the same way as the feature film documentary. *Twenty-Ninth of January,* presenting a day from midnight to midnight in the dead of winter in 1947 Germany, is a "panorama" styled poetic feature in the BBC and emerging German tradition.[27] A "play for voices" more than characters, the words and sounds create an atmosphere hard to forget.[28]

Made less than two years after the defeat of Germany and translated into English for the BBC's Third Programme, this almost aerial vision which takes us over, and into the lives of, a country in ruins, opens with a voice announcing; "This program does not set out to be anything other than a piece of journalism."[29] Strange journalism perhaps, but you can feel its connection to something real, an authenticity even as it turns out to be a kind of performed play (mainly monologues). We become immersed in its evocation of this long freezing night which has descended on the land. The voice, a narration, slowly draws us in: "It's almost 1 [a.m] now, everyone is not asleep...." Yet there is more to unfold; "It's dark down here in the mines; men are lying on their bellies. Slowly they drive deeper into the mountain but the mountain is dead as the grave." We hear something then, a series of piano notes, and voices—What is it? The memory of wind? The voice continues as if it had the advantage of infrared night vision, an ability to penetrate deep into the mountain and into the people's thoughts and dreams. "Up top a wind has come up.... Some are dreaming. Some are in love.... What are you thinking about?" Time passes slowly here but we are drawn in further, "One o'clock already. That was the first hour of the day. The second is even quieter." The voice is casual, almost matter of fact. "It's snowing outside, polar snow falling, we Germans call it.... In town it is so quiet you can hear all the clocks ticking. Up in the attic here the clock has stopped." By now, we are focussing on the real subject of this long day's journey into a German night: "In the camp for displaced persons in the East, a woman lies awake ... and thinks ... if only you couldn't hear everything." Much later, 4.24 pm precisely, our reporter notes, "The sun sets ... Only a few people notice it—the day is snuffed out." Still later, on reflection, the voice offers, "Only the men in the mines don't know it's getting dark." And we go on like this, caught up in this dream of waking, and of not ever being able to sleep. We reach a closure some 60 minutes later as the reporter confides; "It occurred to me, these night thoughts are like evidence in a trial."[30]

In Mitchell's and Schnabel's work, what is discovered and offered is a new ethos of recording. It goes further than the pre-war "democratic" ethos that Scannell described,[31] and comes closer to the radio documentary in its 1960s early *nouvelle vague* form. Mitchell's story is interesting in terms of the development of the radio documentary feature too, because although his pioneering and adventurous work in radio may have been almost forgotten, he exerted a significant influence on the form. Notably, the American Studs Terkel referenced Mitchell's protean montage actuality documentary as a direct inspiration for his belief in the poetry and power of the ordinary voice, the *vox populi,* and created a program made of these voices as pure montage, without the need for narration; it was after experiencing Mitchell's work at the Prix Italia that Terkel embarked upon radio documentaries like his landmark post-Hiroshima montage, *Born to Live* (1961). "I was influenced by Denis Mitchell as well as by Norman Corwin. Sounds need not have a narrator. I got that from Mitchell. Just let the ideas flow from one to the other."[32]

## In the Wake of the Sound Hunters: Golden Age to New Wave

Tony Schwartz was one of a number of amateurs—and I mean this in its sense of someone who is a lover of something—who fell in love with the wild sounds they could collect beyond any studio, creating actuality montages with new technologies they often also helped to develop or modify. CBS's Radio Workshop had supported Corwin's world pilgrimage in 1946 and its rendering into a virtuosic radio series in 1947. And CBS would also air some of Tony Schwartz's idiosyncratic actuality montages, or "acoustic films." His *Sounds of My City,* made for New York station WNYC, won a prestigious Prix Italia award for documentary in 1956. Containing no narration, only sounds, atmospheres, and snippets of interviews recorded from the streets and boroughs of New York, he described it as "the acoustic expression of life."[33] He had collected these sounds over the previous nine years using whatever portable recorders became available. He wrote:

> I have arrived in a time where a new instrument has been perfected: the magnetic recorder. This instrument allowed me to dream of a new and quite different means of expression.... I always carry with me a little portable recorder.... My return home on foot after having dined at a restaurant can furnish an occasion where I might meet a preacher or a street musician. A Saturday morning stroll to the supermarket gave me three or four songs plus children playing with a skipping rope....

Schwartz explained in his essay for the 1956 Prix Italia catalogue how he took over two months to construct this documentary. He concludes: "I do not believe that radio programs and these recordings can be produced hurriedly, as I consider the documentary needs understanding, not simply to offer reality; it needs time and love to arrive at a maturity."

In a much later homage to the man and his many recordings of American life—made in 1999 by the accomplished independent documentary team *The Kitchen Sisters*—Schwartz says he "made" (or rather adapted a machine to make) "the first portable recorder." He recalled; "I brought the VU meter from inside the case to the top so I could look down at it and see how loud things were and I put a strap on it so I could hang it over my shoulder: that was in 1945."[34] While Schwartz's claim to the magnetic portable recorder makes for good radio, it is important here to recall the multiple and divergent views on such foundational moments. It was another young *chasseur de son* in Switzerland who would go on to make waves with a huge breakthrough for radio makers—and much more well known, filmmakers in Europe—with his invention of a truly high quality stand-alone portable magnetic recorder designed to go anywhere in the field (without the need to be connected to a power source such as electricity). After 1957 his battery powered precision machines soon became the equipment of choice for a new breed of filmmaker wanting to record life on the hoof and in the field: "sur le vif" as the *nouvelle vague* cineastes described it. His machines were adopted by many of the pioneers of *cinema verité* and that first celebrated *new wave* we mistakenly seem to associate only with the cinema. The inventor, amateur recordist Stefan Kudelski, called his machine "Nagra" (from the Polish Nagrywa) meaning "He will record."[35]

The development of truly lightweight, high fidelity portable recorders and tape recording machines such as the Nagra allowed new ways of conceiving of a radio program, as much as these tools revolutionized film making. By the beginning of the 1960s a producer could approach a radio program in a similar fashion to film: editing and montaging captured sounds by physically splicing the tape with a razor blade. Another practice, "dubbing," used tape as a way to "cut hard," layer and mix sounds—only here one loaded up multiple reel-to-reel tape players arranged in a room, and played recordings "in" from different machines in sequences. One recorded the resulting composition onto a Master recorder using a mixing desk: (cross) fading, layering, and "cutting." Terkel had in fact done this, working with his sound engineer late into the night to make *Born to Live*.[36] Complicated scenes, sound mixes, and sequences could be constructed with much greater control than had previously been possible in radio's golden age. This also meant less focus on the written feature or using actors:

> We called our new technique "acoustical films". It was not a musical term. It was a visual term.... We felt the competition of TV. In our press campaigns, we had the argument "here you see more than in any TV film ... with your inner sight."[37]

Long "takes" (and stereo which came later) would also provide a depth of field impossible earlier, and offer the auditory equivalent of the tracking shot. Braun put it this way: "The portable tape recorder allowed us to give up our sedentary existence and become nomads and hunters once more.... My God, what a feeling of liberation! We no longer wrote about a subject; we recorded the subject itself. We were acoustic cameras, shooting our sound material in the wild; then combining it into documentary works we called "acoustic films."[38]

The renaissance brought on by new portable recording technologies and magnetic tape in particular would lay the foundation for a whole expanded field of expressive documentary forms in radio in the television age. The Prix Italia established its radio documentary category in 1953, but few countries then entered. By the 1970s the number of participating countries had increased markedly, with most of Europe, the United States, Australia, Japan, and China all there annually. Recalling her early listening apprenticeship in Australia before she had taken up the opportunity to work with the Atelier de Création Radiophonique in Paris, the Australian maker of radio *documentaire de création*, Kaye Mortley, spoke of the revelation she had upon encountering the kinds of new documentary work arriving at ABC Sydney in the early 1970s: "There were all these European tapes which were heavily written onto the tape," she explains. But what does she mean by "written" here?: "I mean the voice and the sound was the message. The medium was the message. They weren't made of texts in particular. They were made of things, which belonged to the domain of sound. They were made outside of studios very often."[39] Mortley was fascinated to see that; "this material could be put together more or less sensitively, more or less intelligently, so what was reality in the beginning deviated towards a type of fiction," and she then understood the importance of the author's immersion "in the material, that the material could be used on the one hand to be itself, but also on the other to express what the author wanted to say." And she adds, "There is the *cinéma d'auteur* and the *radio d'auteur*. Of course there are formulaic documentaries—I really don't mind them—I watch them all the time on TV, perhaps because there are no others. But there are also grand documentaries … things which are closer to fiction."[40]

*Musique concrète* had emerged in French State radio by the end of World War II, and technical as well as artistic experiment was well known and had been also encouraged by RTF's (Radiodiffusion-Télévision Française) Club d'essai (1946–1960). One young recruit who joined the radio in the 1960s was about to be offered the chance to work in a new more open space, the Atelier de Création Radiophonique (ACR). Its goal was to rejuvenate radio in a time of crisis, to gather thinkers, composers, writers, and artisans who might excavate a space from within traditional radio program grids and pioneer an array of forms and subject matter, introduce new sounds and voices to the radio. In what appears as a manifesto, René Farabet proclaimed: "The world is the studio of tomorrow. One great plein-air. To recommence the story from zero."[41]

The ACR made its debut in October 1969. As Farabet described it, the radiophonic arts, performance, even the news were until then "very much confined to the studio, locked up in studios, literature…."[42] Also the radio institution itself was "under siege": "paralysed by strikes."[43] In the midst of this environment of crisis and mood for change, the ACR was offered nearly three hours of time to excavate the spaces of radio, and to move beyond the "dead" studio, outside into the "light" and into the noise.[44] In a certain sense these developments—and unusual emphasis on the art/craft of production: montage, editing, mise en scène, "writing" with the microphone and tape—also helped to focus attention on the producer as author, and away from the writer of a (radio) script. A new *politique des auteurs* emerged, and this produced a new *radio d'auteur*. In this remarkable gesture made possible by managers who also believed in taking risks, unprecedented opportunities presented themselves to the ACR team to construct long form creations made from actualities: radio *documentaires* which created scenes from "wild sound" recordings and nothing much more than air. In the realm of this new type of authorship, a writing with the microphone or micro-stylo, 'microphone-pen', the *documentaire de création* emerges.[45]

At the same time, news reporters everywhere were liberating themselves from insulated overheated studios—released to capture some of this noise and fresh air. In US radio, new developments in public broadcasting offered such chances for renewal. NPR launched *All Things Considered* in 1971; the first program delivered a reporter to Washington to wander amongst demonstrating crowds—everything and anything was recorded as it happened. It sounds like one long scene opening onto another world, and all made possible by a microphone and one reporter with his portable magnetic recorder. Linda Wertheimer, the first show's director would later write: "For all its unedited sprawling, confusing quality, we did what [then host] Robert Conley said we would on that very first day. We put our listeners out there, in the middle of everything...."[46] This kind of development was responsive to the times, but also to the new documentary film movement, Cinema Direct, which had produced its own version of verité (influenced by the French and Canadians) in documentaries like *Primary* or *High School*. The new zeitgeist meant here too one had to get out of the studio, move away from voice of God narration, pen, and typewriter.[47] The imperative was also very much there as in those previous lost moments from the radio vaults—to simply listen.

The journalist Deborah Amos recalls that period at NPR in Washington when she was offered the chance to produce long form audio documentaries for the relatively new program *All Things Considered*. Not only were they listening to American work but their ears were being opened to new international developments: "We listened. We listened to everything we could, stereo documentaries produced at Sender Fries Berlin, news magazine programs from Canada...."[48] In the United States any tradition for this kind of radio had at best been fragmentary, and by the 70s certainly it was not on most people's radar. What memories remained of those CBS documentaries (Corwin, Schwartz, Lomax) or Terkel's *Born to Live* experiment is hard to say. Amos's "golden age," however, is not this, rather it comes when she was given "permission to take risks. That is the definition of the Golden Age. And it didn't matter back then that we seemed like the only ones listening."[49]

In this new wave or golden age, Amos was given the chance to produce one of the most gripping and terrifying pieces of radio I've ever heard: *Father Cares: The Last of Jonestown* (90 minute documentary, 1982) was a rare long form radio "film" based on the found cassettes left by cult leader Jim Jones in Guyana, after his and his "flock's" mass suicide shocked the world. It was the kind of epic labor of love—300 hours of tapes sifted through, with no experts, psychologists, or standard narration—that one had hardly expected to hear coming out of America at that time; and yet there it was, in the tradition of the European longer form feature, *documentaire de création* and "radio film." Uniquely, it mixed the best of the newly revitalizing American reportage tradition (heard with *All Things Considered*) with "new wave" aspects of radio features emerging out of Germany or France, and which Amos had been exposed to through the increased ability of radio programs like this to travel. Just to listen outside the format was now to also take a risk.

Almost everybody there wanted to experiment with the medium, find new ways to use sound, and when we weren't working on a radio piece, we were listening to radio pieces. I remember the first time hearing the Kitchen Sisters take old recordings and remix and edit them into something new and exciting. This was a sound collage, without script, that had the power to evoke emotion simply by juxtaposition and editing choices ... Robert Krulwich [who would go on to make *Radiolab*] was experimenting with theater and the news....[50]

These new *metteurs en ondes* (drawing on *metteur en scene*) or *monteurs* all explored innovative and traditional ways to make expressive documentaries—or "reality fictions" as the Director of the ACR René Farabet described these at an international conference in 1981.[51] In the process, as others were doing at the same time in film culture, they opened up possibilities for an extended field for documentary through sound. Here a new aesthetic might be proposed or a number of possible types of the *documentaire*. Here also one could find "images," but they would come from the creative imaginaries of broadcaster and listener. This is an idea that we hear re-sounded in the current rejuvenation (or as some are re-claiming it, a "new golden age") of the radio documentary in the United States; for example, in the work of Jad Abumrad and Robert Krulwich (of NPR's hugely successful *Radiolab*).

Today we are witnessing perhaps a greater expansion than ever before of creativity in reality radio forms—at least in terms of the numbers of producers making radio documentaries and as found on the internet. A memory is returning to the radio too as archives are discovered anew by producers in search of a genealogy or markers for their practice. What appear to be new forms reveal the continuity—even if it is fragmented—with this past life. This is enabled as programs demonstrate a newfound ability to linger on the internet: as podcasts, or as "radio on demand":

The other interesting thing about media these days is that it can stand perfectly still. In fact it loiters: shows don't simply spill over the airwaves and evaporate; they linger on DVRs, DVDs, various online services.... The value of media product [like *RadioLab*] does not come from being fast. It comes from being timeless.[52]

Sue Schardt, executive director of the Association of Independents in Radio (AIR) recognises great opportunities: "[t]here is, at this time of tremendous consolidation, a creative renaissance underway," but, she cautions: "with very few exceptions, the traditional approach to long form, sound rich documentary-making is at a low point, with little funding and few opportunities of significance in the United States to reach a meaningful audience." She argues the situation has not come by accident: "[it] is the culmination of a 24-year trajectory that began with the first comprehensive national report on the public radio audience: 'Audience (19)88'…. The well-funded, widely supported evolution of public radio's research-driven, news journalism franchise has led the industry to great success in terms of building a significant constituency of core listeners (11% of the American public) and a diverse revenue model drawing from government, foundations, corporations, and average citizens." Paradoxically, with this success, formal conservatism has followed. "This evolution has resulted … in the virtual elimination of experimental work, and minimized opportunity for producers working in any area outside of news reportage."[53]

Against earlier predictions of the medium's use-by-date, the BBC may also be re-discovering radio today as the overlooked "jewel in the crown."[54] And the BBC cautiously appears to be opening to experiment again—and with reality forms, although these are still the exception rather than the rule. We can witness other key public broadcasting institutions and individuals engaging with radio's past documentary culture, as well as with innovations and new propositions for the radio documentary arriving from abroad. It is possible to connect the pioneering "actualities" and golden age "people's programs" with the ordinary voices gathered together in new ways today; for example, in what UK radio critic Gillian Reynolds recently called BBC Radio 4's "new big thing": *The Listening Project*. After attending to one conversation moment between a granddaughter and her grandfather (featured by BBC Radio 4 and captured for the radio and for download), we get a sense of how mysterious even those we think we know well can be. This is not grand drama, and although earth shattering stories might emerge in time, these are not of course promised.

The formula seems simple enough: to offer to anyone "out there" the chance to come in and record a conversation with someone they love; to make possible a dialogue "they might wish they'd had, but never did."[55] Reynolds: "This is communication made into art. Drawn from real life, voices, memories … it becomes a distillation of emotion and experience. In other words it is what documentary and feature makers have done for decades, ever since technology made it possible to record then edit speech." Reynolds reminds us of the artisanal nature and time behind such apparently transparent recordings of actuality: "entwined lifetimes expressed in a few hundred seconds. But that is only what we heard. What they said will have taken up to forty minutes to record, much longer to edit."[56]

BBC Radio 4's *Listening Project* is in fact an example of a new version of a hybrid form somewhere between the documentary feature and oral history collection. It is the product also of the long history of ideas, experiment, creation, and technologies (not to mention people) moving between countries, cultures, and across continents in association with the documentary "project" in radio as it continues to evolve. In this current example, which is not really documentary but certainly something possible because of it, we can trace one of these more recent movements of ideas as we discover the project's direct antecedent and model to be former American documentary radio maker David Isay and his monumental, continually expanding *StoryCorps.*[57] Reynolds traces this more recent British version, launched on Radio 4, but also involving the British Library, as deriving directly from the BBC radio documentary and feature tradition. She traces a lineage that takes us back to the 1930s and that first BBC Experimental Research Unit, as well as to those producers and poets of the real in the North of England at the end of the 30s.

For Silvain Gire, founder and director of *Arte Radio*—a Web-radio station with a difference—it definitely is radio. But a radio made for new ways of listening, and reconnecting with younger audiences more familiar with the iPod or mobile phone than with a transistor radio, digital or otherwise. It is revealing here to know, however, that this radio "station" has been inspired against the odds by those traditions and *auteurs* I have just called up from radio's analogue era, voices that might brush up against us for a moment as almost forgotten visionaries, artisans, and maverick explorers of the sounding world. These past wielders of the *micro-stylo* would render to us voices, events, and places that speak against the ocularcentrism of other media, and for something we still might call "the acoustic expression of life" (Schwartz).[58] According to Gire, formerly a producer and journalist with Radio France's *France Culture*, this "other radio" was largely unknown to a younger generation before the internet arrived. Then in 2002 Gire was invited to create a radio station by the largely publicly funded European cultural television production house, ARTE. The ARTE directors were thinking at first of "real" radio, a transmitter, etc. But Gire would go on to develop instead something "like radio" with young sound engineer and Web expert Christophe Rault.

At the time of writing, Arte Radio comprised 1625 individual pieces (including some audio rich "Web docs"). Gire says this "station" was "founded on the quality of the sound and on the originality of the point of view": "a rather radical editorial project in which ARTE gave us carte-blanche."[59] At first Gire decided to privilege "short forms," as they imagined their younger audiences might not be able to cope with listening to long form documentaries of 30 to 60 minutes, the kind still heard on *France Culture* or most European "cultural radio" stations. Even less did they imagine their audience might appreciate the possibilities explored by the ACR's near carte-blanche some thirty years earlier, with three hours of time on the national state radio service. However, the short form policy soon changed, as audiences turned out to be more than willing to listen to longer pieces—*documentaires, reportages, actualités, créations, fictions, chroniques*—especially when they were sonically adventurous or were composed with rich "wild sounds." As Gire noted, "We said at the time: 'Radio is an art, not only a transistor.'"[60]

Arte Radio is comprised of multiple forms—*reportages*, witness and *bruits pas sages* or literally, sounds which are not so well behaved. The station can be accessed on the Web and also through a mobile App. Although having no real AM/FM/digital broadcasts, it has pioneered multi-lingual co-productions (with BBC Radio and others since 2008). It is acting like a radio station mixed with a production house for movies. As far as I can determine, Arte Radio was the first "radio station" on the Web to offer all of its programs as downloads, effectively creating podcasts before any other "official" radio organization or site. Then they offered RSS feeds: "That was Feb 2005," says Gire, "13 months before Radio France. We were the first professional podcast in France."[61]

Arte Radio does not yet claim to have the large audiences of other radio stations. But this is not what it is all about for ARTE, which provides the funds and resources, or for Gire. It is about creating a culture, a new revitalized culture for creative forms of radio, including documentary. Arte Radio's audience is growing, Gire assures, with figures to back it up; and compared to mainstream public broadcasters these are much "younger": the internet iPod generation. While staying true to the audio forms developed by a long tradition in radio stations in France and elsewhere, Gire says he's not giving in to internet pictures, or transcripts, or to providing too much other than the audio. However, he does recognize that this radio, even if only online, is also becoming a cultural commissioning institution for radio films, diaries, soundscapes, quirky radio writing/essaying, and immersive documentary radio films. It is a production house and yet a magazine, and also curiously a "broadcaster." Its "time shifted" content (podcasts) are there "forever": small deliveries not to a "dead letter department" lost in an inaccessible archive, but available to be opened as they drift and settle within the listener, wherever and whenever he or she chooses to listen. This means Arte Radio has the potential to create dialogues, sustain conversations between the past and the future, offer an "ecology of the pod"[62] to the radio *documentaire de création*, as well as creating a fertile ground for new forms in the present to interact with the old, to mix and create new hybrid forms for the future, just as other written and cinematic art forms have been able to achieve since the book, the library, the video, the DVD.[63]

Multiple festivals for radio creation have emerged in France as they have in Britain and are dedicated to documentary forms (in Belgium also). In addition to Braun's continuing Prix Europa and RAI's Prix Italia, there are prizes such as the Prix Phonurgia Nova (Arles). Arte Radio has won the Prix Europa radio documentary prize multiple times now, although the Italy-based Prix Italia organization at RAI only accepted ARTE's radio entries in 2012, previously refusing to consider their audio programs as "radio."[64] Their audio entry for radio fiction' won the Prix Italia in 2012. Interest in radio docs is growing in other francophone countries, indeed all over Europe.

## Conclusion

Even in crisis then, as television took the limelight after the first golden age of radio, the "feature," radio drama, and documentary forms forged in these years did not disappear from the airwaves—not in the 1960s, the 1970s, or even the

1990s. Despite today's renaissance and re-invention, much of this hard-to-pin-down field of discovery and expression seems still confined to the more marginalised places of the radioscape. In some countries it is hard to track down, if locatable at all, but the work of a few individuals has always managed to rise up out of the endless "featureless" flow of music and babble to be noticed by those searching the horizon for the right signals. Leo Braun recounted how in the beginning he was: "quite a lonely figure" with his "conception of how a radio documentary should be made and not written."[65] Through the IFC and Prix Futura he recalled "looking for rare personalities capable of composing information, writing with the ears, these journalists of sounds—rare birds ready to march in a very different direction of development."[66] Perhaps now these "rare birds" are finding sufficient sanctuary—even new breeding grounds in which to thrive—in public broadcasting stations, on individual programs, or through the new *pod ecology* of the Web.[67]

## Notes

1. Lance Sieveking, *The Stuff of Radio* (London: Cassell, 1934), 28–29.
2. Silvain Gire, "Arteradio.Com," ARTE France, www.arte.com/. This quote accessed March 12, 2005.
3. Michele Hilmes and Jason Loviglio, eds., *Radio Reader: Essays in the Cultural History of Radio* (New York: Routledge, 2002), 2.
4. Robert Peach (Interviewer/Producer), "Other People's Radio," *ABC Radio Two* (Australia: Australian Broadcasting Commission, Archival Recording, September 28, 1977).
5. John Grierson and Forsyth Hardy, "The Documentary Idea." *Grierson on Documentary* (London: Faber, 1966), 250.
6. John Grierson, "The Documentary Producer," *Cinema Quarterly* 2, no. 1 (Autumn 1932), 8. Grierson first used the term "documentary" in 1926.
7. Derek Paget, *True Stories?: Documentary Drama on Radio, Screen, and Stage* (Manchester, UK: Manchester University Press, 1990), 46.
8. Bridson's "Steel: An Industrial Symphony" (1937: British Library No T10157R) made with Auden and Britten and using disc recordings made in a Sheffield steelworks, responded to the classic documentary film *Coal Face* (1935), produced by the GPO Film Unit.
9. D. G. Bridson, *Prospero and Ariel: The Rise and Fall of Radio* (London: Gollancz, 1971), 33.
10. Ibid., 69–70. Co-produced with Olive Shapley.
11. Paddy Scannell, "Radio Documentary: From Profession to Apparatus," in *Prix Italia: The Quest for Radio Quality: The Documentary*, ed. Prix Italia, 33–40 (Rome: Prix Italia; RAI, 1996), 40.
12. Shapley's program, *They Speak for Themselves,* was one of a dozen "actualities" made in 1937–38. It included interviews with the founders of "Mass Observation" and vox pops about the possibility of war. See also Olive Shapley and Christina Hart, *Broadcasting a Life: The Autobiography of Olive Shapley* (London: Scarlet, 1996).
13. Christopher Cook, "Documenting Ourselves," in radio feature *The Mike at Large* (London: BBC Radio 3, 1970s) Audio archive recording, British library.
14. Bridson, op. cit., 99–100. Erik Barnouw supports this view in *Radio Drama in Action: Twenty-Five Plays of a Changing World* (New York: Farrar & Rinehart, 1945), 49: "[p]rograms of this type, using people, not actors … were almost unknown in America."
15. For more on Corwin and the *Columbia Workshop*, see R. LeRoy Bannerman, *Norman Corwin and Radio: the Golden Years* (Birmingham: University of Alabama Press, 1986); Howard Blue,

*Words at War: World War II Era Radio Drama and the Post War Broadcasting Industry Blacklist* (Lanham, MD: Scarecrow Press, 2002).

16. Bridson, op. cit., 99; Michele Hilmes, *Network Nations: A Transnational History of British and American Broadcasting* (New York: Routledge, 2011).

17. Bridson, op. cit., 101.

18. Virginia Madsen and Leonhard Peter Braun, *Peter Leonard Braun Interviewed Collection* (Sydney-Berlin: Personal Collection, 1984–2004; cassette, mini disc). This citation from interview, Sydney, May 7, 1984.

19. Adapted from secret German-developed technology (Magnetophon) discovered by Allied forces at the end of World War II.

20. Jerome Lawrence, "A New Radio Form," *Hollywood Quarterly* 2, no. 3 (1947), 280–81. See also Matthew C. Ehrlich, *Radio Utopia* (Urbana: University of Illinois Press, 2011); Michael Keith and Mary Ann Watson, *Norman Corwin's "One World Flight": The Lost Journal of Radio's Greatest Writer* (New York: Continuum Books, 2009).

21. Op. cit. Jerome Lawrence, 280–81.

22. The first wire recorder was a Valdemar Poulsen Telegraphone of the late 1890s. These and related machines had a limited usage until World War II.

23. A term first used by the Russian experimental and pioneering documentary film maker, Dziga Vertov.

24. Madsen and Braun, op. cit., Braun Interview, Berlin, June 14, 2004.

25. For example, Ian Rodger, in *Radio Drama* (London: Macmillan, 1982), 92–93.

26. Denis Mitchell, "Night in the City," Accessed British Library Archive No. 9CL0028587. This radio feature was later made into a film for BBC television. (*Night in the City: Eye to Eye*, BBC, tx. 14/6/1957).

27. Madsen and Braun interview op. cit. Braun recounts how "the feature" was adopted as a key reality form by the post-war German public broadcasting system: radio documentaries in Germany (thereafter) are referred to as "features," not the earlier German term, "Hör-bilder" (trans. "listening pictures"). See Virginia Madsen, "Radio and the Documentary Imagination: Thirty Years of Experiment, Innovation, and Revelation," *The Radio Journal: International Studies in Broadcast and Audio Media* 3, no. 3 (2005), 189–98.

28. Ernst Schnabel, "Twenty-Ninth of January." BBC version produced by Leonard Cottrell and Laurence Gilliam. Audio Archive Number: T11707WR Adapted by A. L. Loyd. Music: Paul Hindemith. Broadcast January 29, 1948. First broadcast: North West Deutscher Rundfunk (NWDR) Hamburg, April 1947.

29. Ibid, and all quotes following from audio, *Twenty-Ninth of January*. Available British Library.

30. Ibid. Braun regarded this as Schnabel's greatest work and "one of the best things I have ever heard" (Braun to Madsen 2004). It was documentary in the sense that Schnabel broadcast a request on NWDR for listeners to send their descriptions of that one day. His text was created as a montage of some of the 80,000 letters he received from his listeners. In Madsen Braun Interview, Berlin, 2004.

31. Scannell, op. cit.

32. Studs Terkel, *Studs Terkel on Transom,* July 25, 2001, http://transom.org/?p=5163. The program can be heard at: http://transom.org/?p=5163. Mitchell's work was also known to Charles Parker, celebrated in the British radio documentary tradition for his innovative series of "radio ballads" made soon after Mitchell left radio for television.

33. Prix de la Federazione Stampa Italiana. Presented by The National Association of Educational Broadcasters—USA. Tony Schwartz wrote about the making of his 31-minute documentary in Tony Schwartz, "Sons De Ma Ville Documentaire Sonore Par Tony Schwartz, Technique De L'enregistrement," in *Prix Italia Catalogue 1956*, ed. Prix Italia (Rome: Prix Italia, 1956). All quotes from this source. Translated from French by Virginia Madsen.

34. The Kitchen Sisters, "*30,000 Recordings Later*," made for NPR's *All Things Considered*, February 26, 1999. 1' 30" into the recording. Programme available www.prx.organisation/pieces/26842.

35. A homage to this inventor/amateur/sound hunter, Stefan Kudelski, was made by one of the

outstanding proponents of a new wave in French radio documentary, Yann Paranthoën, for the ACR, August 9, 1987: released as *On Nagra*, Paris: (CD) Co-edition Radio France, INA, SCAM, Harmonia mundi, 1993.

36. See also Transom, "About Born to Live with Jim Unrath." June 1, 2011. http://transom. org/?p=16646.
37. Madsen and Braun interview, December 16, 2002, op. cit.
38. From a speech presented to the International Features Conference (IFC), Amsterdam 1999. Reprinted in the accompanying booklet to the *IFC Collection: 30 Years of International Radio Documentaries* (EBU-UER 2004), 4. EBU-UER, "The I.F.C. (International Feature Conference) Collection," ed. Edwin Brys (Geneva: EBU-UER, 2004).
39. Virginia Madsen, "Interview Mortley, Paris, December 29, 2002."
40. Ibid. Also cited in Virginia Madsen, "A radio d'auteur: The documentaire de création of Kaye Mortley." *SCAN* 6, no. 3 (2009).
41. René Farabet, "Recréer Le Monde," *L'Arc* no. 50 (1972), 20,; cited again by R. Farabet, in "L'avenir de la radio," *Dossiers de l'audiovisuel* no. 53 (1994), 15–17. Trans. Virginia Madsen.
42. Virginia Madsen, *Interview with Rene Farabet*. Paris, 1994. Audio recording.
43. Ibid. see also Virginia Madsen, "The Atelier de Création Radiophonique: Propositions for an Expanded Radio Imaginary," in *Radio in the World: Radio Conference 2005*, eds. Bruce Berryman, David Goodman, and Sianan Healey, 471–81 (Melbourne: RMIT Publishing, 2005).
44. Ibid.
45. After the "camera-stylo" or "camera pen," adopted by the French *nouvelle vague* cinema. See Alexandre Astruc, "The Birth of the New Avant-Garde: La Camera-Stylo" (1948) in *The New Wave*, ed. Peter Graham (London: Secker & Warburg, 1968).
46. Linda Wertheimer, *Listening to America: Twenty-Five Years in the Life of a Nation* (Boston: Houghton Mifflin, 1995). Cited in "30th Anniversary Celebration of All Things Considered: The Atc Time," NPR, www.npr.organisation/programs/atc/atc30/timeline/index.html, accessed January 12, 2012.
47. This trope of escaping the studio is common across countries in the 60s/70s period. Peter Leonhard Braun spoke of producers "in blue suits," "like 'monteurs' (people who repair cars)," "because we had to lie down, climb…. We had left our desk, our situation of distinction, our tower of poetry. We were outside now in the cold, in the dirt'." Madsen and Braun interview, 2004, op. cit.
48. Deborah Amos, "Deborah Amos Topic with Rick Davis," *The Transom Review* 2, no. 2 (April 2002), Atlantic Public Media.
49. Ibid.
50. Ibid.
51. "Reality and Fiction in Radio," EBU Radio Drama Conference (March 26–28, 1981), Berlin. Published in Farabet's book, *Bref eloge du coup de tonnerre et du bruit d'ailes* (Arles: Phonurgia Nova, 1994), 73–77.
52. Rob Walker, "On 'Radiolab, the Sound of Science'," *New York Times*, April 7, 2011, Online version.
53. All quotes from Schardt, http://think-tank-leipzig.blogspot.com.au/2012/01/radio-future-nutshell-xxvi.html. The annual Third Coast Audio Festival in Chicago (showcasing American radio documentary culture), plus huge audience downloads and broadcast popularity for programs like *Radio Lab* and *This American Life* reveals however a continuing re-invigoration of the genre.
54. http://www.guardian.co.uk/media/2011/nov/01/mark-thompson-radio-festival-speech.
55. Gillian Reynolds, "Radio 4's 'the Listening Project' Turns Conversations into Art," *The Daily Telegraph*, April 3, 2012. www.telegraph.co.uk> Culture>TV and Radio
56. Ibid.
57. "Since 2003, StoryCorps has collected and archived more than 40,000 interviews from nearly 80,000 participants. Each conversation is recorded on a free CD to share, and is

preserved at the American Folklife Center at the Library of Congress. StoryCorps is one of the largest oral history projects of its kind," David Isay, http://storycorps.org/.

58. Schwartz, op cit.

59. Silvain Gire and Laurent Gago, "Arte Radio.Com 'La Radio Est Un Art, Pas Seulement Un Transistor' Entretien Avec Silvain Gire," in *(Dossier) Mediamorphoses: "La Radio: Paroles Données, Paroles à Prendre,"* ed. Jean-Jacques Cheval (Paris: Armand Colin/INA, 2008), trans. Virginia Madsen: "fondée sur la qualité sonore et l'originalité des points de vue. Un projet éditorial plutôt radical, sur lequel ARTE nous laisse carte blanche!..."

60. Ibid. "On décide de privilégier des formats courts. Nous pensons alors que les gens auront du mal à écouter un long documentaire sur Internet—ce n'est plus le cas aujourd'hui ." "Nous étions "La radio est un art, pas seulement un transistor."

61. Madsen and Gire, *Interview with Silvain Gire (Director Arte Radio/Arte France)* Paris, April 22, 2011.

62. See my discussion in Madsen and Potts, 2010, op. cit.

63. In my interview, op. cit., Gire explains how the station was born out of a long love of "radio de creation." He and Christophe Rault adored the "documentaire de Yann Paranthoën," in France known as the "tailleur de sons" (sculptor, tailor of sound). Internationally known "auteurs" like Kaye Mortley also continue to create dialogues with listeners here, and new, younger auteurs have a chance to develop bodies of work continuing the tradition and revitalizing the culture of audio/radio expression.

64. Op cit. Madsen Gire, 2011. Arte Radio Prix Europa winning radio documentary 2010, "Who Killed Lolita," can be heard on the ABC (Australia) site "Pool" with translation to read as you listen. Go to http://pool.abc.net.au/node/36813

65. Peter Leonhard Braun, *Peter Leonhard Braun Presents the Classics* (Sydney: Audio Arts Department, Australian Broadcasting Corporation, 2001). CD recording.

66. Ibid. Braun is still cited on the IFC website: "Feature-making is no method—no catalogue of tricks—but an attitude towards life," http://ifc2.wordpress.com/, accessed September 15, 2012.

67. See, for example, Josef Trappel, Denis McQuail, and Euromedia Research Group, *Media in Europe Today* (Bristol, UK; Chicago: Intellect, 2011). I note newspapers are also innovating with audio documentary forms, see, for example, the Guardian podcasts (http://www.guardian.co.uk/audio). See also the richly evocative "Hackney podcast" created by Francesca Panetta and volunteers: beautifully crafted programs/journeys which engage the mind and imagination and move the documentary experience to the locative mode, using innovative Apps for the mobile phone, to be listened to in situ as you walk, remapping realities with fiction and wild sound, http://www.hackneyhear.com/ or hackneypodcast.co.uk/.

# Radio's New Histories

# 9

# EL OCTOPUS ACÚSTICO

## Broadcasting and Empire in the Caribbean

*Alejandra Bronfman*

To think about radio in the 1940s Caribbean is to comprehend multiple technologies, listening practices, networks, and audiences in which both domestic and transnational negotiations played a part. In Havana, listeners might tune in to one of dozens of stations from the moment they woke up until deep into the night. They could choose news or they might wait to hear about the love affair on their favorite telenovela. On certain days they might enjoy the strains of a new band or singer, or the voice of a politician making a bid for their loyalty. Ads brought them into a world in which they would be persuaded that Colgate or Palmolive existed to make their lives better. Many would listen at home, on their General Electric or Westinghouse receivers. Depending on their wealth and interest in the medium, they would have bought a large, elegant receiver for their living room, or a smaller more practical one. Or they might listen in one of many cafés or bars with sets whose sounds spilled into the streets. Perennially open windows and doors allowed sounds to flow between homes and sidewalks, so it was difficult to stroll without hearing something on the radio. And one of the city's most popular gathering spots was Radiocentro, a complex that housed the main radio station, and at which crowds gathered to listen to the loudspeakers blasting the day's programming.[1]

In Port au Prince, Haiti, listeners had a choice of two commercial stations, which had sprung up soon after the 1938 demise of the government-owned station. They would have to wait all day for a nightly two hours of recorded music or, on occasion, a live transmission of a performance. They would have heard announcements in French, English, and Spanish, since most of the programming was directed abroad. On occasion, the popular actor Théophile Salnave might have taken the microphone and spoken in Creole, the language most Haitians used on a daily basis. Wealthy residents of the city might skip the local programming altogether and search for sounds emanating from the US, Europe, or Cuba on their shortwave receivers. The less wealthy might congregate around a neighbor's receiver, but they might hear more static than music, since the stations operated on shortwave, so distant listeners heard more clearly than local ones. But they welcomed even these brief and fuzzy musical or spoken interludes as an appealing replacement to the reviled government station that had come to represent the worst of the American occupation.[2]

Meanwhile, residents of Kingston, Jamaica had only recently begun to partake of local broadcasting. Despite a long history of pleas for the construction of a radio station, the city had remained a neglected appendage of the British broadcasting system. The 1940s airwaves included only one local station, which broadcast a few hours daily with a sparse menu that included classical music, educational lectures such as "The Banana" or "Typhoid Fever," notices and news relayed from the BBC, and, most popularly, broadcasts of cricket matches.[3] As in Havana or Port au Prince, wealthier Kingstonians might have tuned in with their beautifully designed Phillips receivers if they wanted to listen to announcers reading local news from the *Daily Gleaner* or catch one of the newer "all Jamaican" programs. They might have welcomed the absence of advertising but bemoaned the limited range of programming. But they knew that they might easily turn the shortwave dial and receive all-day programming, putting up with or perhaps even enjoying the advertising in exchange for continuous music, news, or talk from all over the world.[4]

Extending the notion of radio's "Golden Age" to parts of the world beyond Europe and the US adds new dimensions to and in some ways challenges the narrative in which the 1940s represents a moment of consolidation and the "coming of age" of this relatively new medium. Alexander Russo and others have already complicated this narrative in the context of the US, arguing that the Golden Age was much more variegated and multivocal than previously understood.[5] At the same time, as Michele Hilmes has argued and convincingly demonstrated, reaching beyond national borders in radio history is crucial to understanding the development of the medium. Interactions and exchanges across nations produced broadcasting. The dichotomy of "commercial" vs. "public" around which many debates in early radio hinged, was less a clear-cut distinction than a series of arguments made by American and British broadcasters as they were constructing systems that incorporated elements of both. Creating what she calls a "transnational cultural economy of British and American broadcasting" entailed wary comparisons, accounting for audience demand, and dialogue among the leaders of the broadcasting industry into the 1940s.[6]

A perspective from the Caribbean further decenters these discussions about 1940s radio. Listening to broadcasting in the spaces quite literally in between Britain and the US unsettles the narrative of 1940s radio as uniform or absorbed in nation building.[7] Attention to this region suggests that if broadcasting did propagate, it did so precisely because it took on a variety of formats and parameters, some national, some transnational. Moreover, in some places, the 1940s were not replete with transmitted sound, remaining relatively silent. The major cities of Havana, Port-au-Prince, and Kingston partook of this transnational economy as their governments and entrepreneurs transposed broadcasting to Caribbean particularities. Caught in the middle of both growing and waning empires, the Caribbean was among the first to acquire communications technologies that incorporated the region into zones of commerce and information, yet it often felt the sting of being relegated to the fringes. The hybridity of Caribbean radio was not comfortable. Rather it was highly contested and understood as precisely a site through which to work out conflicts over the politics of empire in the 1930s.

The divergent imperial trajectories of the US and Britain slid past each other in the early twentieth century Caribbean. Britain had established its earliest colonies in the seventeenth century and marked the region in important ways. In Antiguan author Jamaica Kincaid's pointed memory, "I met the world through England, and if the world wanted to meet me it would have to be through England."[8] By the early twentieth century, however, imperial expansion relegated the Caribbean to a marginalized position in relation to the more absorbing potentials of India, Africa, and the Middle East.[9] Jamaica remained a British possession until 1962, but amidst the travails of war and economic struggles, the imperial center of gravity shifted east and Jamaica found itself on the fringe along with other British Caribbean possessions.[10] Labor rebellions of the 1930s resulted in a degree of attention to this region as colonial officials sponsored a flurry of analyses and projects of social reform intended to quiet the unruly subjects who had incited those rebellions. But in some ways it was too late, as another war and increasingly vocal anti-colonialism pushed British rule towards obsolescence.[11]

At the same time, the American presence in the Caribbean greatly expanded in the early years of the twentieth century. If Puerto Rico was the only official US territory, Americans insinuated themselves into Caribbean economies and cultural practices as well as using military occupations to wield power. Throughout the region, residents encountered US expansionism in different ways. The United Fruit Company and the Panama Canal spurred the movement of thousands of workers throughout the region. In 1917, the US purchased the Danish Virgin Islands.[12] Cuba developed "ties of singular intimacy" with its northern neighbor in a variety of ways: occupied from 1899 to 1902, and from 1906 to 1909, it also witnessed expansive US investment in sugar and other industries. Baseball, cinema, and consumer goods circulated freely.[13] Haiti, on the other hand, witnessed a longer occupation (1915–1934) and considerably less investment.[14] Marines were a stronger presence than businessmen, and while US film stars flocked to Cuba's swanky hotels, American anthropologists roamed Haiti in search of exotic forms of blackness.[15] By World War II, when it built military bases in Trinidad and Jamaica, the US was a voluble presence and the source of ambivalence, as Caribbean people acknowledged both its appeal and worried about its increasing clout.[16] Rather than comparing the British and American imperial presences, this essay lingers in the space between them.[17] It is precisely in this space that radio took hold in the region. As such, it serves as another vantage point to study (and challenge) some of the dominant binaries upon which much of the literature on broadcasting rests. US vs. British, commercial vs. state, military vs. civilian, and national vs. transnational all come out sounding slightly different after several stops in the Caribbean.

## PWX, CMQ, RHC Havana

Broadcasting in Havana was the most straightforward iteration of commercial broadcasting. Havana's PWX echoed the format of its US-based partners as soon as it turned on its transmitters in October of 1922.[18] Built by the Cuban Telephone Company, an offshoot of International Telephone and Telegraph, it transmitted via telephone line to its sister station, WEAF in New York, which in turn broadcast within its range. Havana and New York were thus linked via telephone and radio sooner than New York and other parts of the US.[19]

This was an extension of a longstanding relationship with the US since the nineteenth century, which included flows of goods and capital. As the Spanish empire began to crumble in the face of nationalist opposition, Cubans turned to the US as a source of what they perceived to be modern alternatives to Spain's authoritarian constraints. By the same token, Americans saw in Cuba an opportunity to invest, profit, and spread their influence. All of this entailed an exchange of people, as Cubans attended American universities, and Americans traveled to Cuba as administrators and technicians of growing enterprises.[20] Capital also moved towards Cuba. While the majority ended up in the sugar industry, a considerable quantity also flowed to the communications networks that supported business and commerce. The telegraph and telephone networks had been installed by Spanish companies, but in the wake of the US occupations of 1898 to 1902 and 1906 to 1909, US-based capital took greater control and created the Cuban Telephone Company. The brothers Hernand and Sosthenes Behn subsequently bought this and added it to their growing telecommunications empire, International Telephone and Telegraph. Broadcasting was part of this network of capital and communications technologies. The new station served the agendas of the Cuban administration and the interests of ITT. For President Zayas, the opening of a broadcasting station reinforced an ongoing relationship with indicators of modernity and gave his administration a boost in the midst of a political and economic crisis. For ITT, a station in Havana expanded a growing network.[21]

The audience was not quite in place. At the time the station opened, there were only about 100 receivers in Havana, and the initial broadcast was directed at listeners in New York rather than within the city itself. An early period of experimentation with programming included broadcasts of conferences, operas, weather reports, sports events, a great deal of music, and programs from the US. Although many Havanans could not afford receivers, radio listeners began to build their own or gather in public places to catch whatever was on the air.[22] Eventually, GE and Westinghouse repeated a strategy that had increased their receiver sales in the US, designing and promoting receivers as indispensable pieces of furniture for the middle-class parlor.[23]

Despite early experimentation with programming, the revenue-generating structure was never in question. While fully sanctioned and supported by the Cuban government, broadcasting was not under its aegis or control. Radio would pay for itself with advertising. The advertising itself reflected a variety of local, domestic, and international interests, all on the airwaves at different intervals. Large US companies such as Gillette claimed airtime, as did Cuban producers of beer and soap. As US-based advertising agencies opened branches in Havana, Cubans adapted techniques and strategies to local demands, products, and conditions.[24]

Advertising was taken for granted by radio producers, but it generated criticism, as did the generally cacophonous nature of broadcasting. One critic bemoaned the ubiquity of the "jinete satánico" ("Satanic prostitute")[25] and forecast a future in which loudspeakers on street corners would "incessantly bombard helpless cities with hymns to Palmolive soap and Gaitera cider." He objected not just to the advertising but to the ways it signaled a porosity of aural borders. "Latin America" he wrote, "is already suffering the torment of constant entertainment in perpetual English from our big and good friend to the north. When we begin to receive broadcasts from China and Europe, we'll be in Babel, with visits to the insane asylum."[26] Other critics worried about the ways that broadcasting was bankrupting live performances, disrupting family life ("the children won't go to bed"), and wreaking havoc on courtship as lovers neglected their partners in their seduction by the "octopus acústico" ("acoustic octopus").[27]

The anxiety, of course, indicated the medium's growing popularity. Cubans' relative wealth and their readiness to adopt a variety of listening practices meant widespread access: at home for the better off, but also in public spaces, where open windows and doors allowed anyone walking past to partake of the sounds emanating from interiors. Loudspeakers remained in cafés and plazas even after the push towards privatized listening. By the late 1930s advertisers estimated that 45% of Cubans listened to radio on a regular basis.[28]

Cuban broadcasting grew robustly in the 30s and 40s as Havana became what Yeidy Rivero has referred to as the "media capital" of Latin America by the late 1940s. Infusions of capital and expertise as well as the ability to tap into consumerist desires and the seduction of melodrama created a vibrant network system based in Havana. Announcers and musicians were professionalized and personnel unionized. Eventually, Cuban programming, most notably serial detective stories and dramas in addition to music, became widely known throughout the region, so popular that writers and producers were invited to travel throughout Latin America to share their expertise. For Latin Americans, the 1940s signaled, beyond North American broadcasting, the flooding of their airwaves with Cuban *novelas*, music, and advertising. Poised to take advantage of both local and transnational capital and programming, Cuban broadcasting flourished and took on an imperial dimension, creating a kind of counter-empire to rival the US.[29]

## HHK, HH2S, HH3W Port-au-Prince

If the US flexed more military muscle in Haiti than Cuba during this period, its sway over broadcasting was much more tenuous. Midway during the US occupation (1915–1934), William Cumberland and George Fouche Freeman, two officials of the occupation government, purchased and built a station, which they envisioned using for educational purposes. Newspapers in the US had been proclaiming the successes of broadcasting as an educational tool, and Cumberland and Freeman planned to replicate that in Haiti. The idea was that talks on farming could be broadcast to rural listeners in the hinterlands as a way to update their methods and increase productivity. Cumberland and Freeman hoped that these broadcasts would be appealing and welcomed by Haitian farmers and filled the two weekly broadcasting hours with talks (apparently in Creole) as well as some announcements in English and French. The non-commercial station opened in 1926 and operated with shortwave, which limited the audience to better-off residents of Port au Prince or distant listeners. The implementation of the educational strategy required the dissemination of receivers in rural areas, an ambitious plan imperfectly realized.[30]

The local press immediately understood the station and broadcasting plans as an extension of US imperialism and attacked both the occupation and the Haitian government, which they understood to be lackeys for the regime. Ernest Chauvet of the *Nouvelliste* was the most vocally opposed, pointing to the lack of receivers in rural areas, the unproven claim that broadcasting was effective for rural education, and the amount of Haitian taxpayer money that had been spent on a potentially useless plaything for the US occupation. The government responded rather defensively by hesitating to invest additional funds and continuing to broadcast as cheaply as possible. According to John Huston Craige, the Marine who took over the station after its initial clumsy attempts at instruction and uplift, the format changed to a piecemeal assembly of interviews with the local elite and music—whatever he could scrape together given his limited funding—in English and French, directed mostly abroad. The powerful station enjoyed a measure of overseas success, as evidenced by the cards received from Canada, the US, and other places.[31] After Craige came a succession of directors who ran the government-owned station mostly as a kind of public relations medium, with music and interviews intended to impress listeners abroad with pleasing music or astute intellectuals' thoughts on a variety of topics. When they played records from the US and Cuba, however, many Haitians bristled. The music appealed to listeners abroad and some Haitians, but for other Haitians "the menacing invasion of jazz from records and the popularity of son, danzon and boleros" signaled a profound threat to their national music.[32]

The government continued to have an interest in promoting broadcasting as an educational endeavor, and devised a project that would install 150 loudspeakers all over the country, many of them in the agricultural schools it had created as part of a vocational school project. Intending to educate Haitians in more "practical" ways, the occupied government had created schools dedicated to teaching Haitians "technical skills" such as farming or mechanics alongside more traditional schools organized around the liberal arts.[33] This idea generated even more criticism from different sectors. Critics accused the US occupation and the puppet government it controlled of destroying an established culture of learning and replacing it with a plan to create a servile population. Moreover, the disproportionate amount of resources devoted to this project confirmed US disregard for the Haitian educational system. Any sign of misspent funds provoked anger and protest among students at those schools. The conflict exploded in an incident in 1930 in Cayes. Students began a strike, demonstrating against, among other things, the "radio invasion of rural schools."[34] When the strike spread to other institutions, Marines faced down crowds on the verge of rioting and met them with violence. Ten people died, and in the wake of this incident both occupier and occupied began to push more firmly for the US to leave the country.[35]

In this context, the broadcasting project was all but abandoned. By 1932, Donald Heath, the American consul in Port au Prince, outlined the failures of the venture:

> The Haitian government, several years ago, contemplated installing public address stations in fourteen towns throughout Haiti through which programs of music and educational talks would be brought to the masses. These stations were to be set up in the public squares or in the market place of each town and the programs sent via telephone to the amplifiers. Of the fourteen stations proposed, only eight were installed, and today, only two of the eight are operating intermittently. It has been ascertained that the country people evince no interest in the programs offered. This fact has tended to discourage attempts on the part of the government to continue the programs.[36]

Government-run, educational radio was in this context understood as imperialist and patronizing, and at the same time mocked for its inability to enact any of its programs. When it tried to act most like an educational, state-sponsored institution—non-commercial, dedicated to instruction and uplift—was when it was most roundly dismissed as the "bad joke of an incompetent occupation."[37] When it dropped the educational intent and aimed to entertain it enjoyed relatively more success. American visitor Edna Taft offered a description of her visit to HHK on a Friday night devoted to music:

> Afro-American victrola records were played before the microphone: meringues, beguines, rumbas, tangoes, bambucos, interspersed with humorous Creole monologues by a popular Haitian raconteur.... Presently another of radio's impressarios dashed from the room to drive downtown and get another set of gramophone records from the store... outside, peering in, was a vast crowd of Port-au-Prince's lower classes, making a gay fiesta of HHK's regular night on the air.... Clad in their dress-up clothes, the young girls show bright in bright purples, yellows, pinks and blues, they promenaded back and forth, arm in arm on the greensward, or they sat in groups on the lawn....[38]

Despite its occasional success as a visual and aural spectacle, the government-run station was perpetually short of funds. Forced to diminish air time from two weekly hours to one, and unable to secure new owners, the station eventually closed its doors.[39]

Commercial radio was understood by Haitian elites in this context as a positive development that put broadcasting under Haitian control and freed the constraints imposed by the government owned station. In 1935 Haitian businessman Armand Malebranche opened station HH2S, built by a colleague and engineer, Edouard Gentil, who drew on his experience building a station in Puerto Rico the previous year. Malebranche sought out local music groups and domestic sponsors for his nightly, hour-long broadcasts. Since it was a short-wave station, he understood that audiences would be mostly distant and broadcast in English, Spanish, and French. M. Widemaier, an amateur radio operator, built a second station, HH3W, later that year. This station also understood its mandate to be the broadcasting of local musical performances, and its personnel roamed the streets of Port au Prince looking for suitable sites from which to broadcast. These more populist stations enjoyed greater success than the government station.[40]

The subsequent history of Haitian broadcasting is very difficult to tease out of the fragmentary evidence that remains. By 1941, however, a public seemed to be taking shape. In January of that year, Edward Sparks, the interim Chargé d'Affaires at the US consul wrote to the Secretary of State in Washington, DC, with the following report:

> I have the honor to report that five young Haitians were arrested on January 11 by the Haitian police charged with operating a radio transmitting station in Pétionville which had broadcast propaganda directed against President Vincent and the Haitian Government. Those arrested include

Jean Wiener, an employee of the Electric Light Company, René Moravia, an employee of the Haitian Government Radio Station; Ernest Woolley, a chauffeur; Augustine William, a young mechanic and radio repair man; and Emile Chancy engineer and former employee of the Haitian Public Works Department.[41]

The letter went on to report that the men were in jail and faced court martial, accused of sending out propaganda violently critical of President Vincent. The size, demographics, or location of the public these five men imagined is not clear in the records, nor is any evidence regarding the frequency or effect of these broadcasts, but perhaps we can speculate that if these men risked arrest to broadcast oppositional messages, they must have imagined a sizable enough audience to have some kind of effect. They must have taken as a starting point that radio was the most effective medium with which to reach large numbers of people.

The files from the Office of the Coordinator of Inter-American Affairs (OCIAA) offer further evidence of Haitian listening practices. Founded in 1940 under the aegis of the Good Neighbor Program and run by Nelson Rockefeller, the OCIAA's intended purpose was to soothe US–Latin American relations with cultural exchanges.[42] In 1942 the Cap Haitien Committee on Haitian American Rapprochement of the OIAA discussed and decided to begin broadcasting a program designed to appeal to what they called the "Haitian lower classes." The program, entitled "Le quart d'heure de Frère Hiss" would feature conversations between two fictional characters, Frère Hiss, a peasant, and Maître Jasmine, an urban intellectual. They would discuss news of the war each week and its implications for daily life.[43] This Creole-language program, broadcast on HH3W, apparently met with great success. Subsequent reports from the committee over the next few years make note of the popularity of the show. They include letters received from listeners, photographs of groups of Haitians gathered in barber shops and cantinas to listen, and in the most resounding (if somewhat self-serving) endorsement, a letter from Théophile Salnave, a renowned radio personality and voice of Frère Hiss, commenting on the program's success. According to him, it was clearly heard as far north as Port-de-Paix. He also claimed that "between four and five hundred peasants are reached through one radio only." In an attempt to verify these claims, the secretary of the local committee took it upon himself to "cruise through the downtown area of the city several Saturdays during the broadcast, and found that indeed, three quarters of the operating sets were tuned to the program." In addition, he found that "in places where the radio was in a store, and easily heard from the street, there were small groups of five to ten people stopped and listening in."[44] If the occupation government had failed to generate much interest in radio, the commercial stations that followed seem to have fared better. And once they created an audience, it became possible for US-government sponsored radio to re-enter the broadcasting scene. Produced by an office of the US government, reliant on Haitian writers and actors, relayed on Haitian commercial radio, a Creole program intended to foster enhanced neighborly relations between the US and Haiti by offering news and commentary on the war in Europe serves as an example of the complex ways Caribbean radio created sonic space between empires.

## ZQI Kingston

As the Cuban airwaves became more crowded with music, *novelas*, news, and political commentary, and stations in Haiti competed for the loyalty of listeners with dueling programs, Jamaicans could only observe from the sidelines. Local elites sought to compensate for the absence of a local station by seeking out programming abroad. A 1938 announcement in the literary magazine *The West Indian Review* noted a new collaboration between it and station HH2S in Haiti, featuring "a daily programme in English ... for the benefit of listeners in Jamaica and the British West Indies." The announcement stated explicitly its interest in pursuing a commercial model: "advertisers who are interested in having announcements included in this broadcast are invited to communicate with the Advertising Department."[45] In 1939 Violet Allwood, a social reformer and member of the local elite, travelled to Havana to survey the state of their broadcasting. "My embarrassment was considerable," she recalled, "when I admitted we had no broadcasting station." Frustrated with the slow pace of negotiations over the acquisition of a local station, Allwood sought out other ways to fill airtime. In Cuba she arranged for relays of "the best NBC programs from the Cuban stations" from the Cuban Transatlantic Radio Corporation, which rebroadcast programs from the US. CTRC director Walter Graff responded positively enough for her to push for him to substitute the Spanish language ads (designed for Cuban audiences) for English ones.[46]

Meanwhile, the distracted British colonial state in economic crisis proved reluctant to build a local station. The BBC had argued forcefully for widespread dissemination of its Daventry service to the colonies. The author of a 1935 confidential report on broadcasting in the colonies assured government officials that the Daventry service continued "to meet the demands for broadcasting from the home country representative of British tradition and sentiment."[47] But government officials were convinced also of the importance of maintaining control over broadcasting, which meant denying colonies their own stations, if necessary. The reception was not as strong as relayed wireless, they argued, and the "technical" personnel that ran them couldn't be trusted to recognize relevant programming. Moreover, there was the problem of who was to pay for these services. A local committee created in Jamaica in 1934 issued a report in 1937 that estimated costs at about £53,000, rather than the originally projected £5,000. Colonial officials considered that exorbitant, but they also rejected any requests to combine public funding with some commercial revenues.[48] Perhaps they recalled the warnings of the recent BBC report that argued that it might be necessary to find commercial support for local stations, but this could only be regarded as a temporary measure: "Experience has shown that the association of commercial interests with the operation of a service of any type is undesirable."[49] In gridlock, colonial officials and the local committee traded expressions of frustration, as each side blamed the other for the failure to move forward. Officials in Britain downplayed their role and blamed the Jamaicans. "All that remained to be done," wrote one official referring to Jamaican plans for a broadcasting station, "was for the Jamaicans to vote the necessary money and get on with it. Although, however, these arrangements were concluded a year ago we have had no report that any definite progress has in fact been made."[50]

It was only an extended labor rebellion that began with protests over lack of employment opportunities and grew to a violent, island-wide confrontation that jolted government officials out of their complacency. Among other reactive measures, they declared a new support for broadcasting as an expedient way to educate island residents and quiet their rebellious dispositions.[51] The broadcasting station that opened in 1939 was firmly in government hands. Broadcasting one hour per week, the programs offered what local reformers imagined the populace needed. Infrequent and dull programming, combined with a lack of receivers in the country, resulted in a halting beginning for Kingston's ZQI.[52]

Broadcasting took hold slowly and unevenly. Projects to distribute low-cost radio sets faltered in the face of a perpetual lack of funds. And when receivers did arrive, a malfunction might put them out of commission for years. Written correspondence between distributor for RCA and owner of a radio repair shop, Stanley Motta, and the director of a community center in rural Jamaica records the two-year long process during which they had to wait for a part to arrive from Europe, immersed in war. Once the part did arrive, the community center could no longer afford to pay for the repair.[53] The weather and terrain also posed obstacles. A 1956 report about broadcasting described the problem: "before 1947 the listener suffered acutely from the difficulties of obtaining good quality reception in an area subject to severe atmospheric and other interference...."[54] Jamaica was particularly difficult both because of "difficult mountainous terrain" and frequent "interference by foreign stations encroaching on the allotted frequencies."[55] Still, some evidence suggests the presence of an audience. If small and fickle, it was not entirely missing. By 1946, ZQI records point to the increasingly interactive nature of broadcasting, as announcers responded to song requests and announced birthdays on the air.[56]

A government-owned station in Kingston met a very different fate than it had in Port au Prince. In Haiti, local elites had either enjoyed the programming meant to signal their participation in a cosmopolitan community of radio listeners, or protested its imperialist implications. When it reached non-elites, they too had understood broadcasting as a wasteful and potentially threatening extension of the US occupation. The Port au Prince station had come to stand in for an unpopular occupation, and as such served as a concrete target of nationalist rage. In Kingston, on the other hand, local elites were given control of the station and regarded it as theirs. The reaction, by non-elites, to whom most of the programming was directed, was a distinct lack of interest. Rather than rage, they responded with disregard.

Towards the end of the 1940s the station was not able to sustain itself. Revenues from licensing receivers (after the British model) failed to produce enough income, and neither the local nor the imperial government was willing to contribute enough funds to sustain its operations. The newly formed Jamaican Broadcasting Company proposed a successful bid and prepared to take over the station.[57] But the plan met with a great deal of local resistance. Some critics objected to the details of the plan, arguing that the JBC only had profits in mind rather than improving Jamaica's broadcasting conditions. "If Jamaica is to give away her radio rights," argued Vere Johns, "let it be for something worthwhile. Are we going to be satisfied with a small station (such as Trinidad and British Guiana have) and permit its operators to make a huge profit out of advertising? I think not."[58] Former BBC announcer and Jamaican celebrity Una Marson offered a dire analysis of the impending dangers: "It is all well and good," she wrote,

> for American Radios to herald the merits and demerits of bathsalts or champagne mintsticks or chewing gum, but in Jamaica where at present and maybe for years to come the economy of the country impels us to turn over a penny a dozen times before we spend it, gay and glamorous advertising coming into our cornmeal porridge and salt-fish fritters for breakfast can only be a snare and a delusion.[59]

It was difficult, however, to maintain a pure opposition to advertising. As one letter to the *Gleaner* noted, while the Cuban and Dominican stations had a "positively appalling" amount of advertising, there were fewer on the "Voice of Guatemala," and "when you hear them, you don't mind."[60]

The 1940s closed with the confirmed transfer of ZQI to commercial management. In the end, even the fiercest opposition had resigned itself to the predicted transformation of Jamaican broadcasting. An editorial in the *Daily Gleaner* optimistically framed the compromise: "there is no reason why commercialism and competence, advertising and art, should not be happily wed in the programmes of Radio Jamaica."[61] But it was not a particularly happy marriage. In a context of rising nationalism, critics expressed dissatisfaction with both British and American contributions to their broadcasting system. The British government, had, after all, declined to fund their broadcasting station. And ironically the Jamaican Broadcasting Company, which would introduce commercial radio, was supported with British capital.[62] Yet if this was presumably a new era in broadcasting, the voice of radio retained much of its reformist and condescending tendencies, ignoring a majority of Jamaicans in its focus on urban middle-class tastes until the 1960s.

## Radio between Empires

Caribbean broadcasting drew from two themes to produce three variations. In Kingston, local radio, transposed with a great deal of delay, remained within a centralized paradigm. It retained this inheritance even through changes necessary to make it financially viable. The compromises that brought radio into the 1950s both relied on and eluded British and American models and in so doing had limited appeal. The contrapuntal experience in Port au Prince witnessed the embrace of commercial broadcasting in an effort to counter radio as introduced and controlled by local government at the behest of the US military regime. Haitians enjoyed domestic music but resisted jazz and Cuban music, two icons of "Golden Age" radio. One of the popular Creole voices on Haitian radio was sponsored by a US government agency. And Havana wholeheartedly embraced the US commercial model of broadcasting, eventually using it to generate a broadcasting empire of its own. Thus the radio industry rendered Cuba, often imagined as a victim of US imperialism, an agent of media imperialism.

Each case complicates the dichotomies within which many radio histories remain. While Jamaicans warily adopted a combined public and commercial formula, Haitians inverted the normative framework in which commercial broadcasting was understood as a corrupt and tainted version of the purity of public media. On the other hand, the notion that Britain and the US were somehow equal players in the struggle over the shape of broadcasting was belied not just by an overwhelming US presence in the region but also by a British reluctance to implement broadcasting until very late in the day.

The Caribbean cases examined here might be understood as the manifestations of some of what Hilmes calls the "messy and transgressive" transactions that generated the culture of broadcasting.[63] A regional focus makes clear the uneven spread of communications technologies. The stories here do not suggest that the Caribbean was blanketed with full-blown, completely interconnected circuits, but rather that voluble, dense media contexts existed alongside zones that remained electronically silent. If neglected by historians, broadcasting mediated the experiences of ordinary Caribbean people—of politics, of consumerism, of their relationship to their bodies, domestic and public spaces, nation, and empire. It did so in ways that often reproduced or reinforced social inequalities. I hope these stories can begin to record unwritten radio histories of the region.

## Notes

1. Reynaldo González, *Llorar es un placer* (Havana: Editorial Letras Cubanas, 2002); Oscar Luis López. *La radio en Cuba* (Havana: Editorial Letras Cubanas, 1998); Alejandra Bronfman, "'El naciente público oyente': Towards a Genealogy of the Audience in Early Republican Cuba," in *State of Ambiguity: Civic Life and Cultural Form in Cuba's First Republic,* ed. Steven Palmer, José Antonio Piqueras, and Amparo Sánchez (Durham, NC: Duke University Press, forthcoming).

2. David Hartt, *Broadcasting in Haiti, Its History, Penetration, Social Role and Perspective* (PhD Thesis, Florida State University, Tallahassee, FL., 1977); Jean Fouchard, *La Meringue: danse nationale d'haiti* (Quebec, Canada: Editions Leméac, 1973); Gage Averill, *A Day For the Hunter, A Day for the Prey: Popular Music and Power in Haiti* (Chicago: University of Chicago Press, 1997).

3. Jamaican Archives and Record Department, Spanishtown (JARD), ZQI Log Book, 1935–41, Gifts and Deposits, 7/199 #1.

4. The *Daily Gleaner* regularly listed shortwave broadcast programming available in Jamaica in its column, "Radio News." See, for example "Radio News," *Daily Gleaner,* June 15, 1938.

5. Alexander Russo, *Points on the Dial: Golden Age Radio Beyond the Networks* (Durham, NC: Duke University Press, 2010).

6. Michele Hilmes, "Radio Nations," in *Atlantic Communications: The Media in American and German History from the Seventeenth to the Twentieth century,* ed. Norbert Finzsche and Ursula Lehmkuhl (New York: Berg Press, 2004); Hilmes, *Network Nations* (New York: Routledge, 2012).

7. On Latin America, see, for example, Joy Hayes, *Radio Nation* (Tucson: University of Arizona Press, 2000); Robert Claxton, *From Parsifal to Perón: Early Radio in Argentina, 1920–1944* (Gainesville: University of Florida Press, 2007). Important exceptions are Bryann McCann, *Hello Hello Brazil* (Durham, NC: Duke University Press, 2004) and Christine Ehrick, "'Savage Dissonance': Gender, Voice, and Women's Radio Speech in Argentina, 1930–1945," in *Sound in the Age of Mechanical Reproduction,* ed. David Suissman and Susan Strasser (Philadelphia: University of Pennsylvania Press, 2009).

8. Jamaica Kincaid, *A Small Place* (New York: Farrar, Straus and Giroux, 1988), 33.

9. L. J. Butler, *Britain and Empire: Adjusting to a Post-Imperial World* (London: I. B. Tauris, 2002).

10. Thomas Holt, *The Problem of Freedom: Race, Labor and Politics in Jamaica and Britain, 1832–1938* (Baltimore: Johns Hopkins University Press, 1991), Epilogue; Daniel Headrick, *The Invisible Weapon: Telecommunication and International Politics, 1851–1945* (New York: Oxford University Press, 1991).

11. Mary Chamberlain, *Empire and Nation Building in the Caribbean: Barbados, 1937–66* (Manchester, UK: Manchester University Press, 2010); Jason Parker, *Brother's Keeper: The United States, Race, and Empire in the British Caribbean, 1937–1962* (New York: Oxford University Press, 2008).

12. Gilbert Joseph, Catherine LeGrand, and Ricardo Salvatore, eds., *Close Encounters of Empire: Writing the Cultural History of US-Latin American Relations* (Durham, NC: Duke University Press, 1998); Alfred McCoy and Francisco Scarano, eds., *Colonial Crucible: Empire in the Making of the American State* (Madison: University of Wisconsin Press, 2009); Harvey Neptune, *Caliban and the Yankees: Trinidad and the United States Occupation* (Chapel Hill: University of North Carolina Press, 2007); Lara Putnam, *The Company They Kept: Migrants and the Politics of Gender in Costa Rica, 1870–1960* (Chapel Hill: University of North Carolina Press, 2001).

13. Louis A. Pérez Jr., *Cuba and the United States: Ties of Singular Intimacy* (Athens: University of Georgia Press, 2003); Pérez, *On Becoming Cuban: Identity, Nationality and Culture* (Chapel Hill: University of North Carolina Press, 2007).

14. Roger Gaillard, *Les blancs debarquent* (Berkeley: University of California Press, 198); Hans Schmidt, *The United States Occupation of Haiti, 1915–1934* (New Brunswick, NJ: Rutgers University Press, 1995).

15. Kate Ramsey, *The Spirits and the Law: Vodou and Power in Haiti* (Chicago: University of Chicago Press, 2011); Mary Renda, *Taking Haiti: Military Occupation and the Culture of U.S. Imperialism, 1915–1940* (Chapel Hill: University of North Carolina Press, 2001); Averill, *A Day For the Hunter*; Laurent Dubois, *Haiti: The Aftershocks of History* (New York: Macmillan, 2012).

16. Neptune, *Caliban and the Yankees*; Pérez, *On Becoming Cuban*.

17. For a comparative approach, see Ann Stoler, "Introduction," in *Haunted by Empire: Geographies of Intimacy in North American History*, ed. Ann Stoler (Durham, NC: Duke University Press, 2006).

18. González, *Llorar es un placer*; López. *La radio en Cuba*; Bronfman, "'El naciente público oyente'."

19. José Altshuler and Roberto Díaz, eds. *El teléfono en Cuba, 1849–1959* (Havana: Sociedad Cubana de Historia de la Ciencia y la Tecnología, 2004); Omar Pérez Salomón, *Cuba: 125 años de telefonía* (Havana: Editora Política, 2009); Thomas O'Brien, *The Revolutionary Mission: American Enterprise in Latin America 1940–1945* (New York: Cambridge University Press, 1996).

20. Marial Iglesias Utset, *Las metáforas del cambio en la vida cotidiana: Cuba, 1898–1902* (Havana: Ediciones Unión, 2003); Gillian McGillivray, *Blazing Cane: Communities, Class, and State Formation in Cuba, 1868–1959* (Durham, NC: Duke University Press, 2009).

21. Altshuler and Díaz, eds., El teléfono en Cuba, 1849–1959; Salomón, Cuba: 125 años de *telefonía*; O'Brien, *The Revolutionary Mission*.

22. Bronfman, "El naciente público oyente"; Steve J. Wurtzler, *Electric Sounds: Technological Change and the Rise of the Corporate Mass Media* (New York: Columbia University Press, 2007).

23. Wurtzler, *Electric Sounds*.

24. Yeidy M. Rivero, "Havana as a 1940s–1950s Latin American Media Capital," *Critical Studies in Media Communication* 26, no. 3 (August 2009), 275–295.

25. Jinete means "jockey," or "rider," but it is also slang for prostitute in the Cuban context.

26. Julian Power, "Torre de Babel" *Carteles* (April 1923), 38, 43.

27. Alberto Guigou, "El radio y el amor" *Carteles* (May 1923), 36, 44.

28. González, *Llorar es un placer*, 102.

29. Rivero, "Havana as a 1940s–1950s Latin American Media Capital."

30. David Hartt, *Broadcasting in Haiti*.

31. John Huston Craige, *Black Bagdad: The Arabian Nights Adventures of a Marine Captain in Haiti* (New York: Minton, Balch, 1933), Ch. 9.

32. Jean Fouchard, *La Meringue: danse nationale d'haiti* (Quebec, Canada: Editions Leméac, 1973), 152.

33. Leslie Buell, "Black Haiti: A Republic of Many Revolutions," *New York Times,* December 15, 1929, p. 26; Schmidt, *The United States Occupation of Haiti.*

34. Hartt, *Broadcasting in Haiti*, 9.

35. Schmidt, *The United States Occupation of Haiti*; "All Quiet in Haiti; New Marines Help," *New York Times*, December 10, 1929, p. 3; "15 Arrested in Haiti for Curfew Violation," *New York Times*, December 12, 1929, p. 9.

36. National Archives and Records Administration, Washington, DC (NARA), RG 84, *Records of Foreign Service Posts, Consular Posts, Port au Prince, Haiti*, Vol. 149, 1932; Donald Heath, Letter to All-American Service Inc., Radio Publishers' Listeners Official Radio Log.

37. Hartt, *Broadcasting in Haiti*, p. 5.

38. Hartt, *Broadcasting*, 28, citation is from Edna Taft, *A Puritan in Voodoo Land* (Philadelphia: Penn Publishing, 1938).

39. Hartt, *Broadcasting*, 31.

40. Hartt, *Broadcasting*, Chap. 2.

41. NARA, RG 151, 838/3550, Memo No. 1185, "Political Arrests In Haiti."

42. Gisela Cramer and Ursula Prutsch, "Nelson A. Rockefeller's Office of Inter-American Affairs

and Record Group 229," *The Hispanic American Historical Review* 86, no.4 (2006), 785–806; Cramer, "How To Do Things With Waves: United States Radio and Latin America in the Times of the Good Neighbor," in A. Bronfman and A. G. Wood, eds., *Media, Sound and Culture in Latin America and the Caribbean* (Pittsburgh: University of Pittsburgh Press, 2012).

43. NARA, RG 229, Entry E-114, Volume 8, Box 1405, File "Special Radio Programs," Letter to Nelson Rockefeller, November 16, 1942.

44. NARA, RG 229, Entry E-114, Volume 1, Box 1402, File "Radio Correspondence, Outgoing," Letter to Nelson Rockefeller, June 10, 1943.

45. *West Indian Review* 4, no. 11 (July 1938), 2.

46. "Outstanding U.S. Radio Programmes to be Relayed to Island From Cuba," *Daily Gleaner*, March 29, 1939.

47. National Archives, Kew Gardens (NA), CO 323-1338-5, British Broadcasting Corporation, "Introductory Memorandum on Broadcasting and the Colonial Empire," 5.

48. JARD, 1B/5/77/205, "Wireless Broadcasting Scheme—Jamaica—Report of Committee."

49. NA, CO 323-1338-5, British Broadcasting Corporation, "Introductory Memorandum on Broadcasting and the Colonial Empire," 14.

50. NA, CO 137/823/7, "Jamaica 1938, Miscellaneous, Sir S. Cripps."

51. NA, CO 137/823/7 "Jamaica 1938, Miscellaneous, Sir S. Cripps," 7–9.

52. JARD, ZQI Log Book, 1935–41, Gifts and Deposits, 7/199 #1.

53. JARD, Semi Public 3/24, Jamaica Social Welfare Commission 2077: Guy's Hill Community Centre.

54. Central Rediffusion Services Ltd., *Commercial Broadcasting in the British West Indies* (London: Butterworths Scientific Publications, 1956), 48.

55. Central Rediffusion Services, Ltd., *Commercial Broadcasting in the British West Indies,* 53.

56. JARD, 1B/5/99, ZQI Log Book, 1935–41, Gifts and Deposits, 7/199 #1; April–October 1941, Vols. 6–8, 1944–1947.

57. "JBC Shapes Plans to Take Over," *Daily Gleaner,* February 8, 1950, 1.

58. Vere Johns, "Let Us Clear the Air On Broadcasting Issue," *Daily Gleaner,* July 13, 1949.

59. Una Marson "Why Commerical Radio?" *Daily Gleaner,* June 25, 1949.

60. Norris Smith, "Letter to the Editor," *Daily Gleaner,* June 25, 1949.

61. "Radio Jamaica," *Daily Gleaner,* July 11, 1950, p. 8.

62. This reflected the growing clamor for commercial radio in Britain, as well as an opportunity for resentful businesses to circumvent the non-commercial monopoly of the domestic BBC. I am grateful to Michele Hilmes for pointing to this connection.

63. Hilmes, *Network Nations*, 25.

# 10

# PORTIA FACES THE WORLD

## Re-Writing and Re-Voicing American Radio for an International Market[1]

*David Goodman and Susan Smulyan*

Radio soap operas and other serial dramatic programs arose in the United States as a form of national programming, providing a common denominator of lucrative commercial entertainment for radio networks and large corporations. Their national popularity represented a significant achievement in a large and diverse nation, one that attested to the skills of the writers and producers of these new kinds of radio shows. Legendary U.S. soap producer Frank Hummert claimed that "our stories are about the everyday doings of plain, everyday people—stories that can be understood and appreciated on Park Avenue and on the prairie."[2] That broad appeal across class, ethnic, and even gender lines was the basis of the spectacular success of radio soaps at home.

American radio shows were designed for the U.S. market, which is to say they were made for a large, culturally and socially diverse population spread over a continent and more. In what had for decades been a high immigration society, successful commercial entertainment in the 20th-century U.S. had to be produced in a way that created rather than presumed a common background. Radio soap opera did this by using stories of daily life with a slow pace and much repetition of key points that provided, for persistent listeners, highly satisfying rewards as they accumulated a remarkable stock of "inside" knowledge of characters' lives and histories. Herta Herzog's pioneering 1941 psychological study of American soap opera listeners stressed the individual gratifications the serials provided—both the catharsis and the lessons in life were welcomed by individual listeners.[3] In a fluid, changing, diverse society, common entertainment worked to build bonds of common experience—trading stories about baseball games or what Jack Benny said or how Portia was dealing with life—where none had existed before.

What is less commonly realized is that those absorbing, world-creating, inclusive characteristics of the American radio soap opera also made it a highly exportable cultural form. American radio serials, unlike Hollywood films, were not initially conceived and produced with an international audience in mind.[4] American radio history has most often taken the nation as its focus, noting the moments that radio brought the nation together and its situation within a national policy frame.[5] This article recuperates the forgotten history of the international connections between commercial radio broadcasters in English-speaking nations after World War II. These commercial broadcasters operated alongside non-commercial broadcasters such as the BBC, which sent programs around the Commonwealth and whose imperial presence, as Simon Potter has shown, complicates any simple story of national and transnational radio.[6] We seek to problematize the national and even nationalist frame of much radio history, thus extending the study of what Lawrence Levine optimistically dubbed the "folklore of industrial society" from the national to the international context.[7]

Much work on "Americanization" focuses on the deliberate attempts of the United States to project itself abroad through agencies such as the U.S. Information Agency and the Voice of America and the reception of American cultural products in other nations: the history of the complex process by which "indigenous cultures adapted to and resisted American cultural products."[8] Commercial cultural exports such as Hollywood film have also received attention, particularly where (as with Hollywood) the export was economically central to the American industry itself.[9] Historians have seen World War II and its immediate aftermath as a moment when the United States government and commercial interests worked to consolidate and expand markets for cultural products.[10] Radio has not been studied in this international cultural export/Americanization context, however, and there is little history written about the commercial export of recorded American radio programs from the 1930s.[11]

Our focus here is an American cultural export trade hidden even further from historical view: the transformation of American radio serial scripts—lightly re-written but completely re-voiced in Australia—into successful export commodities in the 1950s and 60s. Taking place during the Cold War, when U.S. government attention focused on using cultural products as propaganda and at a time when Americanization and cultural imperialism were topics of heated debate in many nations, this export trade occupied a curious position. It might well have been more vigorously denounced as Americanization by stealth if the process had been more widely understood. But these popular programs entered other national radio soundworlds as neither clearly American nor Australian. Histories of Americanization naturally gravitate toward the most obviously and distinctively American products that proclaimed their Americanness—the export of jazz, Coca Cola, and Mickey Mouse.[12] That the re-voicing of radio serials could so easily defuse concerns about Americanization tells us something significant about sound, form, and content in cultural export. Perhaps we have all missed the deeper significance of the export and import of cultural forms in all the noise about, and resistance to, particular cultural products.

## Transcriptions

Historians' preoccupation with radio's national role relates to the emphasis placed on radio networks—the transformative 1930s technology that allowed a whole nation to be addressed simultaneously via wired land lines. The programs discussed here circulated instead on transcription disks, the better quality recorded disks made specifically for broadcast. Transcriptions had the capacity to extend a program just as far across space as wired networks, but in a series of temporally asynchronous local broadcasts. Alexander Russo points out that, despite constant network assurances that the best radio was "commercial, national, live," transcriptions occupied a significant place in prewar American radio because they allowed more flexible possibilities for local and regional advertisers, audiences, and stations. The big networks even went into the transcription business themselves as a defensive measure.[13]

It is likely that Australian radio used transcriptions even more frequently than American radio in the 1930s: the great distances, low population density, and high cost of landline transmission all contributed to the utility of transcriptions in the Australian context.[14] There was, however, a crucial difference. In the United States almost all radio transcriptions were American productions; in Australia many were imported from the United States and from the BBC, and that changed the cultural dynamic. If networks spoke to nations, transcriptions flowed between them. The successful export and adaptation of radio programs, had it been more widely noticed and discussed, might have thrown into doubt the prevalent nationalist assumptions that successful radio programs had to be cultural products crafted within a nation and finely adjusted to suit the particularities and peculiarities of the national temperament.

The majority of Australia's imported transcriptions, especially of those that played on the commercial stations that had the largest audience, were American. The story of their importation begins in 1933 when A. E. Bennett, managing director of Sydney station 2GB, traveled to the United States and purchased a large number of American transcriptions, including *Chandu the Magician*, a 1931 series that had been an early transcription success in the United States. Bennett signed on as Australian agent for the Radio Transcription Company of America and the Freeman Lang Studios. After his return home, he arranged for Freeman Lang's vivacious young assistant, Grace Gibson, to come to Australia in 1934 to help develop the transcription import business.[15] Gibson, born in Texas and educated in California, made the journey. With a population just reaching 7 million by the end of the 1930s, Australia was a relatively small, English-speaking radio market. Eager for content of all kinds, the Australian commercial stations began looking to the United States for entertainment programs, just as the national public broadcaster, the Australian Broadcasting Commission (ABC), from its creation in 1932, sought its imported fare from the BBC. The ABC, with its relays of BBC Empire Service (known from 1939 as the Overseas Service) and broadcasts of BBC transcriptions, took on the task not only of maintaining ties with Britain, but also more generally of sustaining education and cultural programming. A. E. Bennett understood quite astutely that the formation of the ABC in some ways freed up the commercial stations. The national service, he explained, "rightly shouldered the responsibility for educational talks, and left the commercial stations free to look to their own peculiar business—supplying popular entertainment."[16] Finding high demand from the Australian commercial stations for American transcriptions, Gibson and Bennett set up a transcription company—American Radio Transcription Agencies, soon more commonly known by its cable address, Artransa—and Gibson decided to stay in Sydney.

American transcriptions were thereafter used extensively on Australian radio, the number increasing in the mid-1930s with the introduction of cheaper acetate recordings. *Broadcasting Business* explained in 1936 that, because Britain produced few transcriptions, Australian commercial stations were "almost compelled to use American transcriptions."[17] In the 1930s, Australian stations proudly listed many American transcriptions in their programs: Al Pearce and his Gang, George Burns and Gracie Allen, Pinto Pete and His Ranch Boys, and many others became Australian favourites. In 1934, Amalgamated Wireless Australasia (AWA)—radio manufacturer, station owner, and program maker—announced that it would begin importing high fidelity NBC transcriptions, programs such as the Maxwell House Showboat.[18] By 1935, Grace Gibson represented fourteen American transcription companies, had sold 62 different American serials to Australian stations, and had "almost achieved a monopoly of this business in Australia."[19] She succeeded in finding big corporate advertisers to sponsor the broadcasts of several of these serials, including significantly, Lever Brothers, the international soap manufacturers. In 1938 she made a trip back to the United States to buy more shows for Australia and to try to interest American stations in transcriptions produced at 2GB; she thought there was every possibility that "in the near future there will be a regular interchange of dramatic programs between America and Australia."[20]

The flow in the 1930s, however, was almost entirely one way, as American programs gained prominence and popularity on Australian stations. The addition of American radio programs to the stream of American films, recorded music, and comic books was provoking nationalist concern in some quarters that was heightened by the fact that the American radio programs were often very popular. One letter writer to the *Sydney Morning Herald* in 1934 observed that "it is a matter of extreme wonderment that patriotic Australian manufacturers are asking Australian consumers to purchase their goods through the medium of these American records."[21] Australian actress Tralie Russell told an interviewer in 1939 that she thought it was "deplorable" that "so many American radio transcriptions are flooding the ether here ... where is the opportunity for the average Australian?"[22]

It is important to note, however, that there was also a flourishing Australian transcription business in the 1930s, providing original Australian recorded programs for the commercial stations' schedules and work for local actors, writers, and producers. *Broadcasting Business* predicted in 1936 that "the transcription business in the future will lie largely in Australia," claiming proudly that Australian recordings did not require the "intensified listening" that imported ones did, because everything was "pronounced clearly and distinctly."[23] Industry leader AWA became very active in the transcription business, as did EMI. George Edwards and Company, in league with the Columbia Gramophone company, produced transcription recordings, including serials based on Dickens' novels and two series of *Notable British Trials*. The rural comedy *Dad and Dave* was created by the U.S.-based transnational advertising agency J. Walter Thompson in 1937, in an attempt to create a long-running serial that would emulate in Australia the success of *Amos 'n Andy* in the United States. Author Steele Rudd's established characters (already familiar in print, on stage, and on film) offered comparable country bumpkin humour but without the blackface element.[24] Minstrel shows were nevertheless also popular on Australian radio at the time—46 episodes of *Nigger Minstrels* proved "an outstanding radio success" in 1940.[25] In 1938, the British Australian Programmes company aired many transcriptions including an Australian series of *Marie Antoinette* with a cast of 100, and an Australian version of *East Lynne* in 52 episodes. The same year Featuradio Sound Productions in Melbourne sold 52 episodes of *David Copperfield* and of *The Tower of London*, while in Sydney, AWA produced 217 episodes of *Fred and Maggie Everybody*.[26] George Sutton of Featuradio observed in 1937 that there were good opportunities for Australian writers who could write "dramatised adventure and mystery tales" with "'snappy' dialogue and fast moving action adapted to wireless conditions."[27]

## War Stimulates Local Production

The war dramatically changed the business environment for imported radio transcriptions in Australia. Under pressure from the Bank of England, Australia moved to conserve its reserves of sterling and dollars by reducing non-essential imports, which included radio transcriptions.[28] From December 1, 1939, while there were no restrictions on the importation of transcriptions from the British sterling area, imports of transcriptions for radio play from non-sterling areas were effectively banned, but scripts from non-sterling areas could be imported under special licence.[29] Suddenly, local performance from imported scripts, rather than transcriptions, had become the only possible way of presenting

American material, which was now known to be potentially very popular, on Australian radio.

The result of this unexpected wall of protection was a golden age of antipodean commercial radio serial production. As the general secretary of the Australian Actors Equity reported: "During the period 1940–45 an undreamt of expansion took place in the Australian broadcasting industry." Estimates at the time were that between 10 and 20% of local radio production was performance from imported scripts.[30] The boom lasted into the 1950s. The *Sydney Morning Herald* in 1952 thought that there were 200 people in Sydney—authors, producers, actors, technicians—working on the production of dramatic radio serials, primarily soap operas. Actor Alastair Duncan, who played Dr. Paul in the serial of that name, remembered that in Sydney there were perhaps 30 or 40 actors in regular radio employment, and more who had part-time work.[31]

Visiting the United States in November 1941, Gibson was caught by the outbreak of war in the Pacific, and could not return to Australia until 1944. For these two and a half years, in wartime conditions, she served as managing director of the Radio Transcription Company of America. On her return to Sydney in 1944 she broke with Artransa, founded her own company, and married, all in a week.[32] Her new company, Grace Gibson Productions, began importing scripts of popular American radio programs and re-performing and recording them as transcriptions, which were then sold around Australia, New Zealand, and beyond. It was an extraordinarily successful business model. Gibson was not the only one employing it, but her company was the most prolific and successful practitioner. At its height, Grace Gibson Productions was producing 55 radio serial episodes a week. The company employed an American-style industrial mode of production, but made it even more lean and efficient. Frank and Anne Hummert's famous soap opera factory in New York was considered speedy because it allowed only an hour's rehearsal for each 15-minute episode—other American studios had 90-minute rehearsals.[33] But Grace Gibson Productions manager Reg James explained that she allowed only an hour of studio time in total for a quarter-hour program, including the initial talk with the director, the rehearsal, *and* the recording. James claimed that, because of this rapid production, "Australian actors were recognized as the best sight readers in the world." Gibson thus further streamlined and industrialised production of radio serials, achieving high productivity with relatively low costs; crucially, actors signed away rights to residuals for subsequent sales.[34]

Many of the Gibson shows made from adapted American scripts were very popular in Australia. Some had longer runs in Australia than in the United States. *Portia Faces Life* played for 11 years in the United States (1940–51), but for 16 years (1954–70) in Australia. There were 3544 Australian episodes: episode 1 in Australia picked up the story from after the wartime episodes, at U.S. episode 1967, broadcast there in October 1947—presumably the wartime episodes were deemed too difficult to adapt to post-war conditions. Thus the Australian production must have run out of American scripts after 5 years and continued producing new Australian-written episodes for another 9 years. Grace Gibson bought the rights to the programs, making careful notes on the cost sheets for the programs about how much she paid for each U.S. written script, and separating that cost from the fee to the Australian adapter. *Doctor Paul* ran for 8 years in the United States (1940–45 and 1951–53): in Australia it ran for 21 years (1949–71) and 4400 episodes, so again there were over the whole run many more Australian- than American-written episodes. Writer Richard Lane was employed at first to adapt American *Doctor Paul* scripts; he recalls that the supply ran out in 1956, and that thereafter he was writing original episodes.[35] The result of this ad hoc importation and adaption was a truly hybrid cultural product. The form and style of these shows was no doubt defined by their American origins, but they were then localised: first just in the adaptation and re-voicing, but then even more comprehensively with the shift to scripts entirely written in Australia.

There is no evidence that Australian audiences noticed the transition. A footnote in Meaghan Morris's 1998 *Too Soon Too Late: History in Popular Culture* identifies an Australian tradition in soap production—the argument is that Australian soaps focus on "homely communities" rather than the "rich and beautiful individualists" (this probably a reference to later television soap operas) who feature in American soaps. Morris suggests an Australian genealogy for such communitarian soaps that runs back to Australian social realist literature such as Kylie Tennant's 1941 *The Battlers*—her Australian soap tradition runs from radio serials *Blue Hills*, *Portia Faces Life,* and *When a Girl Marries*, to Australian TV soaps such as *A Country Practice*, *Flying Doctors*, and *Blue Heelers*. That both *Portia* and *When a Girl Marries* were originally American radio soaps, adapted and re-voiced in Australia, before becoming completely locally written, at least complicates the argument about a distinctive local tradition.[36]

## Nationalism

Cultural artefacts flow across borders but not in all weathers. These Australian re-performances of lightly re-written American scripts were produced in a political and cultural climate deeply ambivalent about American cultural products. A combination of indisputable popularity, low-priced availability, and some (frequently exaggerated) cultural differences, placed the import and broadcast of American transcriptions in Australia under constant challenge even before the war ended the trade. In this environment, the re-writing and re-voicing of American scripts created a Trojan horse effect—the re-voiced American shows were not heard as American, and thus slipped under the radar of all but the most alert cultural nationalists.

The leaders of the Actors Equity union in Australia were certainly vigilant cultural nationalists. They had an obvious interest in protecting the jobs of their members, but also in some cases espoused a kind of popular front leftism that saw in authentic local popular culture a vital line of defence against American imperialism. In 1947, Actors Equity stated that its first goal in seeking a continued ban or limitation on the importation of transcriptions and scripts was to "protect the economic interest of employees engaged in the occupation of radio broadcasting"; its fourth goal was "the establishment of a national Australian outlook and the encouragement and establishment of an Australian cultural and artistic tradition."[37] Equity secretary Hal Alexander had joined the Communist Party in the late 1930s.[38] He argued that because "most of Australia's entertainment—films, popular music, musical plays and legitimate plays, has during the last 25 years come from, or originated in, America," Australians had been misled into thinking that "an Australian national tradition and philosophy did not and/or could not exist." Alexander warned that the profit motive had subordinated "art in the radio sphere" to commerce: "This clash of ideas must be resolved within our present social system if democracy is something which really works and is to continue."[39] Radio writer and Equity member William Lynch similarly employed an urgent nationalist rhetoric when he told the Australian parliamentary standing committee on broadcasting that there should be a complete ban on the importation of American radio serials. American serials were, he argued, unwelcome in Australia because they were culturally damaging. "The American radio serial contributes nothing whatever to the improvement of the Australian way of life," he insisted: "It is culturally decadent, intellectually degrading and morally debasing. It is the most powerful agent of social destruction at large in this country."[40] In Australia, despite or perhaps because of the continuing and demonstrable popularity of American popular music, film, and radio, there came from both ends of the political spectrum—Anglophile conservatives and leftist nationalists—an oft-articulated dismissal of the perceived values and influence of American popular culture.

Amidst continuing debate about how and whether import restrictions should be eased, Actors Equity in 1951 launched a vigorous campaign against imported transcriptions. It encouraged boycotts of those companies that sponsored imported transcriptions on Australian stations: "Don't Listen to Imported Radio Programmes! Don't Buy the Advertisers' Goods!"[41] The publicity and political pressure led to an Australian Broadcasting Control Board survey in 1952, which found that while 12% of Australian radio programs were transcriptions, only 1.4% were imported transcriptions.[42] Transcriptions adapted from imported scripts but re-voiced and recorded in Australia would for this purpose have counted as Australian transcriptions. The business model that Grace Gibson had developed so well was not only profitable, it allowed a kind of cultural importation from the United States to continue just under the radar of most Australian cultural nationalists.

One of the major Australian objections to American radio serials had to do with their perceived preoccupation with crime. As Michele Hilmes notes, contrary to some characterizations, in the United States "crime and its resolution played a large role in soap plots."[43] In Australia, however, these crime stories, in soaps as in crime dramas, were often understood as expressions of a national rather than a genre trait. American dramatic serials were, Lynch maintained, full of "gun-play, violence, trickery and intrigue" and "false social values."[44] William Moloney (writer for radio serials such as *Officer Crosby* and later *The Golden Colt*) told the parliamentary wireless committee that American radio drama had a "deplorable tendency to emphasize the subversive elements of crime and violence, which are, I believe, quite foreign to the instincts of most people."[45] This contrasting of American sensationalism with Australian common sense was prevalent in public debate about radio in Australia. The Melbourne *Argus* complained in 1947 that the air was being flooded with "tense, emotional hysteria" in the form of radio serials.[46] Criticism of the violence, preoccupation with crime, and general emotionalism of both radio soaps and crime dramas was of course heard within the U.S. Federal Communications Commission, whose chairman Lawrence Fly had condemned soaps in 1943 as "highly emotional, cheap forms of droolery."[47] But within the United States, these were arguments against commercialism and masculine objections to, or condescension towards, what appeared in soap operas to be a distressingly popular form of feminised and emotional entertainment. In Australia very similar arguments were deployed, but gained from their new context the added overlay of nationalist differentiation—inventing an Australian national persona that was entire of itself and clearly distinct from the American. We can see clearly that it was invention, because the allegedly foreign cultural products at the heart of the dispute—American-originated radio serials—were both popular and generally uncontroversial with Australian radio audiences.

## Re-Writing and Re-Voicing

In this ideological climate, Grace Gibson had to insist publicly that her writers extensively re-wrote the American scripts to make them suitable for Australian audiences. She told the parliamentary committee on wireless that imported scripts had to be "either localized or adapted by Australian writers to overcome overseas localization and characterizations, and are in many instances completely rewritten around the idea of the imported script." Most imported scripts were as they stood, she said, completely unsuited to Australian audiences—"customs, expressions and locale are entirely different" and "situations and characterizations that are entirely natural to Americans are false and unreal to Australians in many cases."[48]

Our research suggests, however, that the changes made in the American scripts for their re-broadcast in Australia were often relatively small and not the significant re-writing alluded to in public debate. Matching up the American versions with the Australian versions presents significant research challenges.

Luckily, one set of scripts, sold by Jane Crusinberry, writer of *The Story of Mary Marlin*, to the Sydney-based Macquarie Broadcasting Service, was sent to Australia, edited in pencil, and then returned to Crusinberry, who included them in her papers donated to the Mass Communications History Collection at the Wisconsin Historical Society.[49] Mary Marlin, a mid-Western single woman at the beginning of the program, struggles to "find love and happiness over thirty." In some ways, *Mary Marlin* in Australia becomes a show both out of time and out of place. It was written and broadcast in the United States in the 1930s and early 1940s; Crusinberry sold the scripts to Australia and the program was broadcast there from the late 1950s. Given these important differences, you might think the changes would be many, but an examination of the scripts shows only a few. Some time and place names did get changed. The show talked of building the Sydney Harbour Bridge instead of the Golden Gate Bridge; the Australians re-wrote some holiday episodes, mainly those featuring July 4 and Thanksgiving. The scripts show that the Australians replaced all the American slang. "What a little brick you are—and nothing but a kid" turns into "You don't know what this means to me. All my life I've waited"; more directly "Land's sakes" becomes "Mercy me," while "You're a peach" becomes "thanks" and "OK" turns into "alright." Other Americanisms disappear, so attorney becomes lawyer, elevators become lifts, dollars become pounds, and fried chicken becomes roast chicken. When Mary's American husband gets elected Senator, in Australia he becomes a Member of Parliament going off to Parliament House in Canberra, without many other changes to either plot or prose. Slightly larger linguistic differences from the American versions of the scripts involved the servants of the middle-class couples who peopled the soap operas. The American Mary Marlin's housekeeper, Annie, has Southern inflections, presumably African American: "Miz Mary" and "Mis Mary"; this was changed to "Mrs. Mary" in the Australian scripts. When Mary moves to New York City (in the Australian version, "the city") during one particularly unhappy moment in her marriage, her Irish servant Nora keeps her brogue in both the U.S. and Australian scripts.[50] These are in general fairly minor changes; considerably less than the major rewriting that the parliamentary inquiries were being assured took place with all imported scripts.

Other programming forms also saw only minor transformations in their emigration from the United States to Australia. Among the Grace Gibson productions, we have matched up several *Night Beat* episodes which change the reporter, Randy Stone's newspaper from the *Chicago Star* to the generic *Daily* and "bologna sandwiches" to "cheese sandwiches"; "elevated train" to "electric train."[51] *Night Beat*, a superior crime series, ran in the United States only from February 1950 to April 1952, but in Australia from August 1950 until July 1959, so again there were more Australian-originated than American-originated episodes. *Night Beat* followed quite a different pattern of importation from *Mary Marlin*: it came to Australia less than a year after it began in the United States and there were from the beginning a mix of adapted and completely Australian-written scripts. The soap operas in comparison seem to have had Australian-written episodes only after all the American scripts were exhausted. Perhaps this was because the detective shows had standalone episode plots that could be mixed around more easily, whereas in the soaps, with their glacially slow developing story lines, continuity and memory of what had happened before was crucial. The Internet Archive holds 76 of the 100 or so U.S. episodes of *Night Beat*, several of which seem to have travelled to Australia with only minor changes, despite the fact that the American version seems deeply embedded in Chicago.

American soap operas made an easier translation to Australian audiences than the comedies or dramas. The most popular programs on U.S. radio were the big comedy shows, which were as fast-paced and as easy to misunderstand as the soaps were slow and repetitive ("drip dramas" the Australian press began calling them). Grace Gibson did import the very popular Midwest-themed comedy *Fibber McGee and Molly* (it was retitled *Chipper Malloy and Connie* in Australia) and another based on the film, *My Friend Irma*.[52] "Being American, when I read them I laughed like mad," Grace recalled, "but when I heard them on the air here they weren't so funny."[53] In addition, Gibson's business manager noted that Australianising shows featuring superheroes did not work because the heroes did not seem "believable" with an Australian accent; Australian audiences apparently believed only in superheroes who lived in America.[54] Critics might scoff at the endless and aimless plots of the soaps, what one *Sydney Morning Herald* journalist described as "dramaturgic goulash, without structure, plot or discernible end," but there was probably less alarm sounded in Australia than in the United States about the cultural effects of the soaps, and the soap operas turned out to be the most easily translated of radio programs.[55]

Gibson herself later said that her company's programs produced from American scripts were not "Australianised" but internationalized: "we just edited them slightly for Australia, to make them sound more Australian. Not Australian, but international. We used to try and produce our shows so they'd be acceptable anywhere."[56] Reg James, the company's long-time business manager, reported that Gibson Productions aimed for a "mid-Atlantic" voice (not "mid-Pacific") in its shows so that they could be sold more easily. The Australian product was designed to be somewhere indeterminately between British and American. Gibson noted that she changed the names of the characters and the cities because "we didn't have it set in Chicago—anyone producing a soap opera wants to produce it so it could happen anywhere so that the people next door think they could be part of the show."[57] Owen Weingott, a versatile actor who played Walter Manning in *Portia Faces Life*, recalled that: "Grace ... would get American scripts out and ... local writers would make any adjustments, you know, if the script ... sounded too ... when I say sounded too American, I don't mean vocally, I mean the shape and the rhythms of the thing were a bit American. Then the local writers would adapt them to the modern thing."[58] There were still enough Australian voices straining after American accents, however, for a Melbourne listener to complain about "the rubbishy mass of fake Americanism, rolled R's, nasality, and Transpacific mannerisms" he heard on his radio.[59] Another Melbourne letter writer asked: "Is Sydney fast becoming an American city, and is the well of pure English becoming more and more defiled, or is it going to dry up all together?"[60] Australian's Wireless Telegraphy Act had been amended in 1927 to include a stipulation that every radio announcer employed by a licensee had to be "of good education, style and personality, and possessed of clear enunciation, as far as possible free from any characteristic dialect," and clarity of diction and accent remained controversial issues through the 1930s and 40s.[61]

These Australian-produced transcriptions performed from adapted American scripts were broadcast on stations around Australia. But then, remarkably, the shows were sold all over the English-speaking world, particularly to Commonwealth countries—New Zealand, but then Kenya, South Africa, Tanganyika, Singapore, Hong Kong, Fiji, Canada, the West Indies, and eventually UK pirate radio. Australian-produced radio soap operas were "the dominant types on Caribbean radio."[62] As Reg James explained, "we'd get our money back out of Australia and our profit came from New Zealand; and New Zealand bought 90% of our product so that was very good."[63] Both Gibson and James travelled the Commonwealth selling the transcriptions. Their ability to produce large quantities of an appealing and familiar product quickly and cheaply opened global markets to them. So a hybrid Australian-American cultural product found an international market.

Did Australians (and others) hear these shows as American or Australian, or as something in between? Commonwealth listeners were, after all, highly experienced at negotiating that in-between territory as they watched American films and listened to American recorded music. Those forms came unmediated while the radio shows were re-performed by Australians, just perhaps as Australians informally re-performed American music or movie speech in playgrounds or among friends, or Australian popular singers recorded versions of American hit songs. To an American listener, many of the voices on the Australian radio of the late 1940s and 1950s sound British, not Australian, with announcers and actors using "plummy" or "posh" accents, not the Australian tones heard in Melbourne streets or on the current commercial television stations. But of course, these accents were also Australian, used by middle-class Australians especially for formal public speech such as radio announcing. In later programs, the diction changed, as broader accents found their way onto the air. Portia and Walter Manning continued to sound like the upper middle-class couple they were (he a journalist, she a lawyer), but Portia's son Dicky and the many criminals Portia met had accents more obviously Australian.[64] When the shows were exported, the speech could again provide an internationally acceptable form of aspirational English diction. A Jamaican woman recalls her childhood listening: "I played all the roles in my fantasies, imitating the voices of actors in the Australian soap operas like *Portia Faces Life*, *Doctor Paul*, or *Life Can Be Beautiful*, which daily were broadcast on the radio. I measured my speech against their accents … I did my best to imitate the English of Portia or Dr. Paul."[65]

Scholars have considered how this cultural brokering happened in film and television, but less so in radio. Richard Waterhouse contrasted the Australian reaction to American film with that to American television: "What had muted the outcry against American films was that many of them were neither about nor set in America. What sharpened the protest against American television was that so many of the American programmes shown here focused heavily on distinctively American themes and characters."[66] Where does radio sit in this contrast? Mid-way chronologically, radio also sat somewhere in between in terms of content because some of the radio shows were about distinctively American themes (particular cities or character types), while some were designed to be moral dramas with more generic appeal.

Perhaps the most American part of these programs was not their content, nor their sound, but the fact that they were produced as commercial vehicles and so easily inserted into other, commercial broadcasting systems which flourished after World War II. The programs sold by Grace Gibson Productions shared a worldview that raised few worries about consumption, and was familiar to large, multi-national corporations. Perhaps the most important factor shared by all the *Portia* and *Dr. Paul* broadcasts, for example, was the sponsor, Lever Brothers, a British firm that also advertised heavily on American radio. Represented by the advertising agency Lintas, in Australia, Gibson had the most success re-selling her programs in countries where Lever Brothers had markets. But, other big soap companies found the programs familiar and years later, Jamaicans could remember the Colgate-Palmolive jingles used to sell Fab detergent on *Dr. Paul* and *Portia Faces Life*.[67]

This transnational radio history needs to be recovered, lest our radio history end up simply repeating the nationalist claims about distinctive sensibilities and unique local preferences that were the content of protectionist debates at the time. As historian Petra Goedde notes, one of the problems with the theory of "Americanization" is that it implies the "existence of a monolithic national culture" which was "homogenous" as well as a passive receiving culture.[68] The remarkable success of the American-originated scripts in Australia, and the apparent ease with which the stories were continued by Australian writers and further exported, give the lie to any simple nationalist reading of either Australian or American radio history.

## Conclusion

Domestic American entertainment radio from radio's golden age had an international history after World War II that needs to be understood as a significant and influential form of American influence and Americanization abroad, alongside the much better remembered international histories of American film, television, and music. In Gibson's case this American influence has been overlooked in part because the slight re-writing and complete re-voicing of these American radio shows produced a radio performance whose intellectual origins in the United States may have been disguised, being both inaudible to listeners at the time and generally unnoticed by historians since. Yet the export of the form as much as the particular content of these radio dramas *was* a significant instance of the post-war Americanization of the world. While much scholarly attention has been paid in recent years to the more obvious forms of Americanization, there is less work that thinks about deeper genre influences; for example, the form of the endless serial which became dominant in the English-speaking world or the American television programs whose forms were often unreflectively adapted in different national contexts.[69]

Recent scholarship has often focused on the localization of cultural imports, their absorption into local cultural practices and eventually traditions. Neither a simple diffusionist nor a simple cultural imperialist framework will help us understand this process. Was Grace Gibson doing "glocalisation" before globalisation became a global preoccupation?[70] Was this Australian industry of adaptation and re-export an early example of "asymmetrical interdependence"?[71] At one level the point we are making is about timing; that these things happened earlier than current scholarship usually acknowledges. An article observes that "it was not until the early 1980s ... that U.S. soap operas achieved international recognition when American primetime soap *Dallas* became a hit in over 90 countries."[72] We have shown that once radio is taken into account that assessment is off by several decades. We knew that American film and music travelled the world, in fact that they were created to do so, but historians have mostly thought of radio (other than the special case of shortwave radio) in nationalistic and place-based terms, as too intimate or culturally specific to work across national borders. Portia and Randy Stone travelled fairly easily from the United States to Australia and then around the Commonwealth as pioneers in global entertainment, transcending their local American settings to become citizens of the world in ways never imagined by their first creators. The recovered history of this form of transnational radio poses challenges to existing frameworks in radio history as well as to the study of Americanisation and its effects.

## Notes

1.  We thank the Australian National Film and Sound Archive in Canberra for the shared fellowship under their Scholars and Artists in Residence program which allowed us to research this chapter in their extensive collections.
2.  Quoted in Jim Cox, *Frank and Anne Hummert's Radio Factory: The Programs and Personalities of Broadcasting's Most Prolific Producers* (Jefferson, NC: McFarland, 2003), 140.
3.  Herta Herzog, "On Borrowed Experience," *Studies in Philosophy and Social Science* 9, no. 1 (1941), 65–95.

4. On Hollywood's internationalism see Peter Lev, *Transforming the Screen, 1950–1959* (Berkeley: University of California Press, 2003), Ch. 7; Desley Deacon, "'Films as Foreign Offices': Transnationalism at Paramount in the Twenties and Early Thirties," in *Connected Worlds: History In Transnational Perspective,* eds. Ann Curthoys and Marilyn Lake(Canberra: ANU E Press, 2006), 139–156.

5. A recent exception is Michele Hilmes, *Network Nations: A Transnational History of British and American Broadcasting* (New York: Routledge, 2011).

6. Simon J. Potter, "Who Listened When London Called? Reactions to the BBC Empire Service in Canada, Australia and New Zealand, 1932–1939," *Historical Journal of Film, Radio and Television*, 28, no. 4 (2008), 475–487; and Potter, "Webs, Networks, and Systems: Globalization and the Mass Media in the Nineteenth- and Twentieth-Century British Empire," *Journal of British Studies* 46, no. 3 (2007), 621–646.

7. Lawrence Levine, "The Folklore of Industrial Society: Popular Culture and its Audiences," *American Historical Review* 97, no. 5 (1992), 1369–1399.

8. Petra Goedde, "The Globalization of American Culture." in *A Companion to American Cultural History* ed. Karen Halttunen (Malden, MA: Blackwell, 2008), 247; see also Emily S. Rosenberg, *Spreading the American Dream: American Economic and Cultural Expansion, 1890–1945* (New York: Hill and Wang, 1982).

9. Kristin Thompson, *Exporting Entertainment: America in the World Film Market, 1907–1934* (London: British Film Institute, 1985).

10. Thomas Doherty, *Projections of War: Hollywood, American Culture and World War II* (New York: Columbia University Press, 1993); Thomas Guback, "Shaping the Film Business in Postwar Germany: The Role of the U.S. Film Industry and the U.S. State," in *The Hollywood Film Industry*, ed. Paul Kerr (New York: Routledge, 1986); Susan Smulyan, *Popular Ideologies* (Philadelphia: University of Pennsylvania Press, 2007), 82–115.

11. For two exceptions see, Bryan McCann, *Hello, Hello Brazil: Popular Music in the Making of Modern Brazil* (Durham, NC: Duke University Press, 2004) which describes a similar phenomenon where Brazilian musicians "covered" American songs, producing a musical form that was heard as Brazilian. Then commercial broadcasters, operating from Europe through Radio Luxembourg and Radio Normandy, played transcriptions of British programs, recorded in London, and broadcast back into the United Kingdom. The format of British commercial radio was influenced by American commercial broadcasting as described in Sean Street, *Crossing the Ether: Pre-War Public service Radio and Commercial Competition in the United Kingdom* (Eastleigh, UK: John Libbey, 2006).

12. See for example Penny von Eschen, *Satchmo Blows Up the World: Jazz Ambassadors Play the Cold War* (Cambridge, MA: Harvard University Press, 2004); Uta Poiger, *Jazz, Rock and Rebels: Cold War Politics and American Culture in a Divided Germany* (Berkeley: University of California Press, 2000.

13. Alexander Russo, *Points on the Dial: Golden Age Radio Beyond the Networks* (Durham, NC: Duke University Press, 2010), 79.

14. See Craig Nugent, "A History of the Australian Radio Transcription Industry," http://www.australianotr.com.au/transhistory.asp; Bridget Griffen-Foley, *Changing Stations: The Story of Australian Commercial Radio* (Sydney: University of New South Wales Press, 2009), 211–222.

15. "They Said They Wanted to Meet Pinto Pete!," *Australian Women's Weekly,* March 9, 1935, p. 16.

16. "Will Search for Radio Talent," *Australian Women's Weekly,* August 24, 1935, p. 18.

17. "Australian Transcriptions Coming to the Fore," *Broadcasting Business*, February 13, 1936, p. 6.

18. "American Recordings," *The West Australian*, November 14, 1934, p. 3.

19. "An American Girl Sells Sixty-Two Radio Serials," *Australian Women's Weekly*, March 2 1935, p. 25.

20. "Sydney Girl Flies Across America," *Australian Women's Weekly,* March 5, 1938, p. 32.

21. "Why American?" *Sydney Morning Herald*, September 7, 1934, p. 6.

22. "Tralie Russell," *Rockhampton Morning Bulletin,* June 28, 1939, p. 14.
23. "Australian Transcriptions Coming to the Fore," *Broadcasting Business,* February 13, 1936, p. 6.
24. Steele Rudd was a pseudonym used by author Arthur Hoey Davis.
25. John Potts, *Radio in Australia* (Sydney: New South Wales University Press, 1989), p. 53; "Nigger Minstrels on the Air Tonight," *Brisbane Courier Mail,* November 1 1940, p. 12. Use of the term was declining only slowly in Australia: the National Library of Australia's Trove database of digitized newspapers records 81,000 hits for "nigger" in the 1920s, 32,000 in the 1930s, but then 10,000 in the 1940s, and 5,000 in the 1950s.
26. *Broadcasting Business Yearbook 1939,* pp. 106–113.
27. *The West Australian,* April 20, 1937, p. 9.
28. Kosmas Tsokhas, "Dedominionization: The Anglo-Australian Experience, 1939-1945," *The Historical Journal* 37, no. 4 (December 1994), 863, 870; Potts, *Radio in Australia,* 66–73.
29. Testimony of Raymond Foster Filbey Hall, Department of Trade and Customs, in *Record of Evidence of Parliamentary Standing Committee on Broadcasting, 18th Parliament, 1947–48,* 211.
30. Hal Alexander, general secretary of Actors and Announcers Equity Association of Australia, in *Record of Evidence of Parliamentary Standing Committee on Broadcasting, 18th Parliament, 1947–48,* 128, 232.
31. "Soap Opera– New Social Opiate', *Sydney Morning Herald,* October 4,1952, p. 7; Alastair Duncan interview, #000073, Australian National Film and Sound Archive, Canberra, Australia, hereafter cited as NFSA.
32. Phillip Mann, "Soap Opera's Leading Lady," *Sydney Morning Herald,* February 6, 1949; James Murray, "The Guide Interview: Grace Gibson—A Texan Who Gave Australia Some Great Radio Drama," *The Sydney Morning Herald,* August 12, 1985; "New Grace Gibson Studios Opened," *Broadcasting and Television,* May 9, 1952; "Amazing Grace," *The Mercury* (Hobart, Australia), November 25, 1987; "National Film and Sound Archive—Women in Early Radio," n.d., http://www.nfsa.gov.au/the_collection/collection_spotlights/women-in-early-radio/grace-gibson.html (accessed June 2010).
33. Cox, *Frank and Anne Hummert's Radio Factory,* 40.
34. Reg James Interviewed by Nick Weare, 2005, Oral History, #678806 NFSA.
35. Richard Lane, *The Golden Age of Australian Radio Drama* (Melbourne: Melbourne University Press, 1994), 272.
36. Meaghan Morris, *Too Soon Too Late: History in Popular Culture* (Bloomington: University of Indiana Press, 1998), 275. *When a Girl Marries* ran in the United States from 1939 to 1957; AWA (Amalgamated Wireless Australasia) bought the scripts and adapted them and the show ran in Australia from 1946 to 1965. As with *Portia,* the Australian adapters elected to skip the wartime episodes, so 500 American episodes were summarised in three or four Australian ones (Lane, *Golden Age of Australian Radio Drama,* 341); for similar claims about British versus American soap operas see, Michele Hilmes, "Front Line Family: 'Women's Culture' comes to the BBC," *Media Culture Society* 29, no. 5 (2007), 5–29.
37. Hal Alexander, general secretary of Actors and Announcers Equity Association of Australia, in *Record of Evidence of Parliamentary Standing Committee on Broadcasting, 18th Parliament, 1947-48,* 230.
38. Drew Cottle, "Hal Alexander (1902–1990)," *Australian Dictionary of Biography,* http://adb.anu.edu.au/biography/alexander-hal-12127/text21403 (accessed February 22, 2012).
39. Hal Alexander, general secretary of Actors and Announcers Equity Association of Australia, in *Record of Evidence of Parliamentary Standing Committee on Broadcasting, 17th Parliament, 1945–46,* 130–131.
40. William Lynch in *Record of Evidence of Parliamentary Standing Committee on Broadcasting, 18th Parliament, 1947–48,* 253.
41. *Actors Equity News* (December 1951), 16.
42. Letter from H. L. Anthony (Postmaster General) to Hal Alexander (Secretary, Actors Equity) October 1953, Australian Broadcasting Control Board records, National Archives of Australia, BA/11/5 Part 1.

43. Michele Hilmes, *Radio Voices: American Broadcasting, 1922–1952* (Minneapolis: University of Minnesota Press, 1997), 161.

44. William Lynch in *Record of Evidence of Parliamentary Standing Committee on Broadcasting, 18th Parliament, 1947–48*, 253.

45. William Moloney in *Record of Evidence of Parliamentary Standing Committee on Broadcasting, 18th Parliament, 1947–48*, 255; Billy Moloney, *Memoirs of an Abominable Showman* (Adelaide: Rigby, 1968), 142.

46. "A Plea for Relief from Those Serials," *Argus,* July 26, 1947, p. 41.

47. "Washboard Weepers," *Pittsburgh Post Gazette,* November 17 1943, p. 8.

48. Grace Gibson and John Alexander Watson representing the Radio Recording and Production Association of Australia to the Australian parliamentary committee on wireless, 1946.

49. Jane Cruisinberry Papers, 1933–1960, Wisconsin Historical Society Archives, Madison, Wisconsin, http://arcat.library.wisc.edu/cgi-bin/Pwebrecon.cgi?BBID=8831 (accessed February 2012), hereafter cited as Cruisinberry Papers, WHS.

50. Most of the small changes are evident in Scripts 1–14, Box 8, Folder 1; for the Sydney Harbour Bridge, see Script 45, Box 8, Folder 8; for a set of scripts that changed the Senate to Parliament, see Box 10, Folder 3; for Nora, see Scripts 15–29, Box 8, Folder 2 all in Cruisinberry Papers, WHS.

51. "Flowers on the Water," American version, recorded March 1950, http://www.archive.org/details/NightBeat (accessed August 2011); "Flowers on the Water," Australian version, recorded August 1950, #205427, NFSA.

52. Reg James Interviewed by Nick Weare, 2005, Oral History, #678806 NFSA.

53. "Amazing Grace," *Hobart Mercury,* November 25, 1987, p. 20.

54. Reg James, Personal Interview with Authors, June 24, 2010.

55. Leicester Cotton, "Soap Opera—New Social Opiate," *Sydney Morning Herald,* October 4, 1952, p. 7.

56. Grace Gibson interviewed by Jacqueline Kent, 1983, Oral History #458180, NFSA.

57. Grace Gibson interviewed by Nick Erby, 1979, Oral History #259182, NFSA.

58. Owen Weingott interviewed by Nigel Giles, October 29, 2000, #467457, NFSA.

59. "A Plea for Relief from Those Serials," *Argus,* July 26 1947, p. 41.

60. "Radio Review," *Argus,* March 29, 1947, p. 18.

61. *Broadcasting Business Yearbook 1939*, 173.

62. Vibert C. Cambridge, "Radio Soap Operas in Global Africa: Origins, Applications and Implications," in *Soap Opera Criticism,* ed. Suzanne Frentz (Bowling Green, OH: Bowling Green State University Press, 1992), 114

63. Reg James Interviewed by Nick Weare, 2005, Oral History, #678806 NFSA.

64. For one early example, see "Portia Faces Life," Episode 1510, audio recording, probably mid-1961, #216466, NFSA.

65. Sistren with Honor Ford-Smith in *Gendered Realities: Essays in Caribbean Feminist Thought,* ed. Patricia Mohammed (Barbados: University of the West Indies Press, 2002), 446.

66. Richard Waterhouse, "Popular Culture," in *Americanization and Australia,* ed. Philip Bell and Roger Bell (Sydney: University of South Wales Press, 1998), 56.

67. Dan Owen, "Garth Rattry too Young to Know," *The Gleaner* (Jamaica) July 19, 2004, http://jamaica-gleaner.com/gleaner/20040419/letters/letters9.html

68. Goedde, "Globalization of American Culture," 252.

69. Discussed in Robert Allen, ed., *to be continued: Soap Operas Around the World* (New York: Routledge, 1995).

70. M. M. Kraidy, "Glocalization as an International Communication Framework?" *Journal of International Communication* 9, no. 2, 29–49.

71. Joseph D. Straubhaar, "Beyond Media Imperialism: Assymetrical Interdependence and Cultural Proximity," *Critical Studies In Mass Communication* 8, no. 1 (March, 1991), 39–59.

72. Melissa Scardaville, "High Art, No Art: The Economic and Aesthetic Legitimacy of U.S. Soap Operas," *Poetics* 37, no. 4 (2009), 371.

# 11

# SOUNDS FROM THE LIFE OF THE FUTURE

## Making Sense of U.S. Radio Broadcasting in France 1921–1939[1]

*Derek W. Vaillant*

In 1930 the award-winning French novelist and critic, Georges Duhamel condemned America's seemingly insatiable appetite for consumer goods and entertainment: "They yearn desperately for phonographs, radios, illustrated magazines, 'movies,' elevators, electric refrigerators, and automobiles, automobiles, and once again automobiles. [Americans] want to own at the earliest possible moment all the articles mentioned, which are so wonderfully convenient, and of which, by an odd reversal of things, they immediately become the anxious slaves." Based on impressions from a 1928 visit to the states, Duhamel's bestselling Scènes de la vie future (Scenes from the Life of the Future) lamented the cultural impact of mass-industrial production, technological modernity, and corporate marketing. The author linked U.S.-style popular consumption practices, including commercial radio listening, to unhealthy attitudes, which were not confined to national territory. Duhamel believed that "America the menace" threatened to engulf Europe. "There are on our continent," he noted, "in France as well as elsewhere, large regions that the spirit of old Europe has deserted. The American spirit colonizes little by little such a province, such a city, such a house, and such a soul."[2]

Duhamel's familiar critique of a technologically bedazzled, consumer-centered American culture and his effort to expose its shortcomings illustrates an important dimension of the global history of communications and culture. The international rise of radio broadcasting elicited self-reflexive commentary that assessed comparative, international technological development, cultural change, and power relations within and across the borders of nation-states. Well before the early 1930s, when semi-regular U.S. shortwave radio broadcasts began reaching France, concerned French citizens wondered about transatlantic connectivity. As observers of U.S. radio from afar, they tried to make sense of the "sounds" of the life of the future. They treated American broadcasting as a technological, material, and symbolic system with inter- and transnational dimensions. Studying it could offer understanding of how and why radio operated as it did in France, and the ways it might or might not develop in the future in dynamic relation to the United States.[3]

This article concentrates on French print journalism reporting on the changing U.S. broadcast landscape of the 1920s and 1930s. From the specific reportage and editorial commentary of *Le Petit Radio* (a booster of the French public radio system), three evocative themes emerge: critical reaction to the "Wild West" of U.S. radio growth, an equivocal response to the celebrated modernism of RCA's Radio City, and claims that radio advertising degenerated culture, and must be limited or eradicated. The ideologically charged treatment of U.S. broadcasting in France that resulted casts fresh light on how ideas associated with "American radio" (and America) took hold within communications policy debates and French culture, as proponents of private and public models for national broadcasting competed for advantage.[4]

To its French critics, American-style radio of the 1920s and 1930s was above all a symbol of capitalist, technological modernity, whose commercial excesses and civic shortcomings stirred strong reactions. Commercial broadcasting seemed a tool of exploitative corporate power that delivered a paralyzing blow to artistic endeavor. To French admirers, however, America's private, advertiser-supported solution to developing broadcasting offered fresh ideas to those who felt suffocated by fusty traditionalism, cultural conservatism, and economic regulation, and dreamed of forging a new era of innovation and consumer choice in entertainment.[5]

## Radio Readers, Radio Watchers

Modern broadcasting in France dates to 1919, when control of radio telecommunications passed from the French military into the hands of the Ministère des Postes, télégraphes et téléphones (PTT), including the famous experimental station at the Eiffel Tower. Over the next decade, stations took to the air, including a public network flagship (Paris-PTT) and public affiliates in major provincial cities. Meanwhile, several private enterprises, including the Radiola electronics firm (Radiola, later Radio Paris), and a daily newspaper, *Le Petit Parisien* (Poste-Parisien), established commercial stations of their own. Exploiting the absence of clear regulatory statutes, additional "unauthorized" private stations also appeared. In 1929 a political compromise was reached, whereby all extant stations were recognized as existing lawfully, but with the condition that all future development of the medium would be public, and under full control of the PTT. Significantly, both private and public stations ran advertising.[6]

During the interwar era, the establishment of France's unusual public/private system made developments in the U.S. extremely relevant. The need for informed discussion of French broadcasting's present state and future prospects prompted the Fédération Nationale de la Radiodiffusion (National Federation of Radio Broadcasting) to establish *Le Petit Radio* (LPR), a weekly newspaper. For the next twelve years, LPR published station information and program features, lobbied for public oversight of French radio, and tracked the development of international broadcasting. Louis Ponchon, the brother-in-law of Marcel Pellenc, a high-ranking PTT official, edited LPR and contributed pieces. Pellenc had long advocated a public monopoly system free of commercial intrusion. Not surprisingly, as the semi-official organ of the PTT national network, an editorial bias favoring the superiority of a public service solution defined LPR. Its nationwide circulation and popular digest of program listings kept readers abreast of the debate in favor of public radio in France, and rendered LPR an important French institution. Its focus on French public radio and policy debates at home and abroad gives scholars a revealing glimpse at how users and developers of French radio perceived America and its radio system. [7]

LPR expressed the position that radio's function be dedicated to promoting what in France was sometimes called le bien générale, loosely translated as the "common good." Not surprisingly, the editorial slant of LPR reinforced French cultural conservatism and supported a broadcast ideal of uplift over mass appeal.[8] The stories and commentaries appearing in LPR marshaled evidence and made arguments intended, one can assume, to persuade readers to support public radio, and to refute the views of France's commercial radio interests that liberalizing French airwaves would benefit the nation.

In order to frame discussion of radio's present and future place in everyday life, LPR paid close attention to developments outside of France. By 1926 England had ratified its commitment to a "public service" monopoly model in the form of the British Broadcasting Corporation (BBC). In the U.S., by contrast, a model of minimally regulated, private, commercial broadcasting was ascendant. Calls for alternatives to the commercialization of U.S. radio failed to win national favor in America, but they attracted passionate scrutiny in LPR. Among the journal's favorite themes when it came to criticizing U.S. radio were the relative weakness of governmental regulation, corporate abuse of power, and the negative effects of commercial advertising on the medium.

### Taming the Wild West

The ways that French public radio journalists and editorialists reported and analyzed the relationship between American radio and the U.S. government revealed a set of assumptions about how the marketplace, political power, and the cultural reach of radio into everyday life should be construed. Unable to listen directly to domestic U.S. broadcasting (though special programs were relayed by the early 1930s), the radio watchers at LPR kept track of developments in the U.S. chiefly by reading U.S. and European periodicals and making visits to the U.S. These journalists saw an obvious "French" dimension to breaking events in U.S. governmental regulation of an expanding industry. Observing public/private dynamics abroad could furnish examples of the (negative) consequences of a privatized system that public monopoly advocates could put to use in French policy and cultural discussions.

By the mid-1920s, the relative ease with which would-be U.S. broadcasters could obtain licenses, the plenitude of active stations, and the finite capacity of the radio spectrum, had combined to produce on-air conflict. Listeners in "over-radioed" parts of the country expressed frustration at station interference. The absence of an active authority to oversee America's broadcast system exasperated many operators and listeners, as well as major corporations, such as the National Broadcasting Company (NBC) and the Columbia Broadcasting System (CBS), which were itching to expand webs of profitable stations under central control. In 1927 Congress passed the Radio Act, which established a bipartisan Federal Radio Commission (FRC). The Act gave the FRC authority to use "public convenience, interest, or necessity" as a guide in its regulatory business, which included managing license, power, and frequency assignments. Played out behind the scrim of Washington politics and closed-door hearings, the local impact of the weeding of broadcast licensees garnered limited critical attention in the mainstream press. Some in education and religion pursued the fight in Washington, but the plight of marginalized communities of listeners went largely unremarked.[9]

In France, however, such regulatory upheaval fascinated the public radio press. It is not known whether these boosters were aware of how small American radio producers struggled vainly to defend their licenses, but news about licensing conflicts, and the evident need to temper the ambitions of private interests resonated in France. Given the debate in France over the way forward for broadcasting, the growing pains exhibited in the U.S. helpfully illustrated the complex interconnection between private enterprise, the public, and the federal government.

Michele Hilmes observes that interwar supporters of England's public broadcast monopoly evoked the specter of "American chaos" to encapsulate the flaws of U.S.-style commercial radio. The disorder frame clarified the "wisdom" of Great Britain in taking a public approach. Criticism of such "chaos" extended to listeners, who by natural inclination or the effect of listening to commercial radio were portrayed as disorderly persons themselves. As Hilmes notes, underlying the progressive claims of public service broadcasting lurked cultural antipathies toward plebeian leisure practices and popular tastes for commercial entertainment (e.g., vaudeville and jazz).[10]

While prejudice against commercial culture and American consumers is discernible in Georges Duhamel's work, and characterized a good deal of the culture of the PTT, a significant measure of criticism meted out by LPR evoked a different image of American radio and the public. Critical observers (some of whom were on the French Left) found a way to critique the U.S. situation without condemning American listeners. Eschewing the pejorative concept of "chaos," LPR commentators preferred to characterize U.S. radio culture as akin to a Hollywood-style incarnation of the "Wild West." In this sense, the "Wild West" had a certain rough charm along with its lawlessness. LPR and other radio magazines found maverick station operators who deviated from their assigned frequencies slightly romantic. In general, though, LPR cast government as the heroic stabilizer of commercial individualism gone too far. It hailed the Federal Radio Commission as "the Police of the Air," and praised the FRC for working in the manner of a Western sheriff, who "has begun to carry out [his] duties in a serious way." The French press tracked the story of broadcasters brought to heel and disciplined. Coverage further implied that there was public discontent simmering beneath the facade of mass satisfaction alleged by boosters of U.S. commercial broadcasting. LPR used the American case as a way to tutor French readers in the importance of governmental regulation of the airwaves and to encourage vigilance in the highly unlikely event that a frontier mentality take hold of French broadcasting.[11]

LPR and other advocates of a public monopoly system for France saved their harshest criticism for private corporations that had, in their minds, cynically appropriated the concept of "liberty" to colonize U.S. airwaves. French critics spoke of "liberté totale," a made-in-America concept of unchecked economic freedom that degraded classical notions of individual, civic, and political liberty. U.S. corporations were the outlaws in this scenario, not the American people. By liberalizing broadcasting, ran the argument; a precious medium lost its protection from market forces, and the public good suffered in the process.

Paul Campargue, one of France's most astute radio journalists, and publisher of the socialist newspaper, *Parole Libre*, deplored the presentation inside of France of what he called "the American radio bluff." Campargue challenged the validity of a national broadcast system, such as America's, that stressed freedom, access, and openness to competition, when, in truth, U.S. corporations controlled the vast majority of frequencies, transmitters, and program resources. Noting that most nations in Europe supported the nationalization of broadcasting, Campargue attacked purveyors of misinformation, such as Paul Brenot, president of the leading professional radio syndicate in France, and a champion of privatization, as promoting a misleading impression of a "paradise American" to the French public.[12]

According to Campargue, too much liberty for private enterprise and a lack of firm government regulation in the U.S. was producing "free radio in name only." He reminded readers that a small handful of corporations controlled the medium and had the power to influence U.S. public opinion to an "unprecedented" extent. Nor did Campargue believe himself alone in objecting to the presence of commercial advertising on France's public and private stations. "If one held a referendum today involving radio listeners that allowed them to choose between the French system, where one pays an indirect tax through tiresome radio advertising, and the German system, where one pays a direct tax for an annual license, a large majority of listeners would opt for the democratic model favored by Germany, and elsewhere in England, Austria, Hungary, Italy, etc."[13] Campargue lacked firm data to back his assertion, but he insisted that the lesson afforded by the U.S. underscored the risks France faced should its commitment to public radio lapse.[14]

From time to time, U.S. broadcast watchers in France expressed the quixotic hope that the American system might yet emulate Europe, and move in a public-minded direction. LPR editorials applauded even the most modest of signs of U.S. listener rebellion against advertising or resistance to corporate control. News reports spoke of a backlash, and one even alluded to "a large revolt against the intolerable abuse of radio advertising."[15] LPR cited authorities, such as the *New York Times*, *Washington Post*, and *Chicago Tribune*, to defend the view that ordinary Americans and the Federal government were concerned about excessive private "liberty" on the nation's airwaves. Though some would lose out in the regulatory shake-up, such as WEVD, the New York station established by socialist Eugene V. Debs, such was the fair price to bring U.S. radio into a better alignment.

Doubt remained, however, among many French observers about the U.S. government's commitment to regulation. When the right-leaning *L'intransigeant* newspaper opined that the election of President Herbert Hoover might foretell a plan to monopolize American radio, it was scolded by LPR. To entertain such a naive fantasy, LPR declared, was to misunderstand the stakes of the battle for the future of U.S. (and French radio) where private monopolies with support from the White House were poised to seize advantage from an unwary public.[16]

Such ideological responses to policy developments in U.S. broadcasting reflected one position in the ongoing struggles between proponents of the PTT's public network model and supporters of private stations in France. Drawing again on the alleged abuse of concepts of liberty, LPR mocked "the friends of the trust and the defenders of 'freedom,' who cynically used defense of liberty as a defense of private gain."[17] French radio might appear hamstrung over public/private development, but LPR editors hastened to point out troubles in American radio, too. America's messy system of hundreds of stations in competition put the lie to the idea that an unregulated system made sense for French radio. To such critics, the American experiment in free radio to date had shown the cost of an "absence of order and method," and exposed the risks of placing minority private interests ahead of public ones.

LPR found a potential champion to tame the "Wild West" in the personage of U.S. Senator Clarence C. Dill (D-WA). Senator Dill advocated vociferously for citizen rights to counterbalance private interest in broadcasting. He had co-sponsored the 1927 Radio Act and repeatedly used his status to warn private interests of overstepping their claims to the national airwaves. From a

French public radio booster's perspective, Dill represented a glimmer of hope for U.S. radio's public character.[18] In spring 1932, LPR reported that a Senate resolution introduced by Dill and James Couzens (R–MI), urging that body to "examine the possibility of nationalizing broadcasting" was spurring the FRC to organize a "vast investigation" into the matter of radio advertising. According to the article, "For a long time now the American public has been protesting against the regime of mercenary broadcasting which delivers programs to commercial firms who pay the fattest advertising contracts." On a more sober note, the article predicted (accurately) that the investigation would most likely produce "meager outcomes" given the power of corporate interests in radio and the sympathies of the FRC toward the commercial sector.[19]

Cases in which the FRC thwarted on-air commercial abuse of radio garnered appreciative comment in the pages of LPR. No incident was quite so fascinating, however, as the notorious case of "Docteur Brinkley," a physician, goat-gland transplantation advocate, and on-air peddler of dubious cure-all patent medicines, known only by their formula numbers ("No. 80," "No. 64," etc.). Brinkley, who had operated a powerful radio station in Milford, Kansas for a number of years, lost his broadcast license after an FRC investigation in 1930. For three and a half hours each day, LPR reported, Brinkley prescribed medicines for ills described in listener letters, which he read over the air. He used his station to promote the Brinkley Hospital and Brinkley Pharmaceutical Company both of which he owned. His efforts reportedly netted him almost $38,000 during one quarter in 1930. A Federal District Court of Appeals ruling upheld the FRC decision that Brinkley's actions did not meet the "public interest, necessity, or convenience" standard of Federal broadcast law.[20]

The case so interested editors at LPR that they quoted directly from the FRC's report: "While it is to be expected that a licensee of a radio broadcasting station will receive some remuneration for serving the public with radio programs, at the same time the interest of the listening public is paramount, and may not be subordinated to the interests of the station licensee."[21] The small victory for proponents of public protection from abuses of radio in the U.S. inspired French advocates of public broadcasting. The outcome proved that even in America, broadcasting could not be completely beholden to private interests, but must also "assume a public character," affirming to French radio watchers that even in what some called "the land of dollars," a conception of broadcasting's purpose had broader meaning than the singular pursuit of wealth.[22]

## Making Waves Out of Radio City

Despite an oppositional posture toward private broadcasting in most respects, the editors of LPR, PTT officials, and countless others in France, shared the world's fascination with the technological wonders of RCA's Radio City Music

Hall. It opened in 1932 at Rockefeller Center in New York City. From its soaring architectural lines, to the glamorous stars it catapulted to fame, to the state-of-the-art facilities of NBC, "Radio City" embodied all that was simultaneously great and unsettling about U.S. radio. Buoyed by a formidable promotion apparatus, "Radio City" became a transnational field of identification, admiration, and reflection that influenced conversations about the future of France's broadcast system.

There were no shortages of French politicians, entrepreneurs, broadcast technicians, and journalists eager to stream through the facility, joining throngs of other visitors seeking excitement and inspiration. "I studied that beautiful structure [Radio City] by day and night and I got from it one of the greatest uplifts of my life," gushed Paris fashion designer Edward Molyneux after a visit in 1936. He predicted that the influence would be seen "as a motif for spring designs."[23] The French government went so far as to honor the Radio City Rockettes, who were invited to perform at the 1937 Paris Exposition. It also honored John D. Rockefeller, who personally accepted a Diplôme de Grand Prix, from the French Consul General.[24]

Not all were content to join in the celebration, however. The U.S.-based French journalist, Raoul de Roussy de Sales, questioned the societal impact of Radio City. He dismissed the assertion of technological determinists, many in U.S. radio's corporate ranks, who saw international broadcasting (one of Radio City's newest enterprises) as smoothing the path for harmony among nations. "The disrupting force of nationalism such as we know it today is so great that modern facilities of communication and the shortening of distances, instead of checking it, seem rather to give it more virulence and more reality."[25] The political acrimony in 1930s Europe would appear to support this contention.

Recalling Duhamel's critique, Roussy de Sales suggested that Americans had succumbed to a kind of technological rapture in which they fancied themselves demigods: "In building your Radio Cities, your Boulder and Grand Coulee dams, you seem to be making a dedication as did those ancient builders to a divinity."[26] Such a perspective squares with numerous critiques of technological modernization, which lie at the heart of twentieth-century writing about technology from a humanistic perspective.[27] Along with the benefits of mass connectivity, Roussy de Sales perceived costs arising from America's love affair with its slickly entertaining media culture, namely the attention drawn away from social issues. "The slum districts of an American city are no cleaner than those in China," he wrote, "only [in France] I never remember seeing a picture of the Bowery; all the photographs we had of America being those of Radio City and other beautiful places."[28]

If Radio City proved an irresistible target for some in France, it inspired others to bring French broadcasting into closer alignment with America. As a teenager in Paris, Marcel Bleustein-Blanchet built a galena crystal radio set. He became convinced of the transformative power of mass communications technology. "The upsurge of radio in my village of Montmartre as in all of the villages of France was a cultural maelstrom," he recalled in a memoir, "sweeping out in a few short years, centuries of traditions and habits, in order to introduce all at once understandings, modes of thought, sensitivities, entirely new behaviors."[29] To his great frustration, however, Bleustein-Blanchet's commercial hopes for interwar French radio confronted resistance. When public and unauthorized stations first sprouted in the French provinces, Bleustein-Blanchet canvassed station managers, offering his services as a publicity and advertising agent. But he found few takers. He watched astonished as the directors of a station in Grenoble launched into a lengthy debate over the legitimacy of bringing advertising to French airwaves. "It dawned on me that day, that even in matters of broadcasting, well into the twentieth century, that we [the French] were still preoccupying ourselves with the Justinian Digest!"[30] In 1926 Bleustein-Blanchet founded Publicis, an advertising and public relations firm. He acquired a two-kilowatt station in Paris, Radio L-L, which, in homage to the New York original he renamed "Radio-Cité." Forging ahead with commercial programming and daylong shows on Sunday to capture French workers and families at leisure, Bleustein-Blanchet wrote, "I was almost comparing my station to Radio City in America!" Inspired further by another media form, American magazines, the entrepreneur developed a musical palace in imitation of Radio City, which opened in Paris in 1935. In mid-November 1937, the first Radio-Cité cinema opened near the Place de l'Opéra and four more were added elsewhere in Paris. Meanwhile, the Publicis firm would grow into one of the largest agencies in the world. [31]

## Advertising: Murderer of Art

As Marcel Bleustein-Blanchet learned firsthand, another concern of French public radio advocates concerned the specific issue of American-style advertising techniques influencing French practices. Both PTT public stations and independent, private stations in France ran advertisements of one kind or another, and advertising on the PTT remained controversial. "Advertising will kill Art" glumly predicted LPR in an item from fall of 1927. In 1931 when Lee De Forest, the Yale-educated physicist and inventor of the audion vacuum tube spoke against advertising as "bad, noxious, and of a type liable to compromise the good reputation and development of radio," LPR registered its pleasure by reporting his remarks on the journal's front page. "You can't say it any more clearly than that," it declared.[32]

Citing authorities ranging from the *New York Herald Tribune*, to *Scientific American*, to the *Christian Science Monitor*, LPR alleged there to be widespread discontent in the U.S. over the use of radio by rapacious advertisers.[33] "The inferiority of American broadcasts is attested to by all those who have had the occasion to study them," declared one writer. Maurice Deumesnil of the *Revue Internationale de Musique* echoed the sentiment by disparaging the shortage of time U.S. stations devoted to major musical productions (i.e., symphonic concerts) in favor of "the bleating of amateurs, by groups without rhythm or harmony, by orchestras as inferior as the music that they play." The article also quoted from various U.S. critics of advertising, including present and former members of the FRC, who believed too much advertising to conflict with the public interest of American listeners.[34]

As was often the case in LPR coverage, a casual French reader might be forgiven for coming away with the impression that a revolution was imminent in the U.S., and that a government takeover of radio was a reasonable proposition. Satisfied American network listeners were never directly quoted or considered in these articles. The publication scrutinized U.S radio not for signs of programmatic achievement or listener contentment (or even of resigned American acceptance of the commercially supported system), but rather for evidence to support a view of the structural flaws in the advertiser-supported model, and the urgent need for France and its government to unambiguously support a public monopoly system. Despite such biased framing, LPR accurately represented a small, but vocal minority in America that expressed public concern about the direction of the medium in ways that added legitimacy to struggles over such issues closer to home.[35]

Since actual listening to U.S. programs was not possible for the vast majority of persons in France in the 1920s, LPR reprinted an excerpt of a continuity script for the weekly NBC music program the Ipana Troubadours to illustrate what it saw as the corrupting power of commercialism permeating U.S. radio programs. The show was described as a typical example of sponsored entertainment on American radio. The section described a segue from the eponymous house band performing the song "Smiles" on piano and violin, to an announcer who declared: "Smile and the whole world smiles with you," before launching into a testimonial of the wonders of Ipana toothpaste.[36] After previewing the songs to be performed by the band, the announcer remarked "All of these will be performed in the best Ipana manner, that's to say with a lot of verve, brilliance, and brio." He added that the Troubadours were sporting vibrant red and yellow costumes to show their affinity for the brightly colored striped toothpaste.[37] Focusing on the ways in which the sponsored message and the concert program became interchangeable, the item asked "How many French listeners would like this presentation, ingenious no doubt, but of limited subtlety? Faced with this example should we continue to recommend the pure and simple application of American techniques?"[38] The question was rhetorical and condescending; the editors and right-minded readers already knew the correct answer: French public radio must resist the advance of such "American techniques" onto national airwaves.

## Conclusion

During the interwar years, Georges Duhamel and other critics of an "American menace" criticized the culture of U.S. broadcasting. They pointed to the lawlessness of the "Wild West" of unregulated stations. They challenged the idolatry directed toward Radio City, and they pointed repeatedly to the invasive tendencies of commercial advertisements. Despite such opposition, however, the 1930s proved to be a golden age for French broadcasting.[39] In 1935, after years of partisan rancor between France's center-right Radical Party and socialists over the concerns of LPR and others on both sides, the PTT banned all advertising on public stations and switched to an annual license fee model for revenue. The PTT network expanded, and program quality on public and private stations alike increased significantly.[40]

Despite the effortful reporting of LPR, French listeners were always at liberty to construct their own conclusions about the sounds of the life of the future. They did so by supporting programs on both France's public and private airwaves (though a majority favored the latter). Critics on the French Left, like Paul Campargue, who had expected "a social revolution" from radio, and had waited for "artistic pleasures and moral profundities," felt mildly disappointed. "On the one hand, there are the state stations, which are led by bureaucrats and which have a life as second-rate as it is precarious. On the other hand, there are the private stations which treat radio as a powerful means to strike it rich."[41] In 1930, Campargue articulated his personal dream for the sounds of the future, namely a suppression of commerce on French airwaves as part of a larger national transformation. "The day when the commercial vendors realize that they are speaking in vain, they will stop their rain of gold in the desert of radio."[42] Overwhelming listener support for commercial stations, such as Bleustein-Blanchet's Radio-Cité and Radio Paris carried the day, however. It would take a new government in the aftermath of the war, occupation, and liberation of France to dissolve the split system, and render French radio a public monopoly. The public/private approach would end, not to be seen again, until a different dynamic emerged during the deregulatory waves of the 1980s when private broadcasting returned in France.[43]

The battle over the future of radio and the precarious coexistence of private and public broadcast stations vividly illustrate the complexity of French attitudes toward American culture and the example it set with radio broadcasting. Peripheral as it might first seem, U.S. broadcasting played a substantive role in radio's development in France. Through observation and analysis of interwar developments in America, French journalists and their readers pondered the life of the future of both the medium and their own society. Programmers absorbed new lessons and techniques and worked to integrate them into existing and new programs and production methodologies. Reactions to the "American menace" as embodied via radio marked an important stage of French realignment in the face of the accelerated ascendance of the U.S. as a great power. The interwoven threads of this history and the questions that radio broadcasting elicited remain relevant today as the U.S. and France develop and engage the multimedia forms, technologies, and systems that connect them in a contemporary era of transnational connectivity and national interdependence.

## Notes

1. The author wishes to thank Michele Hilmes and Jason Loviglio for their editorial suggestions. This research has been made possible with the generous support of the University of Michigan's Office of the Vice President for Research, the Rackham School of Graduate Studies, and the National Endowment for the Humanities.
2. Georges Duhamel, *America the Menace, Scenes from the Life of the Future*, trans. Charles Miner Thompson (Boston: Houghton Mifflin, 1931), 202, 15.
3. On Duhamel's world, see Roxanne Panchasi, *Future Tense: The Culture of Anticipation in France between the Wars* (Ithaca, NY: Cornell University Press, 2009). A foundational work exploring the multi-sited processes of the social construction of radio is Susan J. Douglas, *Inventing American Broadcasting, 1899–1922* (Baltimore: Johns Hopkins Press).
4. I examined the complete run of *Le Petit Radio* (LPR; 1927–1939) at the Bibliothèque Nationale. An annual subscription to *LPR* cost 25 francs and radio set dealers were known to offer new customers a free subscription. See *Le Petit Radio*, April 17, 1927.
5. The wider French radio press, of course, included boosters of private stations and commercialized entertainment. Their views of developments in America are beyond the scope of this study.
6. This effectively meant that France had thirteen fully operational, widely audible domestic radio stations by the end of the decade (excluding Radio Alger). For detailed accounts of these developments, see Caroline Ulmann-Mauriat, *Naissance d'un média: Histoire politique de la radio en France (1921–1931)* (Paris: Harmattan, 1999); Fabrice d'Almeida and Christian Delporte, *Histoire des médias en France: De la grande guerre à nos jours* (Paris: Flammarion, 2003); and Derek W. Vaillant, "Occupied Listeners: The Legacies of Interwar Radio for France During World War II," in *Sound in the Age of Mechanical Reproduction*, ed. Susan Strasser and David Suisman (Philadelphia: University of Pennsylvania Press, 2010). A useful resource for tracking station establishment is Robert Prot, *Dictionnaire de la radio* (Grenoble, France: Presses Universitaires, 1997). I draw the statistic for 1930 stations from Caroline Ulmann-Mauriat, "Après l'enterrement du statut, la coexistence des deux réseaux-public et privé est organisée," *Cahiers d'Histoire de la Radiodiffusion* 64 (2000), 5.
7. "Petit Radio [Le]" and "Marcel Pellenc" in Prot, *Dictionnaire de la radio*, 456–59.
8. Such cultural conservatism proved fundamental to postwar state radio's identity in France. See, for example, the analysis of programs of *Radiodiffusion-Télévision Francaise* (RTF) in the early 1960s in Pierre Bourdieu, *Distinction: A Social Critique of the Judgment of Taste* (Cambridge, MA: Harvard University Press, 1984).
9. Erik Barnouw, *A Tower in Babel: A History of Broadcasting in the United States to 1933* (New York: Oxford University Press, 1966) and Robert W. McChesney, *Telecommunications, Mass Media, and Democracy* (New York: Oxford University Press, 1993).
10. Michele Hilmes, *Network Nations: A Transnational History of British and American Broadcasting* (New York: Routledge, 2012), 57–62. On cultural elitism at the BBC, see Paddy Scannell and David Cardiff, *A Social History of British Broadcasting* (Oxford: Blackwell, 1991). On elite antipathies toward, and popular fascination with the cultural practices and forms of ethnic and racial minorities in U.S popular culture and broadcasting, see Robert W. Snyder, *The Voice of the City: Vaudeville and Popular Culture in New York* (New York: Oxford University Press, 1989); Melvin Patrick Ely, *The Adventures of Amos 'n' Andy: A Social History of an American Phenomenon* (New York: Free Press, 1991); and Michael Paul Rogin, *Blackface,*

*White Noise: Jewish Immigrants in the Hollywood Melting Pot* (Berkeley: University of California Press, 1996).

11. Item, September 17, 1927, 7; "Reglementation," October 22,1927, 3; "États-Unis: La police de l'éther," January 28, 1928, 7. All published in *Le Petit Radio*. All translations are my own, unless noted.

12. Paul Campargue, "Le bluff de la radio Américaine," *Le Petit Radio*, June 11, 1932, 3. Campargue's writings for other publications were often reprinted in *Le Petit Radio*.

13. Ibid.

14. "États-Unis mesures d'ordre," *Le Petit Radio*, September 3, 1927, 7 and "L'encombrement de l'ether aux États-Unis," *Le Petit Radio*, April 21, 1928, 3.

15. "Contre la radiopublicité," *Le Petit Radio*, January 9, 1932, March 2 and 19, 1932.

16. Ibid. and "États-Unis: La 'maladie' de la radio," *Le Petit Radio*, June 30, 1928, 7.

17. Phrase in French is "les amis du Trust et les défenseurs de la 'liberté'."

18. "En Amérique," *Le Petit Radio*, February 3, 1930, 6.

19. "Contre la radio publicité," *Haut-Parleur*, reprinted in *Le Petit Radio*, March 19, 1932 and McChesney, *Telecommunications, Mass Media, and Democracy*, 142–43.

20. *KFKB Broadcasting Ass'n, Inc., v. Federal Radio Commission*, No. 5240, Court of Appeals of District of Columbia, 60 App. D.C. 79; 47 F.2d 670; 1931 U.S. App. LEXIS 3531. The significance of the case and Brinkley's exploits are explored further in Gene Fowler, *Border Radio: Quacks, Yodelers, Pitchmen, Psychics, and Other Amazing Broadcasters of the American Airwaves* (Austin, TX: University of Texas Press, 2002); Jason Loviglio, *Radio's Intimate Public: Network Broadcasting and Mass-Mediated Democracy* (Minneapolis: University of Minnesota Press, 2005); and Michele Hilmes, *Only Connect: A Cultural History of Broadcasting in the United States* (Wadsworth, CA: Wadsworth/Thomson Learning, 2002).

21. Excerpt of FRC ruling quoted in "La notion d'utilité publique et la radiodiffusion aux États-Unis," *Le Petit Radio*, September 17, 1932, 6.

22. Ibid.

23. *Chicago Daily Tribune*, November 19, 1936, 24.

24. *New York Times*, October 5, 1939, 22.

25. Raoul de Roussy de Sales, "What Is This Aloofness?" in *You Americans: Fifteen Foreign Press Correspondents Report Their Impressions of the United States and Its People*, ed. B. P. Adams (New York: Funk & Wagnalls, 1939), 32.

26. Ibid., 92.

27. Thomas P. Hughes, *Human-Built World: How to Think About Technology and Culture* (Chicago: University of Chicago Press, 2004).

28. Roussy de Sales, "What Is This Aloofness?" 229.

29. Marcel Bleustein-Blanchet, *Les ondes de la liberté sur mon antenne 1934–1984* (Paris: Jean-Claude Lattès, 1984), 21.

30. Quoted in Ibid.

31. Ibid., 124.

32. *Le Petit Radio*, November 12, 1927, 4; and "La radio en Amérique du Nord—la publicité," *Le Petit Radio*, September 5, 1931, 1.

33. Anti-advertising radio campaigns in the U.S. emerged out of different historical contexts and involved different constituencies. See, for example, McChesney, *Telecommunications, Mass Media, and Democracy*; Derek W. Vaillant, "Bare-Knuckled Broadcasting: Enlisting Manly Respectability and Racial Paternalism in the Battle Against Chain Stores, Chain Stations, and the Federal Radio Commission on Louisiana's KWKH," *The Radio Journal* 1, no. 3 (2004), 193–211; and Kathy Newman, *Radio Active: Advertising and Consumer Activism, 1935–1947* (Berkeley: University of California Press, 2004.

34. "La Radio en Amérique du Nord—la publicité," *Le Petit Radio*, September 5, 1931, 1. Ironically, this type of observation would be used by U.S. commercial networks to explain why the 1927 Radio Act should limit amateur participation in radio.

35. Ibid.

36. "Les beautés de la radio-publicité," *Le Petit Radio*, June 22, 1929. The announcer's words imply that the song was an arrangement of "When You're Smiling (the Whole World Smiles with You)," written by Mark Fisher, Joe Goodman, and Larry Shay.

37. The *Ipana Troubadors* were the radio stage name of the Sam Lanin Orchestra. http://www.dismuke.org/how/prev7-03.html, accessed July 20, 2007.

38. The article used the term "procédés américaines," which evokes a sense of process, as well as behavior, or even artifice. See *Larousse French English/English French Dictionary* (Paris, 2003).

39. See Jeanneney, *Une histoire des médias: Des origines à nos jours;* Joelle Neulander, *Programming National Identity: The Culture of Radio in 1930s France* (Baton Rouge: Louisiana University Press, 2009); and Philip Nord, *France's New Deal from the Thirties to the Postwar Era* (Princeton, NJ: Princeton University Press, 2010).

40. An account of these political debates can be found in Caroline Ulmann-Mauriat, "L'émergence de la radiodiffusion dans la vie publique française (1921–1931)" (University of Lyon, 1984) and *Méadel, Histoire de la radio des années trente: Du sans-filiste à l'auditeur.*

41. "La publicité tuera-t-elle la radio?" *Le Petit Radio*, June 21, 1930, 3.

42. Editorial, *La Parole Libre*, June 21, 1930, n.p.

43. André-Jean Tudesq and Elisabeth Cazenave, "Radiodiffusion et politique: Les élections radiophoniques de 1937 en France," *Revue d'Histoire Moderne et Contemporaine* 23, no. 4 (1976) and Méadel, *Histoire de la radio des années trente.*

# 12

# TICK TOCK GOES THE MUSICAL CLOCK

## Time Discipline and Early Morning Radio Programs

*Alexander Russo*

In 1947, during a famous fight with NBC, comedian and variety show host Fred Allen described a mythical vice president of "Ah! Ah! You're running too long" who sat in a "little glass closet with a mother of pearl gong." When programs went over time, Allen asserted that this executive would "thump the gong with a mushroom tied to the end of a xylophone stick," taking the program off the air, saving precious minutes and seconds that the executive would then save up and use for his vacation. Allen and Portland, his wife and sidekick, concluded that this executive (and presumably all of network radio) "was living on borrowed time" and "enjoying every minute of it."[1] The aesthetics of time borrowing, from whom, and for what ends, frames this chapter.

The paradoxical and vexed relationship to time evidenced in *The Fred Allen Show* also informed the form and content of the programs that are the subject of this chapter, early morning musical clock shows. The temporal constraints that so chafed Allen were emblematic of the organization of a multi-valent organization schedule of live broadcasts in the network-era of American radio, a dynamic Shawn VanCour has described as a "stopwatch aesthetic." This aesthetic was one where "programs were timed down to the last second to ensure that each aired precisely as scheduled and flowed seamlessly into the next."[2] The stopwatch aesthetic was linked to network operations, discourses of staff professionalism, and aesthetic principles that articulated a desire to "reconcile competing demands of unity and variety" and make shows within the music-variety genre sound distinctive.[3]

At this same moment, but at the margins of the broadcast schedule, the musical clock format was developing its own relationship to the aesthetics of the broadcast stopwatch and to its audiences' routines of everyday life. This chapter considers these programs in terms of their placement in the broadcast schedule and how that position informed their aesthetic structure, mode of audience address, and cultural form. Airing in the early morning, these programs were organized around regular time announcements. These announcements exemplified these programs' cultural form, their role in integrating radio listening into the daily transitions between domestic and public space. Yet these shows also evinced a bifurcated structure that placed these formal constraints at odds with the purported content with rigidly determined regular time announcements and unscripted and loosely organized entertainment elements. While this tension tended to function merely as an organizational principle, there were repeated instances when performers mocked radio's time conventions or failed to adhere to them. These moments undermined the cultural role that these shows were designed to fulfill and allowed the programs to embody and respond to cultural anxieties around industrial-era time discipline. The ability to enact and respond to these anxieties helps explain why the durable format of the "musical clock" remains a staple of morning programming to this day.

## Scheduling by the Clock: Network-Era Radio and Time Discipline

The majority of radio's historical research has focused on nighttime programs that commanded the biggest stars, largest budgets, highest levels of prestige, and widest audiences. However, there is now a growing literature on the temporal organization of the broadcast schedule and the daytime programs, like soap operas and homemaking shows, that played important roles in the cultural impact of radio on the everyday lives of listeners.[4] This literature rightly notes that the radio industry offered shows oriented toward women during the day and toward a male-defined mass audience in the evening, reflecting the cultural assumptions about everyday activities and the attentive capacities of gendered listeners. These forces also had a temporal dimension, with radio serving both as a "constant companion" to a presumed female housewife during the day and as a means to reconstitute the family unit with the shift to "universally oriented" evening programs.[5] More than this, radio listening practices were part of larger social processes of maintaining domestic ties and reproducing familiar arrangements. As Shaun Moores argues, via Michel Foucault and Jaques Donzelot, radio entered the home and became part of a larger "field of spatial forces in which the family's morality, sexuality, size, and privacy were inscribed." For Moores, radio was part of a process of governmentality, whereby mothers were delegated as responsible for the successful social reproduction of the family unit.[6] In as much as radio programming was organized around the maintenance of individual female identity during the day and a reintegration of the family unit during the evening, we can examine particular forms and genres in order to understand how radio programs structured the rituals of the temporary dispersal of the family into the public on a daily basis. As a companion within the home, radio morning shows built around the musical clock not only served as a source for potentially disturbing and anxiety-producing news in the world "out there" as described by Paddy Scannell, but also as a means of managing that anxiety by displacing it into the routines of preparing the family members for their journeys into that potentially dangerous space.[7]

The musical clock was a sub-genre of a wider genre of morning radio programs. These programs, such as, *The Forty Winks Club, Cheerio Morning Parade, The Don McNeil Breakfast Club, Rambling with Gambling, Jam with your Breakfast,* and *Morning Moods*, among others, emerged as local station mainstays in the 1930s.[8] There was considerable variation in these programs' tone and address; however, one defining feature was the regular announcement of the time, often to the point of distraction or interruption of the entertainment portion of the program. It is this aspect of these shows that this chapter will focus on. At its most basic, the musical clock format consisted of music and a time announcement. They initially appeared in the mid- to late 1920s. *Musical Clock* was the title of a program based around announcer Halloween Martin. Sponsored by the Marshall Field department store, this show set a template of music, commercials, and time and weather announcements. The program was sonically spare, with little patter or direct address to the audience.[9] The program's utilitarian title *Musical Clock* serves as a marker of how functional its intent was. Although it featured music, its title does not reference the kinds or styles that were played. The need to announce the time structured that ostensible entertainment content. This inversion not only marks the musical clock as a distinctive format, but it suggests that its cultural form is dependent on its temporal register, rather than by its entertainment function.

With its low cost and universal popularity, the musical clock format could be transported, repeated, adapted, and expanded. By the mid-1930s, radio stations were recognizing that there was a large early morning audience.[10] Indeed, as I've argued elsewhere, "The Musical Clock's" appeal was so great that in 1934, the original version of the show caused NBC to break with its ban on phonograph record policy so that it could move the program to one of its own stations.[11] In addition, the company produced transcription discs for affiliated stations to put on their own versions.[12] By the late 1930s, *Variety Annual* noted that they were an "early morning feature on a great many stations."[13] Musical clocks were often promoted by stations as a low-cost option for smaller sponsors and many of the programs were so-called "participation shows" with multiple advertisers.[14] They were exempt from the limits on commercial time dictated by the National Association of Broadcasters' code of conduct, so as "spot advertising" became more popular with sponsors, musical clocks became a valuable part of stations' economic model. In this emergent model of broadcast advertising, companies placed short announcements on multiple stations and programs. Musical clocks were frequently used by these sponsors.[15]

Although they were popular, musical clocks embodied a dilemma for stations that aired them: they were far too easy to ignore. While the industry reassured itself (and advertisers) that audiences paid attention to evening programs, it saw daytime programming as a potentially more difficult challenge.[16] Discourses that manifested anxiety around distracted listening were presented in studies like the one conducted by Halsey Kellogg and Abner Walters of the Wharton School of Finance in 1932. They asked "whether the housewife can be receptive to advertising while she is working about the house."[17] The answer, these authors concluded, was only "probably" and they recommended the creation of daytime programs that either appealed strongly enough to "housewife interests" to outrank housework or that offered musical programs that did not require sustained attention. Kellogg and Walters found that housewives wanted less talk and more music. Some were interested in dramatic programming, but only in the afternoon, after, the respondents said, the bulk of household activities had been completed and more attention could be given to it. One trajectory of these studies was the growth of daytime serials that had slow developing plots and narrative redundancy that coincided with "rhythms of reception" linked with daytime labor.[18] However, the dilemma of morning musical programming remained as sponsors believed it was far too easy to allow music to "merely serve as background" and for advertising messages to be ignored.[19] However, there was a solution, to link popular music listening with other household tasks; the acts of getting up, eating breakfast and leaving (or getting family members out of) the house.[20]

One example of an expansion of a musical clock format to a morning show was Fort Worth station KFJZ's morning show *Quality Time*.[21] Organized around the integration of daily activities and the listening experience, the show's format consisted of musical selections drawn from the NBC Thesaurus transcription library, shortwave-delivered news bulletins, a "Thought for the Day," and "Interesting Facts about Texas." It was created around an assumption that the audience listened as part of a morning routine, one the KFJZ Program Manager Elbert Haling described as: "reading the paper, eating breakfast, or preparing for work." The show avoided comedy because "humor of a too subtle nature is not the best breakfast food in the world."[22] A "brief buzzer attention signal" preceded each news period to grab the attention of distracted listeners. The show's four sponsors were linked to morning activities and included a refrigerator dealer, a coffee company, a drug store, and a supermarket.

*Quality Time* used principles of segmentation and repetition rather than the prevailing standard for homemaking shows of variety and balance. Both involve the combination of elements, but with the latter programs, segments were not repeated and thus required the attention of the listener. Because morning shows repeated segments, listeners did not have to feel as though they must stop their activities to pay attention. There is little suggestion of a high degree of variety in the program itself. The newsbreaks were not significantly different from one another and the aural news flash reminders could perform two roles. They

linked activities in the domestic space to wider world events, explicitly prioritizing the news events as important and therefore asking the listener to set
aside activities important on a domestic scale for knowledge about events on a
national or global scale. At the same time, the news buzzers could also inform
the listener that if they had already heard the newsbreak, they had a certain
amount of time during which listening was not required.

Although *Quality Time* replicated network programs in its division of sponsorship into quarter hours, sponsors were directly linked to daily activities performed while listening—eating, drinking coffee, and getting ready for work.
This suggests that the advertising continuity was tightly integrated into both
the program content but also daily activities and purchasing decisions. Here
local stations possessed an advantage over networks. Because the latter extended
across several time zones, they were forced to be more general in linking programming to daily activities and the tighter deadlines of pre-work and school
routines could not be addressed with the same specificity.

"Musical Clock" elements were present in parts of programs whose announcers were known for their hosts' personas and intimate conversational styles. One
model of this approach was Arthur Godfrey's *The Sundial*, which aired in the
early morning on NBC's Washington, DC affiliate WMAL starting in 1933.[23]
Arthur Godfrey was known for his casual, intimate delivery of musings on
everyday events and of his repeated deviation from sponsor-supplied ad copy.
In the broadcast of September 21st 1939, Godfrey's vexed relationship to time
strictures is clear. The station went on the air at 6 am and the first half hour
consisted solely of popular recorded music (mostly big band or show tunes) and
time announcements every several minutes. At 6:30, Godfrey begins to add
news, weather, and various announcements to the ringing bell that introduced
a time announcement. This transition is heralded by the introduction of his
intimate delivery, distinguished from the impersonal time announcements of
the proceeding half-hour. While Godfrey is relaxed and intimate, his purpose
is clear. The first thing the listener hears is the ring of a bell, then Godfrey saying "It's nineteen minutes to seven o'clock. Generally fair and cool today, the
man says. You've to come on get up. You've got to come on get up. You got to
come on. You've got to come on. You've got to come on get up. [yodels] How
do you like Pepsi Cola mother?" The ruminations on the value of Pepsi Cola
continue for a full minute until another gong sounds, prompting Godfrey to
give another time announcement and another musical selection to start. The
gong and attendant time announcements provide the structure for the program
and link Godfrey's address to "Mother" to her presumed tasks, waking the
rest of the household and starting the morning routine. This sense of purpose
did not necessarily carry over to Godfrey himself as the performer was well
known for arriving at the studio only minutes before his show was due to
start.[24] An inattention to time carried over to this episode as well. As it neared
its end, Godfrey delivered several commercials back to back, after announcing,

"Here we are again with two minutes to go and nineteen sponsors. Life is so sad." Despite the lament, only one more commercial was delivered before the end of the show. There is an irony here, the first part of the program was solely devoted to time, but the latter part completely lost its temporal structure. Indeed, many of these musical clocks possessed just such a problem: the rigorous need to constantly announce the time interfered with the internal flow of the program.

## Keeping Time and (Not) Maintaining Order

Musical clock programs became a mainstay of radio broadcasting in the latter half of the 1930s. Stations embraced the format as more desirable time slots filled with sponsored programs and as stations realized that they could profitably program for slots they had previously regarded as marginal.[25] By the early 1940s, radio morning shows were a staple of network and independent stations. Especially in major markets, pre-9 am slots that had previously been written off by the industry were now considered valuable and competitive. One traditional explanation for the newfound popularity of late-night and early-morning radio was that the conversion to a wartime economy meant more workers were on the night shift, awake, and available to advertisers.[26] However, there is evidence of competition between stations before the start of the war. By April 1941, every station in the New York metropolitan area had its own variation on the news, music, patter, and clock program that aired between 7 and 8 am. WOR had news reports and John Gambling's *Musical Clock*; WJZ aired a show called *Breakfast in Bedlam*; WABC's version was titled *The Morning Almanac*; WNYC had *The Sunrise Symphony*; WHN had a generically titled *News, Popular Musical and Weather*; and even WEVD, owned by Socialist Labor Party newspaper *The Forward,* had a musical clock and Jewish comment show.[27] By the early 1940s, morning shows were such an established part of the airwaves that New York City audiences could tune into competing morning shows tailored for specific tastes and interests. The second half of this chapter examines cases of two morning show personalities, Ralph Dumke and Ed East. At times partners and at others competitors, these individuals, their comedic styles, and their programs represent formal templates that continue to this day. Moreover, they extend the presence of the time announcement into a third decade.

East and Dumke were former vaudevillians and partners in a longstanding routine called *The Sisters of the Skillet,* a parody of homemaker programs. The show (which also went by the moniker *Quality Twins*) featured a range of characters that gave nonsensical "advice" to an audience ostensibly composed of housewives. First airing on WGN in 1928, the characters made regular appearances on the *Rudy Vallee* program and on occasion the bit extended to a standalone series. They had intermittent runs on NBC, Blue, and CBS from 1930 through 1938 (usually as a summer replacement). Because of this sporadic presence, *Sisters of the Skillet* aired in both daytime and evening slots as both a sponsored and sustaining program.[28]

After the partners split, East got work as an announcer on the audience quiz show, *Name it and It's Yours*.[29] He gained his own show on WJZ with the program *Breakfast in Bedlam,* a half-hour show that ran under various names from 1939 to 1945, between 7 and 8 in the morning. After two years, he partnered with his wife Polly who became part of *Breakfast in Bedlam* as well as several other programs, such *Ed East and Polly* from 1941 to 1944 and *Ladies Be Seated* in 1943 and 1944.[30] The show consisted of music, skits, listener contests, and banter between Ed, Polly, and an off-mic engineer named Walter. A typical show featured popular music, birthday announcements, weather, and terrible jokes (one example: rheumatism: nature's effort to establish a weather bureau) was part of the stock-in-trade for musical clock programs. In addition to playing foil for East's antics, it was Polly's job to call out the time every few minutes and announce upcoming bits. In so doing, Polly replicated the role of presumed female audience member: minding the time, ensuring the proper sequence of events that would get the household members out the door.[31] Additionally, East and Polly represent a variation on the "Mr. and Mrs. Breakfast" model of casual cosmopolitanism that become popular on the air in the 1940s.[32]

East's partner, Ralph Dumke, was also a popular presence on New York City radio morning programming during this period, eventually becoming a cross-town rival to his former partner. After the demise of *Sisters of the Skillet*, Dumke had several stints as a voice actor in daytime serials. In 1941 he got a regular gig with a show on WEAF called *Studio X*. Although it was initially slotted at 6:30 pm, the half-hour show was soon moved to mornings, where it aired Monday through Friday between 8 and 9 am (it changed position several times). The show drew upon the established radio variety style but with reduced expense and scale. There was patter between Dumke, his straight-man announcer, Budd Hulick, and the off-mic sound engineer, Gerney as well as a variety of skits, repeated gags, and recorded music. There were in-jokes about the preceding show, Pat Barnes' *Morning in Manhattan* and its soporific pace (although more relaxed than *Studio X*, that show also featured time announcements).[33] A common element of these shows, birthday announcements, was also present (and suggests a diverse mixed age and gender audience). Most importantly, every couple of minutes, the show had a chime or running gag that updated the time.

Dumke and Hulick often clothed their time announcement in the characters they voiced. These characters, such as a gruff old man or an upper class woman from tony Greenwich, Connecticut were often identified as radio performers lost in Rockefeller Center and were used as segues into skits that parodied established conventions of daytime radio. For example, in a program from June 1941, they sent up daytime serials when the "great dramatic guild group players club of America" had a segment of Southern Hospital.[34] In this skit, the hero,

Dr. Smutz has been pushed out of a plane by his rival Dr. Unthank. Dr. Smutz lands safely in a hay bale, which Unthank promptly sets on fire. Fortunately, the proverbial farmer's daughter, Little Nell, rapidly milks the family cow and uses the milk to extinguish the fire. She is entranced by Smutz but the tension does not last long. Unthank continues his air attacks and in his zeal crashes his plane into the barn. The skit ends with expository faux-cliffhanger dialogue by Hulic: "Will Dr. Smutz and his beautiful wife escape with their lives? Will there be anything left of them? Will there be anything left of the barn? Will there be anything left for tomorrow's episode? You betcha. Join us then for another thrilling episode of [sfx gong] Southern Hospital." Preceding Bob and Ray's, "Mary Backstayge, Noble Wife, a play on *Mary Noble, Backstage Wife*, by the better part of a decade, this skit suggests the ways that morning variety shows addressed an audience conversant with, but also potentially alienated from, the melodrama of daytime serials. Unlike morning shows that explicitly addressed "mother," adults and children of both genders were addressed by *Studio X*.

*Studio X* also drew on the routines of *Sisters of the Skillet*, repeatedly parodying homemaker programs. In this way, it resembled *The Wife Saver,* a popular NBC network program that was developed at the same time as *Sisters of the Skillet* but had a much more successful nine-year run. *The Wife Saver* was one of only a few daytime comedy programs in this era. Jennifer Wang argues that its longevity was due to its adherence to the form of daytime radio (short form skits, jokes that assumed a distracted audience, and use of integrated commercials) even as its content parodied those conventions.[35] As I will argue below, *Studio X* enacted a similar logic around anxieties about and failures in time discipline. In the above episode, for example, Dumke read a fake letter that gave advice for getting your husband to work on time. It consisted of step-by-step instructions on giving a hot-foot. Likewise, in a December 1942 program, a guest identified as "Mary Margie McBudd" described how to make a coffee pie with gelatin, sugar, and old coffee made with "chicory and peanut shells."[36] This was a clear reference to Mary Margaret McBride a well-known star of her own daytime homemaker show as well as to the ways that the homemaker genre focused on helping families cope with rationing of food staples during the war. Unfortunately, the skit was prematurely wrapped up as, even with the frequent time signals, the show ran long—a not uncommon occurrence on *Studio X*.

McBudd was a frequent character, often giving advice of questionable merit, like how to make ice. However, given the program's obsession with time, the October 29, 1942 episode stands out because it mocked McBride's tendency to improvise her commercials over a number of minutes.[37] In this skit, Mary Margie arrives with the news that after a year, she has a "comment." Dumke asks: you mean a commercial? Displaying an ignorance of the ways that programs become sponsored, she requests and receives permission to read the spot for Stardust slips, a real sponsor and manufacturer of women's undergarments. Although Hulick reads the ad in drag by impersonating McBride's voice, the copy itself is delivered in a straightforward manner with no mockery of it, at least the first time through. Upon the conclusion of the spot McBudd starts to repeat its copy. Dumke interjects telling the audience, "Well hold on, they only bought a minute. She will keep right on going. Right on plugging this for five minutes if we don't do something. Ladies and gentlemen, we interrupt this announcement to bring you a program." McBudd continues talking (even giving the price of the slips) Dumke tells Gurney to get "it" started and then commenting, "He hasn't done that yet." The "that" is a transcribed commercial for Sheffield Milk, a New York City dairy distributor, introduced via the mechanism of a knock on the door, the entrance of Mr. Sheffield, again voiced by Hulick. This spot is immediately followed by another door knock and the final time announcement indicating the end of the show.

This chaotic sequence demonstrates the failure of "stopwatch" aesthetics on several levels. The knocks on the door were an attempt to integrate into the program transcribed commercials, which did not match the tone or style of the rest of the show. Although "McBudd' was supposed to start to repeat the copy, the Sheffield transcription was not ready to bring the skit to a close. Gurney either missed his cue or was having technical difficulties. It was necessary for McBudd to improvise at the end of the skit/commercial, which was supposed to merely satirize McBride's practice of ad-libbing and personalizing commercials, even as their own show did the same thing. Adding to the ambiguity of this sequence, Gurney's incompetence was a repeated source of humor on the show. Earlier in that same program, for example, featured an extended riff on *Studio X's* collective failure to start on time. However, as I discuss below, it is not clear whether this is a skit about the lack of professionalism by the *Studio X* crew or if it is an actual mistake. The recording begins with Gurney doing a crossword aloud. Hulick asks him for help getting spot announcement number two cued for broadcast.

*Dumke:* Hey, are they kidding us. Did Gurley make the announcement?
*Hulick:* I thought he was working the crossword puzzle.
*Dumke:* So did I.
*Gurney:* Are we on the air?
*Dumke:* I dunno [sic] fellas.
*Hulick:* We must be.
*Dumke:* Let me look at my watch, I wound it last Saturday. Well now it's stopped. I guess we got a little time, why don't you rehearse?
*Hulick:* Let me uh.
*Dumke:* Gurney! Gurney!
*Gurney:* Yes, sir.
*Dumke:* Let's rehearse some of those numbers.

*Gurney:*  You mean those stinkeroos. This is supposed to be my all request day. I'll get that Gurloch [the previous engineer] yet.
*Dumke:*  We'll be on in a few minutes, I suppose they will let us know. Why don't you play something on. [sic]
[Up-tempo swing music plays for less than a minute, abruptly ending, followed by silence.]
*Dumke:*  Bud, that was the signal we are on.
*Hulick:*  Oh we are?
*Dumke:*  Good morning ladies and gentlemen.
*Hulick:*  Good morning and greetings from Studio X.
*Dumke:*  Welcome from good old Studio X. How are you this morning Bud?
*Hulick:*  Oh it depressed me getting way down here in this deep dark...
*Dumke:*  Well what's the matter.
*Hulick:*  I don't know. When are they going to give us a decent studio to work in? A production man to hit cues?
*Dumke:*  We got to get our time right here. I wish they'd buy us a watch don't you?
[Theme song plays]
*Gurley:*  Its eight minutes after eight.

After listening to this recording, it is impossible to tell whether the initial dialogue was background chatter caught by the recording process leading up to a standard opening but not part of the on-air broadcast, a mistake in intra-studio communication that put pre-show chatter on the air, or a self-referential skit mocking the conventions of their own show. In some ways, that lack of clarity is the point. Whether off-air, a mistake, or a joke, the situation turns on time, in this example and in numerous others, Dumke, Hulick, and Gurney repeatedly fail in their battle with time discipline. Dumke may claim to need a working watch, but such laments suggest a distance or even resentment over having to build his program around time signals. However, with NBC, as with E.P. Thompson's description of English factory towns, there can be but one clock.[38] At an airtime of 8 am, doubtless no small portion of the audience was wondering about their own abilities to meet the cues and deadlines of their morning routines and their movement (to paraphrase Irving Goffman) from backstage to front, as they left private spaces and entered public ones. Even as the form of *Studio X* was designed to ensure adherence to industrial age work schedules, the content of the program enacted repeated failures to achieve proper time discipline.

While *Studio X* used recurring characters to make its time announcements, the show's successor favored a more extreme time format. The program, entitled *Two-Minute Man*, was launched after Hulick's departure in 1943 (and perhaps due to the exhaustion of skit-based material). The fifteen-minute show featured musical recordings of varying genres but took its name from the repetition of the time every two minutes. As in *Studio X,* Dumke announced the time in both his own voice and as various characters. There were fewer skits but this didn't seem to help the show remain on time. Indeed, the more stringent requirements to announce the time every two minutes introduced more chaos and incongruity into the show. Dumke frequently would interrupt songs, abruptly segue from a comedy bit to a time announcement. Aesthetically, the musical clock motif resulted in a highly fragmented aural flow as skits and songs were frequently interrupted by the sound of the gong that preceded time announcements and the announcements themselves. Indeed, this structural imposition made the show sound highly disorganized, perhaps mirroring the imagined harried domestic routines of the audience.[39] Moreover, the show seemed to replicate the formal necessity of a structuring time signal that proved so essential to the musical clock genre. The presence of the time announcement ensured both Dumke and the home audience, presumably, would be kept "on time."

Musical clock programs represent a variation on the features of daytime homemaker-oriented programs. This variation is important for what it can tell us about the economics, aesthetics, and cultural form of a distinctive radio genre. Like other morning programs, musical clock programs represent antecedents of the now-commonplace participating sponsorship and magazine advertising format.[40] Like many other musical clock programs, *Studio X* and *Breakfast in Bedlam* had multiple sponsors.[41] *Studio X* was simultaneously sponsored by Lever Brothers, The American Cigarette & Cigar Company, and R.C. Williams, a New York-based grocery and liquor wholesaler. NBC sponsorship records indicate 31 separate advertisers for *Breakfast in Bedlam*. Consisting of both local and national companies, there is no single common denominator in the sponsors. Indeed, they varied from Aetna Insurance to the Westchester Playland Amusement Park. There are local accountant and maid service firms and the National Association of Engine and Boat Manufacturers. As morning programs developed, stations extended the program times from 30 to 60 to 120 minute or longer. The magazine style advertising format and the equally segmented entertainment divisions allowed for the development of music and news block programming formats, the forerunner to the radio formats which dominated radio in the second half of the 20th century.

Second, the relatively marginal position of musical clock programs demonstrates the need to periodize listening practices. In our contemporary moment, when morning drive time is the lifeblood of radio, the lack of attention paid to these programs may strike us as absurd. Still, that fact makes musical clock shows important test cases for understanding ways the radio industry developed its own "low-theory" of audience subjectivity, to use John Caldwell's term, as well as the ways that radio moved from being a primary medium—where one gave it complete attention—to a secondary medium, where one listened while doing something else. In this sense, this paper also takes up calls by Susan Douglas, David Goodman, and Kate Lacey for archaeology and periodization of listening practices.[42] Musical clocks were part of a process by which listeners and broadcasters developed models of listening that informed their relationship to the production and reception of programs. Paddy Scannell has argued that radio broadcasters learned to use intimate, direct address, and informal speech to create a "communicative ethos" of broadcasting. This ethos is defined by the appropriation of informal modes of interpersonal talk that characterize face-to-face encounters to produce a feeling of "co-presence." That audiences responded to these techniques is clear. Still, even though musical clock performers "align[ed] their behavior, their performance, to the nature of the places in which listening … take[s] place," other elements serve as reminders of the ways that modern communication technologies imposed time discipline upon their audiences.[43] The crux of musical clock programs lay in the simultaneous informality of performance aligned with an ever-present disciplinary reminder for the listener. Even as the repetition of show elements allowed for distracted listening, that distraction only goes so far and is reined in by the reminder of the need for the reproduction of labor—whether leaving the house for work or getting family members to work or school, thus ensuring they will maintain, reproduce, or advance their social position. Musical clock programs blur our now established understanding of radio's role in the macro and micro processes of everyday life. This understanding is based on a distinction between daytime programs as an aid to female domestic labor and evening programs as a means of facilitating leisure; a distinction that facilitated recuperation and a return to the workforce the next day. These programs functioned as entertainment that both aided and undermined that impetus toward social production via time discipline. They regularly enacted failures of time discipline; starting late, running long (and requiring sped up or cut off final skits), or openly mocking the industrial requirements that they stay on time. In these cases, the shows had it both ways, with their form enforcing audience and performer discipline even as their content undermined it.

Finally, these shows display a striking formal similarity to contemporary morning radio formats. Washington, DC's WTOP, among others, promotes "News and Weather on the Eights." In so doing, it acts as the heir to the formatting constraints of musical clocks. (For WTOP this lineage is more than metaphorical: its license and transmitter location is also a direct descendent of WJSV, Arthur Godfrey's DC station.) Likewise, *Studio X* and Ed East's programs resemble the "morning zoo" style programs that have dominated US "drive time" radio for the last several decades, albeit with much tamer humor. The morning programs of the 1930s and 1940s adapted models of radio variety shows to the reduced budgets, variable advertising models, and audiences' busy schedules in the early morning hours of the broadcast day. The intermixture of live and recorded music with skits and gags, banter between on-mic announcers and off-air production staff, and the presence of recurring characters (even as these characters were voiced by only one or two performers) are all structural elements that characterize contemporary morning shows. So, when Howard Stern and Robin Quivers banter with Gary the Producer, they are acting within the constraints of a genre that extends back to *Studio X* and other morning shows. While our contemporary versions may be more crass in their comedy choices than would be acceptable during the network era, the form has its roots in the musical clocks of the network era.

## Notes

1. Fred Allen, *Treadmill to Oblivion* (Boston: Little Brown, 1954), 214.
2. Shawn VanCour, "The Sounds of 'Radio': Aesthetic Formations of 1920s Radio Broadcasting" (PhD diss., University of Wisconsin - Madison, 2008), 252.
3. Ibid.,254.
4. Michele Hilmes, *Radio Voices: American Broadcasting, 1922–1952* (Minneapolis: University of Minnesota Press, 1997); Katherine Lacey, "Towards a Periodization of Listening: Radio and Modern Life," *International Journal of Cultural Studies* 3 (2000), 279–88; Shaun Moores, "Box on the Dresser: Memories of Early Radio and Everyday Life," *Media Culture Society* 10 (1988), 23–40; Susan Smulyan, *Selling Radio: The Commercialization of American Broadcasting, 1920–1934* (Washington, DC: Smithsonian Institution Press, 1994); Jennifer Hyland Wang, "Convenient Fictions: The Construction of the Daytime Broadcast Audience, 1927–1960" (PhD diss., University of Wisconsin—Madison, 2006), 144–51. For other primary evidence see Frank Arnold, "High Spots in Broadcast Technique," *Broadcast Advertising,* May 1929, 6; Eve M. Conradt-Eberlin, "Making Friends with the Home-Makers," *Broadcast Advertising,* September 1930, 5.
5. Sean Moores, "The Box on the Dresser," 37. See also Hilmes, *Radio Voices,* 97–129.
6. Moores, "Box on the Dresser," 26, 35.
7. Paddy Scannell, *Radio, Television, and Modern Life* (Cambridge, MA: Blackwell, 1996), 161–62.
8. For an overview of these programs see Philip Leiberman, *Radio's Morning Show Personalities: Early Hour Broadcasters and Deejays from the 1920s to the 1990s* (Jefferson, NC: McFarland, 1996).
9. Arnold Passman, *The Deejays* (New York: Macmillan, 1971), 51.
10. Le Roy Mark, "Reaching the 'Bacon and Egg' Market," *Broadcast Advertising,* August 1930, 5; Julian Bentley, "Large Listening Audience at 6 A.M.," *Broadcasting,* March 1, 1934, 11.
11. The readings of *Quality Time* and Arthur Godfrey in the context of domestic routines that follows initially appeared in a longer version in Alexander Russo, *Points on the Dial: Golden Age Radio beyond the Networks* (Durham, NC: Duke University Press, 2010), 157–60
12. Michael Biel, "The Making and Use of Recordings in Broadcasting before 1935" (PhD diss., Northwestern, 1977), 702; Mark Woods, "Minutes of the May 22 Control Board Meeting," May 22, 1934, Folder 784, Records of the National Broadcasting Company, Library of Congress, Washington, DC (hereafter NBC Records LOC); C. Lloyd Enger, "Memo to Frank Mason," December 34, 1934, Folder 527, NBC Records LOC; C. Lloyd Enger, "Memo to William S. Hedges," December 34, 1934, Folder 527, NBC Records LOC.
13. *Variety Annual, 1937–1938* (New York: Variety Publications, 1937), 356.
14. "WFBR Advertisement," *Broadcasting,* August 15, 1938, 59.
15. "Griffin Mfg. Co., Brooklyn, N.Y." Broadcasting, January 1, 1938, 39; "Royal Goes Spot," Broadcasting, September 15, 1938, 20. For a history of spot broadcasting see, Russo, *Points on the Dial,* 115–50.
16. For a discussion of the devaluation of the female audience see Wang, "Convenient Fictions," 102–103. For a discussion of anxieties around distracted radio listening see David Goodman,

*Radio's Civic Ambition, American Broadcasting and Democracy in the 1930s* (New York: Oxford University Press, 2011), 16 and Russo, *Points on the Dial*, 158–61.

17. Halsey Kellogg and Abner Walters, "How to Reach Housewives Most Effectively," *Broadcasting*, April 15, 1932, 30.

18. Tania Modleski, "The Rhythms of Receptions: Daytime Television and Women's Work," in *Regarding Television: Critical Approaches —An Anthology*, ed. E. Ann Kaplan (Frederick, MD: University Publications of America/American Film Institute, 1983), 67–75.

19. Orrin E. Dunlap, Jr., *Radio in Advertising* (New York: Harper and Brothers, 1931), 157.

20. I distinguish popular from classical music because, as David Goodman argues, classical music was a central site where broadcasters sought to create active listeners that conformed to its idealized "civic paradigm." Goodman, *Radio's Civic Ambition*, 116–80

21. For the broader context in which *Quality Time* emerged see Russo, *Points on the Dial,* 160–61.

22. Elbert Haling, "Quality Time in Fort Worth," *Broadcasting*, August 15, 1936, 44.

23. Arthur J. Singer, *Arthur Godfrey: The Adventures of an American Broadcaster* (Jefferson, NC: McFarland, 2000), 40–43.

24. Granville Klink, Godfrey's engineer, speculated that one reason the performer often ribbed the Virginia State Police on-air was that they frequently ticketed him for speeding on the way to the studio. Quoted in Singer, *Arthur Godfrey*, 54. See also Ernest L. Schier, "Arthur Godfrey's Gags Begin Listeners' Days." *The Washington Post,* April 4, 1943. Accessed September 21, 2012, http://search.proquest.com/docview/151638291?accountid=9940.

25. See Russo, *Points on the Dial*.

26. Keith Jones, "Music in Factories: A Twentieth-Century Technique for Control of the Productive Self," *Social & Cultural Geography* 6 (2005): 723–44.

27. "Radio Today," *New York Times*, April 23, 1941, 42, accessed February 21, 2012, http://search.proquest.com/docview/105509740 See also, Bill Jaker, Frank Sulek, and Peter Kanze, *The Airwaves of New York: Illustrated Histories of 156 AM Stations in the Metropolitan Area, 1921–1996* (Jefferson, NC: McFadden, 1998).

28. John Dunning, "Quality Twins," *The Encyclopedia of Old Time Radio* (New York: Oxford University Press, 1998), 557.

29. As a side note, Dumke and East reunited in 1949 to produce a television version of *Sisters of the Skillet* for KNBH. The show received positive reviews and a limited sustaining run but failed to obtain a sponsor. Alan Fischler, "Review of Sisters of the Skillet," *Billboard*, November 12, 1949, 9. East passed away in early 1952 but Dumke's career continued for another decade. "Obituary: Ed East," *Billboard*, January 26, 1952, 49. "Ralph Dumke, 64, Performer, Dead," *New York Times*, January 6, 1964, 47.

30. John Dunning, "Ladies Be Seated," *The Encyclopedia of Old Time Radio* (New York: Oxford University Press, 1998), 387.

31. "Eddie East Variety Show," November 1, 1939, NBC Radio Collection, RWA 287 A2-B1, Recorded Sound Reference Room, Library of Congress, Washington, DC (Hereafter NBC Radio LOC); "Breakfast In Bedlam," August, 7, 1940, NBC Radio LOC, RWA 4690 B2X; "Ed East Jingles," August, 14, 1940. NBC Radio LOC, RWA 4692 B3. See also, "Ladies Be Seated," Billboard Aug 23, 1943, 10

32. Hilmes, *Radio Voices*, 283 and Donna Halper, *Invisible Stars: A Social History of Women in Broadcasting* (New York: M.E. Sharpe, 2001), 114.

33. "Morning in Manhattan," October 3, 1940, NBC Radio LOC, RWA 4862 B1-2; "Morning in Manhattan," October 5, 1940, NBC Radio LOC, RWA 4885 A2.

34. "Studio X," June 2, 1941, NBC Radio LOC, LWO 16675 29b4-5.

35. Jennifer Hyland Wang, "No Jokes: The Marginalization of Comedy in Early Daytime Radio" (Paper presented at annual conference of the Society for Cinema and Media Studies, Boston, MA, March 22, 2012).

36. "Studio X," December 9, 1942, NBC Radio LOC, RWA 3643 B1.

37. "Studio X," October 29, 1942, NBC Radio LOC, RWA 3643.

38. E. P. Thompson, "Time, Work-Discipline and Industrial Capitalism," *Past & Present* 38 (1967), 56–97.

39. "Two Minute Man," March 1, 1943, NBC Radio LOC, RWA 4085 B1.

40. See Hilmes, *Radio Voices*, 271–90 for an account of the historical erasure of the role of women like Mary Margaret McBride in establishing the magazine format.

41. "Studio X," NBC Index Card Files, Recorded Sound Reference Room, Library of Congress, Washington, DC (Hereafter NBC Index); "Breakfast in Bedlam," NBC Index.

42. Douglas, *Listening In: Radio and the American Imagination* (New York: Times Books, 1999); Lacey, "Towards a Periodization"; Goodman, Radio's Civic Ambition.

43. Scannell, *Radio, Television, and Modern Life*, 12.

# CONTRIBUTORS

**Ece Algan** is an Associate Professor at California State University, San Bernardino. Her research focuses on the relationship between cultural politics and media and technology use. She has conducted fieldwork research on local radio, emerging communication technologies, and youth for almost a decade in Southeast Turkey. Her work has been published in several media and communication journals and edited collections, and earned many awards, including a Top Paper Award at 2011 NCA, Top Faculty Paper Award at the Global Fusion 2009 Conference, and the James E. Murphy Best Faculty Paper Award in 2003. She serves on editorial boards of *Journal of International Communication* and *Global Media Journal*'s Mediterranean Edition.

**Alejandra Bronfman** is an Associate Professor in the Department of History at the University of British Columbia. Her current research records the unwritten histories of radio and related sonic technologies in the Caribbean. *Talking Machines: Caribbean Media and Publics* pays particular attention to new media, including telegraph, telephone, and broadcasting and their relationships to capital flows, imperial projects, and regional political mobilizations. She is the author of *Measures of Equality: Race, Social Science and Citizenship in the Caribbean* (2004), *On the Move: The Caribbean Since 1989* (2007), and co-editor of *Media, Sound and Culture in Latin America and the Caribbean* (2012).

**Dolores Inés Casillas** is an Assistant Professor in the Department of Chicana and Chicano Studies and a faculty affiliate of Film and Media Studies at the University of California, Santa Barbara. She has published essays on radio humor, immigration broadcasts, and language politics. Her manuscript under contract with New York University Press examines how immigration politics and Latino immigrant listeners have shaped the growth and character of Spanish-language radio throughout the twentieth century.

**David Goodman** teaches American history at the University of Melbourne in Australia. He is the author of *Radio's Civic Ambition: American Broadcasting and Democracy in the 1930s* (2011) and "Distracted Listening," in David Suisman and Susan Strasser (eds.) *Sound in the Era of Mechanical Reproduction* (2010). He and Susan Smulyan shared a 2010 Scholars and Artists in Residence Fellowship at the Australian National Film and Sound Archive, where they undertook research on early interactions between Australian and American commercial radio.

**Michele Hilmes** is a Professor of Media and Cultural Studies and Chair of the Department of Communication Arts at the University of Wisconsin-Madison. Her work focuses on media history and historiography, particularly in the area of radio and creative soundwork. She is the author of several books in this field, including *Radio Voices: American Broadcasting 1922–1952* (1997), *Only Connect: A Cultural History of Broadcasting in the United States* (4th ed., 2013), and *Network Nations: A Transnational History of British and American Broadcasting* (2011).

**Bill Kirkpatrick** is an Assistant Professor of Media Studies in the Communication Department at Denison University. Publications include articles in *Critical Studies in Media Communication, Television & New Media, Radio Journal*, the *Journal of the Society for American Music*, the *Journal of Popular Culture*, and several anthologies. He is currently working on a book project on cultural approaches to media policy. Research interests include U.S. broadcast history and policy, media and disability, and citizen-produced media.

**Kate Lacey** is a Senior Lecturer in Media and Cultural Studies at the University of Sussex. She has published widely on the history and theory of broadcasting, and is author of *Feminine Frequencies: Gender, German Radio and the Public Sphere 1923 to 1945* (1996) and *Listening Publics: The Politics and Experience of Listening in the Media Age* (2013). She was a founding member of the Radio Studies Network, serves on the editorial board of *The Radio Journal: International Studies in Broadcast and Audio Media* and sits on the UK Radio Archives Advisory Committee.

**Jason Loviglio** is an Associate Professor and Director of Media and Communication Studies at the University of Maryland, Baltimore County. He is the author of *Radio's Intimate Public: Network Broadcasting and Mass-Mediated Democracy*. He is co-editor (with Michele Hilmes) of *Radio Reader: Essays in the Cultural History of Radio*. He has published articles on the cultural politics of US public radio. He serves on the editorial board of *The Radio Journal: International Studies in Broadcast and Audio Media*.

**Virginia Madsen** is a Lecturer in Media Studies at Macquarie University in Australia. She worked for many years both on staff and as an independent producer for the ABC's national radio networks, Radio National (RN) and ABC Classic FM, and was a founding producer of the ABC program "The Listening Room." She has published articles on sound and auditory culture in *The Historical Journal of Film and Television* and *The Radio Journal: International Studies in Broadcast and Audio Media* as well as in several edited volumes. Her current project is *The Other New Wave: Filme Sonore and the Documentary Imagination*.

**Elena Razlogova** is an Associate Professor of History and a Co-Director of the Centre for Oral History and Digital Storytelling at Concordia University in Montréal. She has published articles on US radio history and on public opinion about Guantanamo detentions. She was an executive producer on a digital project *Gulag: Many Days, Many Lives*. Her book, *The Listener's Voice: Early Radio and the American Public* came out from the University of Pennsylvania Press in 2011. She is currently working on a history of the "morality of snitching" in the United States and the Soviet Union during the cold war.

**Alexander Russo** is an Associate Professor in the Department of Media Studies at The Catholic University of America in Washington, DC. He is the author of *Points on the Dial: Golden Age Radio Beyond the Networks* (2010), and has published on localism and radio formatting in satellite radio, aural attention in the reception of postwar transitcasting, the idea of liveness in sound-on-disc transcriptions, and the role of race in *The Green Hornet*.

**Susan Smulyan** is a Professor of American Studies at Brown University and the author of *Selling Radio: The Commercialization of American Broadcasting* (1994) and *Popular Ideologies: Mass Culture at Mid-Century* (2007), and co-editor of *Major Problems in American Popular Culture* (2012). She has worked on three web projects: "Whole Cloth: Discovering American History Through Science and Technology"; "Freedom Now!: An Archival Project of Tougaloo College and Brown University"; and "Perry Visits Japan." Susan was an Arts Faculty Visiting International Scholar, School of Historical Studies, University of Melbourne and currently chairs the Board at New Urban Arts, a mentoring program for high school students.

**Derek W. Vaillant** is an Associate Professor in the Department of Communication Studies at the University of Michigan in Ann Arbor. He holds a PhD in history from the University of Chicago. He is the author of *Sounds of Reform:*

*Progressivism and Music in Chicago, 1873–1935* (University of North Carolina Press, 2003). His work has appeared in *American Quarterly, French Politics Culture & Society, Technology & Culture*, and *The Radio Journal,* as well as in the anthologies *Radio Reader* and *Sound in the Era of Mechanical Reproduction.* He is completing a book on U.S.-France broadcasting and aural culture in the twentieth century.

# INDEX